A Great Plac

"Gripping. Of all the CIA's strange adv et war in Laos may have been the most ed a true drama with an improbable and colorful cast. An eye-opening, carefully researched, and wrenching yarn of what can go wrong when East meets West."
—Evan Thomas, author of *The Very Best Men: The Daring Early Years of the CIA*

"Superb! Joshua Kurlantzick joins the ranks of preeminent Southeast Asia chroniclers like David Halberstam, Neil Sheehan, and Stanley Karnow. . . . *A Great Place to Have a War* is rich and jarring in its historical insight, fast in its pacing, and gripping in its read. You won't want to put it down."
—Douglas Waller, author of *Disciples: The World War II Missions of the CIA Directors Who Fought for Wild Bill Donovan*

"This eminently well-written and well-researched book deserves deep reflection and wide readership. From moral and human perspectives, the book makes chilling reading."
—*Forbes*

"At the heart of Kurlantzick's deftly paced book are conflicted CIA operatives and the Hmong—led by the charismatic General Vang Pao—who did the bulk of the fighting on behalf of the U.S. But what the book does best is examine the CIA's transformation from an intelligence-gathering organization to a war-fighting one."
—*NPR*

"The war's entire compelling tale can be found in the lucid prose and revelatory reporting of Joshua Kurlantzick's new book."
—*The Economist*

"Accurate and informative."
—*The Wall Street Journal*

"Joshua Kurlantzick's story of the CIA's secret war in Laos brilliantly illuminates one of the most obscure yet harrowing chapters of the Vietnam conflict. . . . This is a cautionary tale of arrogance, recklessness, and unrestrained power that, tragically, finds echoes in many of today's battlefields."
—Joshua Hammer, author of *The Bad-Ass Librarians of Timbuktu*

"[Kurlantzick] shows how critical it is for American leaders to be clear-eyed about their purposes and honest with their public before embarking on a war that will inevitably take on a gruesome momentum of its own."
—*The New York Times Book Review*

"This riveting read belongs in the pantheon of works such as Jane Hamilton-Merritt's *Tragic Mountain* and William M. LeoGrande's *Our Own Backyard*. Highly recommended for those wanting insight into the Hmong people and Cold War thinking."
—*Library Journal*

Also by Joshua Kurlantzick

Charm Offensive: How China's Soft Power
Is Transforming the World

The Ideal Man: The Tragedy of Jim Thompson
and the American Way of War

Democracy in Retreat: The Revolt of the Middle Class
and the Worldwide Decline of Representative Government

A Great Place *to* Have a War

America in Laos and the Birth
of a Military CIA

Joshua Kurlantzick

Simon & Schuster Paperbacks

New York • London • Toronto • Sydney • New Delhi

A Council on Foreign Relations Book

Simon & Schuster Paperbacks
An Imprint of Simon & Schuster
1230 Avenue of the Americas
New York, NY 10020

First Simon & Schuster paperback edition January 2018

SIMON & SCHUSTER PAPERBACKS and colophon are registered trademarks
of Simon & Schuster, Inc.

For information about special discounts for bulk purchases,
please contact Simon & Schuster Special Sales at 1-866-506-1949
or business@simonandschuster.com.

The Simon & Schuster Speakers Bureau can bring authors to your
live event. For more information or to book an event, contact the
Simon & Schuster Speakers Bureau at 1-866-248-3049
or visit our website at www.simonspeakers.com.

Manufactured in the United States of America
10 9 8 7 6 5 4 3 2 1

Library of Congress Cataloging-in-Publication Data
Names: Kurlantzick, Joshua, author.
Title: A great place to have a war : America in Laos and the birth
  of a military CIA / Joshua Kurlantzick.
Other titles: America in Laos and the birth of a military CIA
Description: New York : Simon & Schuster, [2017] | Includes bibliographical
  references and index.
Identifiers: LCCN 2016005352 (print) | LCCN 2016021281 (ebook) | ISBN
  9781451667868 (hardcover) | ISBN 9781451667882 (pbk.) | ISBN 9781451667899
  (E-Book)
Subjects: LCSH: Vietnam War, 1961–1975—Campaigns—Laos. | Vietnam War,
  1961–1975—Secret service—United States. | United States. Central
  Intelligence Agency—History—20th century.
Classification: LCC DS557.8.L3 K87 2017 (print) | LCC DS557.8.L3 (ebook) |
  DDC 959.704/38—dc23
LC record available at https://lccn.loc.gov/2016005352

ISBN 978-1-4516-6786-8
ISBN 978-1-4516-6788-2 (pbk)
ISBN 978-1-4516-6789-9 (ebook)

The Council on Foreign Relations (CFR) is an independent, nonpartisan membership organization, think tank, and publisher dedicated to being a resource for its members, government officials, business executives, journalists, educators and students, civic and religious leaders, and other interested citizens in order to help them better understand the world and the foreign policy choices facing the United States and other countries. Founded in 1921, CFR carries out its mission by maintaining a diverse membership, with special programs to promote interest and develop expertise in the next generation of foreign policy leaders; convening meetings at its headquarters in New York and in Washington, DC, and other cities where senior government officials, members of Congress, global leaders, and prominent thinkers come together with CFR members to discuss and debate major international issues; supporting a Studies Program that fosters independent research, enabling CFR scholars to produce articles, reports, and books and hold roundtables that analyze foreign policy issues and make concrete policy recommendations; publishing *Foreign Affairs*, the preeminent journal on international affairs and U.S. foreign policy; sponsoring Independent Task Forces that produce reports with both findings and policy prescriptions on the most important foreign policy topics; and providing up-to-date information and analysis about world events and American foreign policy on its website, www.cfr.org.

The Council on Foreign Relations takes no institutional positions on policy issues and has no affiliation with the U.S. government. All views expressed in its publications and on its website are the sole responsibility of the author or authors.

For Caleb and Jonah

Contents

A Great Place
to Have a War

Chapter 1

Baci

BILL LAIR HELD OUT HIS LANKY ARMS, THE SLEEVES OF his button-down shirt rolled up to the shoulder. Smoke wafted through the one-room building with mud floors and walls made of corrugated metal and thatch. Besides an open stove in the back of the room and a simple wood table in the middle, there was little other furniture in the building. Lair had been given a low wooden bench to sit on, and he struggled to fold his legs under it. Most of the other people inside the building stood or squatted on the muddy ground.

Lair was surrounded by men and women from the Hmong hill tribe, one of the largest ethnic minority groups in the Southeast Asian nation of Laos, the landlocked country wedged, like a fishhook, among Myanmar, Thailand, Cambodia, China, and Vietnam. They had come for the *baci*, the Thai and Laotian ceremony in which people are symbolically bound through the tying of strings around each other's wrists and forearms. The ceremony had been going on since the late afternoon, and Lair already had at least twenty white strings tied around his arms. His arms would be covered in strings by night. There seemed to be no end to the mass of people crowding through the door of the house and waiting to see the American with the thick Clark Kent glasses, who spoke Lao with a Texas accent. Behind the Texan, women loaded up simple metal plates with pig parts, sticky rice, and fruit, and handed them to Lair, nodding at him to eat. The Hmong women mostly waited to eat until men were finished. Three shamans chanted just behind Lair. Many Hmong believed that when they chanted, the shamans literally entered another world. The men writhed and sang and spat as if possessed.

Vang Pao, a military officer in the anti-communist forces and the leader of this group of Hmong, paced among Lair, the doorway, and the shamans, directing the event. Lair could not see all the people outside the hut, but he estimated that at least five hundred Hmong had come to the *baci*. Vang Pao's battlefield successes had helped him ascend from a modest background—his family had not been clan leaders—to become one of the most powerful Hmong men on the anti-communist side. He would soon be the most powerful Hmong leader in Laos.[1]

Vang Pao claimed to be leading an army of nearly five thousand irregulars against the Vietnamese and Laotian communists. But Lair saw not only young men who might be fighting types but also younger women, children, and older Hmong. Some of the older Hmong men and women had come to the *baci* dressed in what Lair believed was their finest attire: baggy black trousers, embroidered black vests, and strings of silver ornaments.

It was the winter of 1961. Lair had already lived in Southeast Asia for more than a decade, and he had attended *baci* ceremonies before. Groups throughout Southeast Asia had *baci*s all the time. *Baci*s were held, and strings tied, when new homes were built, when relatives relocated, when babies were born, when men and women were married off, when visitors arrived from far away. A village of Hmong might hold fifteen or twenty *baci* ceremonies in one month, if many auspicious events occurred at one time.

But this was not a normal *baci*. Bill Lair had spent his decade in Southeast Asia as a clandestine operative for the Central Intelligence Agency, and he had become known within the agency for his knowledge of the region, his language skills, and his extensive contacts. Behind his shy, aw-shucks demeanor, his plain shirts and plain face, lurked a fierce man who had fought through France and Belgium with an armored division in the Second World War and had devoted his whole life to the CIA. Lair had flown up to the central highlands of Laos, where the Hmong lived on peaks and high mountain plateaus, not just to have strings tied around his wrists—though he understood that ceremony mattered in a place where there was no written language, and oral agreements were the rule. He had flown up, his pilot twisting around high peaks and limestone cliffs and dense forests, to inaugurate a bold plan that the agency would call Operation Momentum.[2]

Operation Momentum was a plan to arm and train the Hmong under Vang Pao to fight in the growing civil war in Laos, which pitted communist insurgents called the Pathet Lao, backed by North Vietnam, against Laos's government and its non-communist allies such as Vang Pao and his men. The war in Laos had raged on and off almost from the time Japan surrendered in World War II in 1945, leaving in Southeast Asia former French colonies where local leaders battled to determine the future. France's loss to the Viet Minh, the Vietnamese independence forces, in 1954 had left Vietnam divided, with the Viet Minh's leaders in control in the north, and a vacuum of power in Laos. (The Viet Minh was led by communists, but the coalition fighting France for independence also included some non-communist nationalists.) Laos's weak central government had maintained control of only parts of the country. The civil war in Laos, which had been going on for nearly a decade, had flared up intensely. Conservative and communist Laotian forces now struggled to control Laos, as well as other countries in the region.

And in Washington, Laos increasingly appeared, at least to American officials, to be part of a broader effort by international communist forces to dominate Asia—and the world. It did not seem to matter to American leaders that Laos was so small it had only one major city, Vientiane—the capital, which was basically a muddy village—or that most people in Laos lived on subsistence farming and had little idea of the differences between communism, democracy, and other political systems.

As a French colony, Laos had mostly been ignored by Paris. But President Dwight D. Eisenhower and his staff, attuned to the domino theory of one country after the next falling to communism, saw Laos as a bulwark—a nation where the United States could make a stand to prevent communism from spreading west out of China and North Vietnam into Thailand and India and beyond. A pro-Western Laos would place a state between Vietnam and Thailand, a critical US partner, and would make it easier for the United States to support non-communist forces in Vietnam. In one of the most famous moments of his presidency, at a press conference in April 1954, Eisenhower had publicly enunciated this domino principle as a reason for supporting France's continued struggle against independence forces in Vietnam.

"You have a row of dominoes set up, you knock over the first one, and what will happen to the last one is the certainty that it will go over very quickly," Eisenhower said. "So you could have a beginning of a disintegration that would have the most profound influences" if Indochinese countries fell to communism.[3] Even after the French loss in Indochina, the Eisenhower administration had made clear the importance of Indochina to US security; a paper issued by the National Security Council in December 1954 stated that it was the United States' objective to "defeat Communist subversion and influence" in Indochina.[4] Over the course of the 1950s, with Vietnam divided and half controlled by a communist party, Eisenhower had come to see Laos as another critical domino. He personally followed reports about Laos day by day during the final year of his presidency.[5] He warned his successor, John F. Kennedy, that Laos was the most pressing foreign policy issue in the world. In fact, the day before Kennedy's inauguration, Eisenhower organized a foreign policy briefing for the president elect, with issues to be addressed in what Eisenhower considered their order of importance to American security. Laos came first—and only after Laos was discussed was the president elect briefed on the looming

US-Soviet standoff in Berlin, on Cuba, and on the global strategic nuclear arms race.[6]

Agency headquarters had approved Lair's plan to train and arm the Hmong, which he had outlined in an eighteen-page cable, almost instantly upon receiving it in the winter of 1960–61. The White House took a personal interest in the plan for the operation. After the CIA's Far East division and its director signed off on Lair's idea, the plan was approved by President Eisenhower's staff, on one of Eisenhower's last days in office in January 1961. It helped that Lair had already run a successful CIA training program for Thai commandos in the 1950s. Some of those Thais would join him in running Operation Momentum, and in fighting Laos's civil war; Bangkok would eventually send thousands of its men to fight in Laos. The CIA leadership had signed off on starting with a training program for a thousand Hmong men and then expanding from there.[7] The operation was budgeted at around $5 million US, but by 1962, it would grow to over $11 million. That was only the start for an undertaking that would command $500 million annually by the end of the decade, with Vang Pao controlling a force of over thirty thousand soldiers.[8] A budget of $500 million in 1970 dollars was equivalent to *$3.1 billion* in 2016 dollars, for an operation in a country that today has less outward trade with the rest of the world than Luxembourg does.

Vang Pao had spent his entire adult life fighting: fighting the Japanese, fighting with the French against the Viet Minh, and now fighting with the government against the Pathet Lao and its backers in Hanoi. Like many of the Hmong, he was intensely proud of the group's freedom. Many Hmong had originally migrated south from China into Southeast Asia, and they traditionally migrated through the mountains, hunting and practicing swidden, or slash and burn, agriculture, and governing their affairs through a kind of communal consensus building. The group repeatedly fought any powers, including the French at first, who tried to control its society. Historian Mai Na M. Lee, an assistant professor at the University of Minnesota Twin

Cities, notes that the Hmong fought for centuries—against the Chinese, the French, and others—to maintain their independence and try to win a state for their people. Although they never gained their own state, they forced these powers to give them a measure of autonomy.[9] Like many Hmong, Vang Pao resented any outside control of the hill tribe's affairs and feared that a government managed by Vietnamese communists would turn Laos into a much more centralized state, starving the Hmong of their freedoms.

Vang Pao had developed a personal animus toward the Vietnamese as well. The long French Indochina War had lasted from 1946 to 1954, as France tried desperately to hold on to its Indochinese colonies. During that war, and then during Laos's on-and-off civil war, Vang Pao had watched many of his friends, aides, and allies be killed by the Vietnamese and their allies. The fighting in the French Indochina War was fierce; many of the French soldiers came from the Foreign Legion, a force of professional soldiers drawn from all over the globe that was known for its willingness to take enormous casualties. The Viet Minh, meanwhile, were brutal not only toward captured enemy soldiers but also toward civilians. Fighting with the French and then with Laotian anti-communist forces, Vang Pao himself had repeatedly shot, bombed, and stabbed to death Vietnamese troops in Laos.

———

The Hmong leader had organized the *baci* to inaugurate Momentum and introduce Lair to clan leaders in the hill tribe. He roamed the muddy house, encouraging everyone to eat and drink more, and talking, rapid-fire, in Lao, in Hmong, and in the French he had learned from French officers. Vang Pao was moving constantly—gesturing, introducing Lair to clan leaders who had come for the *baci*, telling stories of the French Indochina War, commanding some of his men to find Lair more drinks. He commanded his wives—like many powerful Hmong men, he had multiple wives—to bring food to guests who were not eating at that minute. (Vang Pao had married women from different Hmong clans to unite several clans behind him.) As a musician played the thin Hmong bamboo mouth pipe and stomped his feet on the mud floor, Vang Pao himself tied the final string around Lair's wrist, binding him metaphorically to the tribe. Vang Pao led Lair toward the shamans, who waved pungent incense candles around their heads and blessed the nascent cooperation.[10] Locally brewed rice alcohol flowed liberally. Vang Pao's men handed balls of sticky rice to Lair, to make sure that the Texan had something in his stomach to absorb all the liquor.

Circles of Hmong men stood together, dancing the slow, hypnotic *lamvong*, a Laotian folk dance in which people slowly twist their wrists from side to side while swaying together to mournful, minor-key tunes that sound almost like American country and western ballads. Vang Pao laughed and drank and danced the *lamvong*. But during pauses, he also told other Hmong at the *baci*, "We will kill all the Vietnamese who come near. Now we can kill many more."

During a private meeting between Lair and Vang Pao, just before the *baci*, the two men had gone over the details of the operation: how the Hmong would receive arms and supplies in airdrops; how Vang Pao could help identify places to set up simple airstrips in mountain valleys; how the CIA might handle training programs for capable Hmong soldiers. But Vang Pao also made a request. Here the Hmong leader's account of the meeting diverges from Lair's. "I asked Bill Lair to promise me that America would not abandon us [the Hmong] no matter what happened," Vang Pao said.[11] Some Hmong sources claim further that, as the two men decided to start the operation, Lair presented Vang Pao and the Hmong with a written agreement from the American government pledging a kind of alliance, starting with a promise that the United States would soon ship the Hmong five hundred firearms.[12] Several of Vang Pao's aides, who were at the meeting with the Hmong leader, say that Lair told them, "If the Hmong people lose, we [the United States] will find a new place where we can help

the Hmong people."[13] American government sources do not corrob-
orate any of these claims, and Lair did not remember making these
statements.[14]

Later, years after the end of the Laos war, Vang Pao would tell anyone who asked him about Laos that, no matter what was said when he
agreed to the operation, no matter whether the two sides had made
any written agreement, the United States had made a lasting commitment. After all, the US government, over time, would push the
Hmong to broaden their battle beyond simply protecting Hmong villages and to help America's interests in Vietnam. That war did not involve the Hmong directly; yet Vang Pao's men played a major role by
tying down and killing not only the small groups of Pathet Lao communists but also regular North Vietnamese troops who might otherwise have been killing Americans.[15]

And the United States would unleash a bombing campaign on
Laos unlike any other in modern history, bigger even than the bombings of Japan and Germany in the Second World War. This campaign
would become central to the Laos operation, though the American
bombing sorties, supposedly designed to weaken the North Vietnamese and cut their supply lines through Laos and into South Vietnam, would kill more Laotians than anyone else.[16] Over the course of
the war, US bombing of Laos would become so intense that it aver-
aged one attack every eight minutes for nearly a decade.[17] The country would be left with so much unexploded ordnance that, in the
three decades *after* Laos's civil war ended in 1975, the leftover bombs
would kill or maim twenty thousand Laotians.[18]

Together, Vang Pao believed, all of these American actions put
the United States in the debt of the Hmong, who fought in lieu of
American soldiers and suffered as badly under the wanton bombing as other people in Laos did. Many CIA operatives who worked in
Laos did believe that the United States had made a significant promise to the Hmong, even if no formal treaty existed. One former CIA
station chief in Laos, Hugh Tovar, who oversaw the operation in the

early 1970s, admitted that, from the first days that Lair and Vang Pao planned the operation, the United States had done nothing to discourage the Hmong from thinking that America had a lasting obligation to them. "The Hmong committed themselves [to the United States] believing that the United States was fully committed to see them through in the fight," Tovar wrote.[19] "Most Americans [working in the secret war] were viscerally convinced that we were indeed so committed."[20]

In the months after that first *baci*, even before Operation Momentum had grown into a giant undertaking—the biggest in CIA history—Lair and Vang Pao often discussed a contingency plan if the whole war turned bad. If the Hmong losses became unbearable, Vang Pao would take his wives, and his officers, and all the Hmong who had fought with him, and migrate wholesale across the Mekong River, which divides Laos and Thailand. Thai northeasterners often spoke Lao rather than standard Thai, and many had actually come from Laos. Lair even, on several occasions, discussed this option with the station chief in Vientiane, and with the head of the Far East division. Still, no one above him at the agency actually granted permission for this bailout option to ever become reality.[21] The CIA men declined to tell Vang Pao that the bailout plan had no formal approval.

The *baci* for Bill Lair might have seemed like an ancient ritual, taking place in huts with no modern amenities and guided by shamans. But although Laos was geographically remote from Washington, this kingdom with a population smaller than that of Los Angeles now sat at the center of America's foreign policy universe.

The briefing given John F. Kennedy just before his inauguration in January 1961 was not unique. On multiple occasions during the presidential transition period, Eisenhower took aside the incoming president and warned him about the dangers to America's position in the world if

Laotian and Vietnamese communists took over Laos.[22] The growing effort in Vietnam would be threatened, and the United States would look weak throughout Asia if Washington allowed Laos to be taken over and could not protect South Vietnam and Thailand. In fifteen years, this tiny country would be ignored by the United States and the world again. Yet Eisenhower and Kennedy spent considerable parts of their briefings on Laos. Laos was the "cork in the bottle. If Laos fell, then Thailand, the Philippines, and of course Chiang Kai-shek [Taiwan] would go," Eisenhower said during one of their transition meetings.[23] At a National Security Council session near the end of his administration, Eisenhower warned his advisors similarly, saying, "If Laos were lost, the rest of Southeast Asia would follow, and the gateway to India would be opened [to communists]."[24]

Eisenhower's fears—his obsessions about Laos, really—reflected a broader worry about the small kingdom among American leaders. It already had become a coveted prize by the 1950s, although the country would not enter the American public's consciousness until 1960. As far back as the early 1950s, when the Viet Minh had invaded Laos and nearly overrun the country, some American officials had seen how Laos, its long spine running across Southeast Asia, essentially protected the rest of the continent.[25] American partners such as Thailand also viewed Laos as an essential buffer against the spread of communism; the Thais would send whole divisions to war in Laos.[26] Reflecting American officials' growing interest in Laos, the *New York Times* devoted more than three times the newspaper space, in column inches, to Laos in 1960, the year Kennedy was elected, than it did to Vietnam.[27] The *Times* had devoted more space to Laos even though the administration of Eisenhower's predecessor, Harry S. Truman, had allowed France to try to reclaim its Indochinese colonies after World War II, and the Eisenhower administration had played an essential role in keeping France fighting as long as it did in Vietnam by paying for over 75 percent of the French war effort. "Although it is hard to recall that context today, Vietnam [at the beginning of Kennedy's term] was a peripheral crisis," reported the Pentagon Papers, an analysis of the US war in Indochina commissioned internally by the Office of the Secretary of Defense and eventually leaked to the American public. "Even within Southeast Asia, [Vietnam] received far less of the administration's and the world's attention than did Laos."[28]

After France gave up its attempt to keep its Indochinese empire in 1954, the Eisenhower administration had made a series of decisions that increasingly involved the United States in Vietnam, allowing the South Vietnamese government in 1956 to cancel elections planned for both North and South, and sending military advisors to train the South Vietnamese. The White House did not seem to have made similar commitments in Laos.

Yet Laos had not truly been ignored: in 1959 and 1960 Eisenhower actually spent more time with his National Security Council discussing Laos than he did Vietnam, at least according to declassified records. By the end of the 1950s, the CIA had built up its station in Laos so that it dwarfed the actual foreign service component of the American Embassy in Vientiane. "Already in 1958 . . . they [the CIA] had half the [Laotian] ministers on their payroll," recalled Christian Chapman, who served as the chief political officer at the US Embassy in Laos.[29] The agency also had created its own private front airline, Civil Air Transport, which operated across Asia, including in Laos.[30]

President Kennedy held the first foreign policy–related press conference of his administration about Laos in March 1961. Indeed, no foreign policy issue consumed more of the initial months of Kennedy's presidency than Laos, according to Kennedy's biographer Robert Dallek.[31] "It is, I think, important for all Americans to understand this difficult and potentially dangerous problem [in Laos]," Kennedy began at the March press conference. As he spoke, the president stood in front of a map of Laos with menacing—although somewhat factually incorrect—blotches on it that were supposed to represent the Laotian and Vietnamese communists' expanding territory in the country.[32] "[Laos] has been steadily before the administration as the most immediate of the problems that we found upon taking office," Kennedy declared. "Laos is far away from America, but the world is small . . . [Laos's] own safety runs with the safety of us all."[33]

With Eisenhower and then Kennedy paying so much attention, American analysts would scramble to learn about the tiny kingdom. The US Embassy in Laos began to expand and would become a vast complex. The United States helped broker the 1962 Geneva accords, signed by the United States, the Soviet Union, North Vietnam, South Vietnam, and China (among other countries), which committed all outside powers to respecting Laos's neutrality and not sending forces into the country. Then all of the signers ignored the accords. The US government maintained the fiction of the accords, however. Washington opted instead for a covert war in Laos, the first such secret, CIA-run war in American history.

Operation Momentum started small in 1961. At the beginning, the war was to have a light footprint: just a few CIA officers training and arming Hmong, bloodying the Vietnamese and Laotian communists with guerilla attacks, and then vanishing. The Hmong would fight for themselves and for their land and freedom, with American training and weapons. In Laos, remembered Richard Secord, a US Air Force officer who served in Momentum on loan to the CIA, "the war . . . was the reverse image of the war in Vietnam. In Laos, we [the anti-communist forces] were the guerillas. The Pathet Lao and the North Vietnamese army held some of the towns and most of the roads."[34] (In truth, the Pathet Lao and North Vietnamese held roads in Laos in the northeast and east, but not in central and southern Laos until late in the war.) In South Vietnam, the South Vietnamese army and the United States held the roads and the towns but often could not stray more than a mile from the road without risking being attacked by communist forces.

But as Laos became a bigger priority for the agency, the program would balloon in men and budget. More and more Americans would arrive. It would grow into a massive undertaking run by CIA operatives on the ground, and by the agency and its allies in the Lao capital and back in Washington. The United States would build a vast proxy army of hill tribes in Laos—mostly Hmong but also several other ethnic minorities—that would number in the tens of thousands.

Overall, by the end of the war in 1975, some two hundred thousand Laotians, both civilians and military, had perished, including at least thirty thousand Hmong.[35] These casualties comprised about one-tenth of the total population of Laos at the beginning of the war. Nearly twice as many Laotians were wounded by ground fighting and by bombing, and 750,000 of them—more than a quarter of Laos's total population—were refugees. Over seven hundred Americans died, almost all of them CIA operatives, contractors, or US military men working on loan to the CIA, although many of the American deaths would not be revealed to the public for decades.[36]

In the most heavily bombed part of the country—a high, strategically located plateau in the middle of Laos, called the Plain of Jars, the American bombing runs almost never paused. Of the roughly 150,000 people who lived on the Plain of Jars before the 1960s, only about 9,000 remained at the end of the decade.[37] After the war, one-third of the bombs dropped on Laos remained in the ground and undetonated.[38]

The secret war would transform the lives of American operatives and the hill tribes they fought with just as clearly as it would devastate the lives of Laotian civilians. And above all, the war would transform the CIA.

Although the agency had existed for fifteen years before the Laos operation began in earnest, it was a relatively small player in the American policy-making apparatus before the Laos war. The agency concentrated on intelligence and political work, like trying to overthrow foreign governments believed unfriendly to the United States, and not on managing whole wars. But a US government that had assumed global responsibilities in the years after World War II faced an American public that, following the bloody stalemate in the Korean War, which killed roughly 36,000 Americans while resulting in a shaky cease-fire at the 38th Parallel in Korea, had little desire to send American troops to fight more foreign wars. A secret war, and one that utilized relatively few Americans, was a safer choice politically.

Meanwhile, in 1961 the CIA's leaders desired a much greater role for the agency, but they could never match the US military's influence over policy toward Europe or Northeast Asia. Now they saw a unique opportunity to increase the agency's powers. The CIA found in Laos a country where it already had amassed influence, in the heart of a Cold War battlefield, and which had been largely ignored by the American military. These CIA leaders saw that an inexpensive—in American money and lives, at least—proxy war could be a template for fights in other places around the world, at a time when presidents were looking for ways to continue the Cold War without going through Congress or committing ground troops.

Laos would be a dramatic innovation for the CIA; a transformative experience. The agency had never mounted a significant paramilitary operation before the secret war, let alone one as massive as the Laos operation would become. In fact, no spy agency anywhere in the world had launched such a massive paramilitary operation, including air strikes, such large contingents of forces, and the overall management of battle strategy at times. The Laos war would prove the dividing line for the CIA; afterward, its leadership would see paramilitary operations as an essential part of the agency's mission, and many other US policy makers would come to accept that the CIA was now as much a part of waging war as the traditional branches of the armed forces.

Indeed, the experience that the CIA gained in paramilitary operations in Laos would serve the agency well, and in many other parts of the globe. Although it mounted other large paramilitary operations after the Laos war, none of these operations employed over a hundred thousand people, even at its height. None involved the massive airpower of the Laos war, either. Laos war veterans would lead future CIA paramilitary operations in the Americas, South Asia, and other regions, as the agency focused increasingly on killing rather than spying. Having Laos experience would be seen within the agency as desirable for paramilitary officers looking to move to other locations around the globe. The shift begun in Laos essentially culminated in the years after September 2001, when the CIA focused intensely on paramilitary operations. By the 2010s, the CIA oversaw targeted killing missions all over the world, ran proxy armies in Africa and Asia, and helped manage its own drone strike program designed to kill members of the Islamic State in Syria (ISIS) and other parts of the Middle East.

The CIA now has become such a central part of war fighting that even the other large US government agencies, which during the early era of the Cold War tried tenaciously to block the CIA from gaining more influence in Washington, have largely accepted the CIA's massively expanded war-making duties—the duties it took on first in Laos. Occasionally, a Cabinet official such as Donald Rumsfeld, secretary of defense under President George W. Bush, has tried to take back war powers from the CIA, with little success; though Rumsfeld attempted to beef up military intelligence's ability to conduct operations overseas, the CIA blocked him until it was allowed to oversee the Pentagon's intelligence operations.[39] Rumsfeld relented. The resigned acceptance by heads of other Cabinet agencies of the CIA's massive, growing paramilitary capabilities is *the* biggest sign that a militarized CIA has become a permanent part of the American government.

In the early 1960s, most of the CIA leadership was "all for a war in Laos," recalled Robert Amory Jr., who served as the agency's deputy director. "They thought that [Laos] was a great place to have a war."[40]

Chapter 2

The CIA's First War

LAOS WOULD PROVE SO SUCCESSFUL—FOR PRESIDENTS,
and for the CIA, that is—that it would become a template for a new
type of large, secret war for decades to come. The CIA, which originally had employed only a handful of warriors—to train foreign military forces and pilot CIA supplies, mostly—would eventually become
like another branch of the US Special Forces. The CIA, indeed, would
become a paramilitary organization whose primary purpose was killing and war fighting.

Still, after the final withdrawal of US diplomats and aid from Vietnam in 1975, the Laos war seemed forgotten by most Americans. And
despite efforts by historians and journalists to find out more about the
Laos war, the CIA refused to declassify reports and cables issued by its
clandestine operatives in Laos, and, for years, many former Hmong
and CIA fighters avoided talking to anyone about their experiences.
Revelations about CIA abuses that emerged in the mid-1970s, as congressional committees found out that the agency had tried to assassinate foreign leaders and had spied on American antiwar protestors,
made the CIA even more secretive about discussing its activities with
journalists than it had been before. In the past twenty years, many of
the CIA's contemporaneous reports and analyses of the Laos war have
been released, often as part of now-declassified CIA and air force histories of the Laos operation.[1] Those histories reveal many new details
about the CIA's operations in Laos.

The one truly outstanding popular account of the secret war,

Shooting at the Moon: The Story of America's Clandestine War in Laos, first published in 1995 (under a different title) by Southeast Asia historian Roger Warner, had to rely primarily on first-person accounts of the operation, with minimal documentation from the agency. It was a gripping story, but the book said little about how the CIA and American foreign policy changed in and after Laos. Before the CIA's release of its Laos histories, no story of the war could be complete.

Laos's government was also paranoid about controlling information after the end of the war. Perhaps the most repressive regime in the world outside of North Korea, the Laotian government has repeatedly imprisoned both local and foreign journalists simply for reporting in some parts of the country, and jailed any government opponents who dared to criticize the Vientiane regime. For decades, it was virtually impossible to visit parts of Laos and talk to people about their wartime experiences. Hmong-majority areas of the country, where the communist government had committed severe human rights abuses after the end of the war, were kept off-limits to foreigners. Laos's relations with the United States also remained in the deep freeze for decades after 1975; the two countries maintained diplomatic relations but had minimal contact between senior leaders.

The United States and Laos built closer relations during the George W. Bush administration, and in 2012 Secretary of State Hillary Clinton became the first senior American official to visit the country since the war years. Thawing relations between the two nations resulted in some American veterans of the operation visiting Laos, and this seemed to spark their interest in talking more about the war. In the 2000s and 2010s, it also became possible to travel around Laos and interview people about the war, as Laos opened up to the world again. Meanwhile, the Thai government published its own account of the fighting by Thai soldiers in Laos and Vietnam, shedding light on Thai policy and on how US leaders managed the secret war.[2] Increasingly, Thai and foreign scholars began interviewing Thais who had fought in the Indochina wars or made Thai policy about Indochina.[3]

The Hmong who migrated to the United States after the communists took power in Laos in 1975 also have become more willing to discuss the secret war objectively. This kind of discussion was hardly possible in the immediate postwar period, when any Hmong who criticized the war could be ostracized from the Hmong American community. And as the war has faded into memory and many of the key players—both Hmong and American—have died, they have left behind candid memoirs, journals, and other accounts of the secret war and the role of the CIA.

The impact of the war in Laos did not vanish, even though much of the world seemed to move on. And as it becomes easier to pry open old CIA files, to visit Laos and observe the impact of the war on the ground, and to convince the remaining Laos operatives to speak about their time there, we can see that Laos had a transformative impact on how the United States fights wars around the world, on the power of the Central Intelligence Agency, and on the men and women who fought the secret war.

Many of the Americans on the ground in Southeast Asia would end the war utterly shattered. Yet back in Washington, the conflict had a far different impact. The CIA had managed a war fought on the cheap that held the communists in Laos to a virtual standstill for years. The agency had also allowed presidential administrations, both Democratic and Republican, to manage a clandestine war without having to go through Congress for approval. "The CIA in Laos became a kind of archetype," noted Fred Branfman, a long-time aid worker in Laos who later played a role in exposing the secret war.[4] The Laos war became an archetype for agency paramilitary operations—and a new way for the president to unilaterally declare war and then secretly order massive attacks, often using aerial weaponry.[5]

By looking back at the CIA's first real war, we can begin to answer questions about American war making that persist today. Who should have the power to wage war? What happens when these powers shift to the CIA and away from the Pentagon, which, for all its flaws, is far more transparent than the agency? How can a secret proxy war be monitored or eventually curtailed? What happens to the entire idea of war when an attack can be launched remotely, with minimal manpower, and carried out by machines: bombers in the Laos war and unmanned drones today?

The CIA war in Laos raises other fundamental questions about the American way of war as well. To some CIA operatives working in Laos who eventually soured on the operation, Laos became a cautionary tale of what happens when the United States enlists a proxy army, knowing little about it, and does not have a plan for what to do with it if the war is lost. "We had only minimal understanding of the history, culture, and politics of the people we wanted to aid [in Laos]," recalled Richard Holm, who served there as a young CIA case officer.[6]

At the beginning of the operation, both the Hmong and many CIA operatives believed that the fight was to keep a rough kind of freedom, or even democracy, in Laos. Yet as the war went on, and escalated in the size of firefights and the amount of bombing, many American leaders began to see the operation as less about saving Laos and more as a means to kill and maim North Vietnamese, and thus help the war effort in Vietnam. After the end of the secret war, US Air Force brigadier general Heinie Aderholt, who worked with the agency on Momentum, summarized neatly the views of many US officials about America's strategic interests in Laos. "What would have happened if we hadn't gone into Laos? There would probably have been more than ten thousand more Americans killed in South Vietnam, because we tied up ten divisions of first-line North Vietnamese soldiers," Aderholt said. "It's easier to lose your Hmong people than to lose Americans. It doesn't make as bad publicity at home."[7]

The CIA would end up commissioning multiple studies of the war, which the agency considered a success. Yet for all the studies, and all the postwar celebrating inside the CIA, no strategy emerged for handling CIA proxies in the future, many of whom wound up being treated much like the Hmong.

Chapter 3

Vang Pao, Bill Lair, Tony Poe, and Bill Sullivan

SMALL-ARMS FIRE SPLATTERED INTO THE LIMESTONE rocks and muddy ground around Tony Poe, who crouched at the top of the hill overlooking the Laotian village of Ban Hang Non. *Pop, splat, pop-pop-pop!* The firing seemed to be getting closer to Poe's position, which was surrounded by a makeshift network of trenches and booby traps. Heavier mortar fire rocketed in the background from the North Vietnamese and from his own side's mortars.

Groups of North Vietnamese soldiers, in threes and fours, were moving steadily toward the crest of the ridge, covering themselves with bursts of machine gun fire. Poe could see hundreds more North Vietnamese soldiers moving forward. To his left, Hmong fighters let loose with bursts of fire from a recoilless rifle.[1]

Poe stood up and started aiming his M-1 semiautomatic rifle and squeezing off rounds at North Vietnamese who were coming at him, faster now than before. He would shoot, crouch, take quick aim, and shoot again. At the same time, he would yell out instructions to some of the Hmong as if they were training at the firing range he normally ran—helping them sight their rifles and learn how to find an enemy in their sights. Poe ran through two ammunition clips in his M-1, and then looked over the barricade. The incoming fire seemed to have stopped for a second.

Poe moved down the hill thirty feet, to check one of the North Vietnamese bodies. Just as he bent down over it, a flash exploded right in front of Poe, from a bit of scrub, and he was thrown into the air. When he landed, he rushed to get up, his hand on his M-1, but fell again.[2]

Poe tried to stand a second time and almost threw up. He looked down at his torso and found, to his surprise, that he had been shot in his hip and possibly his legs as well. "You feel an electrical shock as the bullet's going through you, but then it hit the bone on the exit, and that's what knocks you all over," Poe explained. "I flipped in the air two or three times."[3] Stunned temporarily, he had not felt any pain up until now—maybe two minutes after the initial flash—but as he saw the blood rushing out of his hip, he almost passed out. He tried moving his legs, but they seemed numb. Poe looked to his left, where the hill sloped down slightly, and a group of five or six North Vietnamese soldiers dressed in jungle camouflage adorned with tiger stripes were panting and running uphill. Poe could feel his mind slipping, and he reached down to the hand grenades he had clasped to his belt and chest. Several Hmong lay dead on the ridge, and at least one of the Thai paratroopers near him was seriously wounded.

The North Vietnamese and Laotian communists had launched a major offensive all around the village of Ban Hang Non during the winter dry season of 1964 and early 1965. Most of the fighting men were North Vietnamese, and they clearly ran the operation, with the Pathet Lao operating in a subsidiary role: after towns were taken, the Pathet Lao would then bring in political officers to win over locals. The North Vietnamese had driven many of the Laotian anti-communist troops out of the surrounding province already when Poe and the Thai military trainers were sent to help stiffen the resistance in and around the town. Poe's battle had started in earnest on January 19, 1965.

Tony Poe, whose real name was Anthony Poshepny but who had shortened his surname years ago to seem more all-American and less Eastern European, had nearly twenty years' experience in firefights by 1965. In fact, Tony Poe had never really held a job that did not involve fighting, and he could not remember a time when he wasn't around guns. When he was just eight, his brother accidentally shot him in the stomach with the family rifle. He had nearly bled to death, requiring multiple transfusions to survive.[4] Poe enlisted in the US Marines in 1942, with the consent of his mother, and been assigned to the 2nd Parachute Battalion.

Poe loved the marines' ethos of constant drilling and the marines' tradition of taking on the most dangerous, possibly bloody assignments. Even decades after he was discharged from the marines after World War II, he continued to wear his marines hat and fatigues almost every day on the job in every Asian hot spot where he worked.[5] His wide body and muscular arms made it relatively easy for Poe to master marines boot camp and then to lug massive amounts of gear up island beaches, which he remembered doing for much of his time in World War II. Charles Davis, a helicopter pilot in Laos for the CIA's contract airline, described Poe, twenty years after the end of World War II, as "a big bear of a man with wide shoulders and the rugged looks of a middle-aged Ernest Hemingway ... He is a true member of the warrior class [who] truly needs to straddle the thin line between life and death."[6]

During World War II, the 2nd Parachute Battalion served as one of the hammers of General Douglas MacArthur's island-hopping campaign, smashing its way up Pacific atoll after Pacific atoll. Poe's own estimations of the extent of his battle experience and his kills could be unreliable, but other battalion marines who served in as many Pacific engagements as Poe wound up in multiple deadly close encounters with Japanese defenders. By the time he arrived in Laos, Poe had been injured in battle at least six times.

When World War II was over, Poe had found himself ill-suited for civilian life. Before the war, that would have been tough luck for Poe, but as the Cold War expanded, the once-isolationist United States suddenly needed a host of professional warriors who could skip from spot to spot wherever required. Some of these men would be employed directly by the US government, in the CIA and other agencies; others, in a new step, would be outsourced to private outfits that provided fighting men, pilots, trainers, suppliers, and other contractors for the CIA and the military.

So instead of giving up fighting and settling reluctantly into American life, Poe followed the current of Cold War American policy in Asia. When the Korean War broke out in 1950, and the Truman administration sent US forces to the Korean Peninsula, Poe signed up for a job training Korean saboteurs and other infiltrators to slip into the North and attack infrastructure. Then when Korea settled into a cold peace, he spent three years training Tibetan and Muslim insurgents who were fighting Beijing as part of a CIA program to harass Mao Tse-tung's regime. Next, Poe helped train guerillas trying to overthrow the left-leaning (though not communist) postindependence government of Indonesia.

In 1961 Poe arrived in Laos to help train the Hmong, who had become the center of Operation Momentum. Poe realized he liked the place a great deal. He was bewildered by the lowland Lao culture, full of veiled threats and incomprehensible politics, where people smiled quietly even when angry, but the Hmong were more straightforward and, he felt, much easier to deal with than lowland people. And Laos, a war that seemed without end, meant a long tour in the field.

That was fine with Poe; he had little desire to go back to urban Western life, or even to enjoy the basic comforts of the twentieth century, like a hot shower. Poe had built a persona around himself as the ultimate hard man. He told people he had advised the young Dalai Lama while training Tibetan guerillas (not true), that he carried a boxing mouth guard in his pocket at all times in case he got into fistfights (maybe true), and that he had killed fifteen men while fighting at Iwo Jima in 1945 (quite possibly true.) In Laos, Poe told Hmong fighters that he would pay a bounty for the severed ears of communist fighters; soon he wound up with several bags full of dried human ears.[7] Poe mailed one bag to the US Embassy in Vientiane to demonstrate how many communists his men allegedly were killing; he recalled that a secretary there opened the bag, after it had been rotting in the steaming hot embassy compound all weekend, and immediately became sick.[8]

Yet despite Poe's bravado and sometime recklessness, which his bosses worried would blow the agency's cover during secret operations, even his harshest critics admitted that he possessed enormous talent for fighting and for teaching men to fight. He still had a job in the CIA simply because of his skill. "Within the agency, you had a lot of guys who admired him," said Bill Lair. "The big wheels at the agency all knew exactly what was happening too [with Poe's ear slicing and other wild antics], and they didn't say a damn word."[9]

———

Now, with North Vietnamese coming at him and dead lying around him, Poe showed that talent for fighting again. He pulled the pin out of a grenade on his belt, waited a second, and then tossed it quickly down the hill. The tiny bomb exploded right in front of several oncoming enemy soldiers. He threw another.[10] Poe glanced again down the hill. The groaning from North Vietnamese fighters below him had stopped. A wisp of smoke curled up toward him.

Still, Poe assumed that more North Vietnamese forces were regrouping farther down near the town; they outnumbered his men significantly, and he had hardly killed all of the communist troops. Bone fragments pushed through the skin on his hip, his stomach leaked blood, and he was out of grenades. He half crawled back to the spot where he and the Hmong had laid fortifications. The Thais who'd been there were all dead, but several Hmong soldiers still manned the post. Poe told them to flee west with the families who'd left the town.[11] He then found the remaining outpost radio and called one of the helicopter pilots based in Thailand to come get him and the most wounded Hmong.[12]

The helicopter couldn't pick them up under fire, so Poe, who had to poke his legs to feel pain and be able to keep walking, led the wounded on a five-mile hike up over a ridge to a safer location. As the American walked through the night, blood leaked out of the makeshift bandages he had wrapped around his legs.[13] When they had reached a safer location, Poe lay down on a makeshift stretcher that he'd helped fabricate and pointed a mirror toward the night sky to reflect light from the chopper and signal the pilot.

Poe's one-man stand had bought some time and allowed many of the Hmong fighters and families from the area to retreat westward. And he had saved himself. The chopper soared west toward Thailand, safety, and a modern hospital. Medics laid Poe out on the helicopter floor as he passed in and out of consciousness.[14]

As the medics probed Poe's injuries, the wounded man sat up suddenly and grabbed one of the doctors, Charles Weldon, by the neck—hard. "Where are we going? Where are we going?" Poe demanded. Told that they were heading toward the hospital in northeast Thailand, Poe screamed, "No! Must go back! Must go back! Turn around! Have to pick up the wounded!"[15] Despite a bullet wound in his pelvis that had left a hole bigger than a quarter, Poe dragged himself to the edge of the helicopter door and gesticulated furiously toward a spot on the ground where he had told seven more wounded Hmong soldiers to wait for evacuation. The helicopter pilot dutifully circled back, picked up the seven Hmong, and lifted off again for Thailand. Once the wounded Hmong had been loaded, Poe lost consciousness completely.[16]

As Tony Poe's firefight erupted, Bill Lair sat in the wooden bungalow that served as the CIA station at Udorn Air Base in northeast

Thailand, close to the border of Laos. Radio dispatches had started to come in from Sam Neua, reporting high casualties and that the Hmong forces were retreating. One radio operator told Lair that Tony Poe had been leading the fighting in the hills. Lair said nothing, his rough, square-jawed face its usual blank mask, rimmed by his bookish, thick spectacles, but it was hard to hide his irritation. Poe was there to train and help command the Hmong fighters from a distance; Lair didn't want him leading the fighting and potentially exposing the deep CIA involvement in the Hmong fighters' anti-communist battles.

Bill Lair had handled Tony Poe for five years now, essentially since the Laos war began. He hadn't asked CIA headquarters for Poe, nor had Poe asked to work on an operation run by Lair, the way that some field operatives would request to serve under bosses they had worked with before. The two men often could not stand being in the same room for more than ten or fifteen minutes. Poe spent many nights eating pig parts, rice balls, and chicken feet, downing local whiskey alongside some of the Hmong officers he liked, and then falling into bed, dropping whiskey bottles on the floor of his hut. At night at Udorn, Lair usually read field reports or write-ups of radio dispatches from Laos and turned in quietly in order to get up very early in the morning and start his daily routine again.

By the time the war in Laos started, Poe and Lair were both CIA lifers, but they had proceeded down different career paths. Poe moved from job to job and from place to place; he knew how to fight and how to teach people to fight. As for Lair, the longer he stayed in Southeast Asia, the more he became convinced that the agency's policy of moving around operatives made no sense—and the less tolerant he became of some of the men sent to work for him who had never bothered to learn much about the place they were going.

James William Lair had grown up in the Texas Panhandle near the Oklahoma border, a place as flat and featureless as the hills of Laos were wild. Lair had grown up around farmers and oil-patch

drillers and cattle drivers, most of whom never left Texas or Oklahoma. Lair had seemed likely to stay as well. Few people in his home-
town of Borger would have predicted during the boy's high school
years—when Lair played basketball and football and did a bit of oil-
rig work in the summer to prepare himself for a life as a driller or an
oil engineer—that Lair would eventually manage a billion-dollar war
in a land ten thousand miles away.

But Lair possessed certain skills that would prove crucial to a
career in intelligence. To begin with, he had a quiet ability to persuade people in face-to-face meetings, and to seem utterly earnest
and convinced of whatever he was talking about.[17] He admired his
grandfather, who raised him after Lair's father basically vanished. His
grandfather, Lair said, used salesmanship to find jobs as a ranch hand
and small farmer, even during some of the toughest economic times
in Texas.[18] That type of salesmanship, Lair reflected, was critical for a
case officer in the CIA, because "If you can't talk [people] into doing
things, you're worthless, and you're of no use to anybody."[19]

With the outbreak of World War II, Lair joined the US Army 3rd
Armored Division, which rolled through France and Belgium and
into Germany. When the war ended, Lair attended Texas A&M University, but he found himself less than enthusiastic about the prospect
of a life in oil engineering or rig work.[20] During his senior year, he
saw a small note posted on an A&M bulletin board about possibil-
ities in what appeared to be intelligence work; Lair attended the information session. When it became clear that the recruitment was for
the CIA, he was hooked: the job offered a way out of his life path and
seemed to promise an outlet for the curiosity and skills of persuasion
Lair believed he possessed.[21] When the CIA offer came, Lair accepted
almost immediately.

After his training program ended, Lair reported to CIA headquarters in the Washington suburbs, where an officer in charge of new
recruits told him he was being sent to Thailand—in one week.[22] Lair
had not chosen Thailand, a Southeast Asian kingdom that had en-

joyed a close relationship with Britain and was building a closer one with the United States. But the agency had assigned him (under the cover of a CIA front company) to train Thais preparing for a possible Chinese invasion of the kingdom. Thailand harbored many Taiwanese soldiers who had fled the Chinese civil war, won decisively by Mao Tse-tung's communists in 1949, and Thailand was run by a group of right-wing generals who promoted virulently anti-Chinese policies.[23] American military assistance to Thailand was expanding rapidly, from $4.5 million in 1951 to $56 million in 1953. The CIA's presence in Thailand was increasing as well.[24]

Lair arrived in Southeast Asia on March 1, 1951.[25] Thailand's smooth diplomats quietly defused the threat of imminent war from Beijing, and Lair could have been transferred to another posting. But Lair did not want to leave. He had put in the effort to learn Thai, a singsongy and fiendishly difficult language in which every syllable could be said in one of five tones, each of which gave the word a different meaning. Lair had realized that the Southeast Asian culture and way of life suited him.[26] Many other Americans in Bangkok, who had come to the country as part of the growing American military alliance or to exploit a booming economy, complained constantly about life in the kingdom. They griped about Thais' reticence to express their innermost thoughts—frankness with anyone but the closest relatives was taboo in Thai culture—the difficulty of understanding Thai colleagues, and how hard it was to maintain a placid, easygoing facial expression even when you were boiling angry. The ability to save face, to stay cool, was a trait valued highly in most of Southeast Asia, including Thailand and Laos, which were not only neighbors but also shared many cultural traits. The Thais called it *jai yen,* or "cool heart."

Lair chose to play by the Southeast Asia way, since it actually suited his natural demeanor. In Bangkok, he adopted what friends came to call the "Lair face."[27] He would listen to CIA briefings or discussions expressionlessly, seeming to blend into the walls. Visiting agency officials sometimes wouldn't notice Lair at first in a meeting in Thailand or Laos, or they would quickly dismiss him because he wasn't aggressive in dealing with Westerners like other CIA operatives in the field. Only after all the Americans had said all they could would Lair begin to talk, his voice slow and full of gravity, able to command the room with his detail and precision.

Lair's bosses in the CIA's Far East division, which ran all of the agency's programs in the Pacific, had indeed wanted Lair to move to another post, but the shy Texan wanted to stay in Indochina. The agency usually tried to move clandestine operatives from one country to the next every few years, to ensure that they did not start confusing the interests of the locals with American interests. But Lair had been able to bend this unwritten rule, since he had convinced the Far East division that the CIA should take advantage of his accumulated knowledge of Indochina, which could be essential as the United States became more involved in the region's conflict. "There was some reluctance to keep me in Thailand, but I convinced them," Lair said later, still proud of his sales pitch from sixty years earlier.[28]

Lair's bosses let him stay to work on a new project: building up Thailand's elite police paratroopers as a force that could be airlifted anywhere Thailand needed. The paratrooper program grew into what Lair remembered as a true partnership in which Lair shared his whole professional life with the Thai policemen. The police paratroopers learned about guerilla warfare, airborne landings, and other tactics of war; in reality, they became like another army unit. Lair learned about the geography of Thailand, Laos, and the whole region, learned more of the language, and learned how to find intelligence sources. Through a CIA front company, the agency gave the police a total of $35 million.[29] Lair ate many of his meals with the Thais and was invited into the homes of some of the paratroopers—very rare in Thailand, where people usually held social events at restaurants and did not even invite their closest friends to their homes.

Throughout the 1950s, as Lair worked with the Thai paratroopers, he started to think more about whether his project with them could be replicated elsewhere. He had heard about the Hmong from CIA operatives coming back from Laos, who reported that the Hmong were by far the most effective fighters in the tiny country, which had been caught in the French Indochina War.[30]

Lair read up on Hmong history and culture, interviewing French officers who passed through Bangkok and CIA operatives who had dealt with the Hmong.[31] He might not have studied the hill tribe like an anthropologist would, but from what he understood about the Hmong, Lair viewed them as essentially democratic, in their own way, building a consensus within their clans and then, ultimately, among many different clans.[32]

Lair had no clear plan yet for what he would do with his growing file of note cards on the Hmong. When France ended its effort to maintain Indochinese colonies in 1954, it signed an accord that called for Vietnam, now split temporarily into North and South, to reunite eventually, with nationwide elections to be held within two years. These 1954 Geneva accords resulted not only in a plan for Vietnamese peace and reunification but also in an agreement that gave Laos full independence. (Laos had already taken control of almost all its affairs save foreign policy.) The Geneva agreement created a commission of neutral states to monitor areas of Laos and help prevent foreign troops from entering Laos and stop flare-ups of fighting, but it did not require the communist or anti-communist Laotian forces to disarm completely. The commission would prove ineffective, divided among communist and non-communist members, and with no real power to do anything if it caught foreign soldiers entering Laos or militaries preparing for battle.

By the middle of the decade, the agency began placing clandestine officers all across Laos. By 1958, the vacuum that France had left by withdrawing most of its economic and military aid to the Laotian government had been filled by the United States.

The Eisenhower administration also had formed the Southeast

Asia Treaty Organization, or SEATO, a collective defense pact that was supposed to resemble NATO in the North Atlantic and which included Thailand and the Philippines.

Lair assumed that the growing American presence in Southeast Asia, which included not only increased aid for the non-communist government in Laos but also American training for the South Vietnamese military, an increasingly close relationship with Thailand's ruling generals, and a mutual defense agreement with Cambodia, would strengthen the freedoms of people in the region. The US presence in Southeast Asia could work, Lair thought, as long as Washington kept a light footprint in the operation. He was unaware that his conception that the United States could intervene in places and be seen as a beacon of democracy closely resembled one major strain of thinking among some American policy makers. Advocates of intervention in Southeast Asia during the Eisenhower administration argued that the United States could promote a democratic future for Asians that was neither communist nor tied to the old colonial masters. Since Japan's rapid sweep through Southeast Asia during World War II had shattered the myth of British and French invincibility, Asians would never accept another colonial power. The United States, however, was a force that could wield influence without being perceived as colonizing.

One leading American intelligence officer and counterinsurgency specialist, Edward Lansdale, who would take over CIA operations in Saigon, famously made this argument. Lansdale had become renowned in policy circles for helping the Philippine government crush a communist rebellion in the 1950s. Leaders in the Philippines, supported by the US government, the former colonial power, achieved this victory partly by winning over the population to supporting a non-communist but also strongly nationalist government, led by Ramon Magsaysay, a World War II hero greatly admired by the poor. After his triumph in the Philippines, Lansdale believed that the United States could foment a similar strategy in other places in

Asia, finding and supporting local leaders who would win over average men and women and undermine the appeal of communism.[33] Lansdale contended that the United States would be a different sort of world power, with local allies who would enjoy legitimacy among the populace, so that the United States would be able to fight communism not only on the battlefield but also in the hearts and minds of average people.[34] He would find out that the Philippines, and Magsaysay, were the exception. The Philippine leaders did indeed combine a great respect for American power and close cultural ties to Americans with genuine legitimacy at home.[35] But the United States could not find many other Asian leaders willing to work as partners who also enjoyed great legitimacy among their publics. To many other Southeast Asians, the United States' vast influence and military strength made it look like a new colonial power, no matter what US officials said.

Bill Lair had not met Lansdale, but he shared the man's essential beliefs: that Southeast Asians could be helped in their fight for democracy as long as Asians led the battles, and that the United States could avoid being seen as a colonial power provided that it did not actually try to take over Asian territory. They were convictions that Lair would maintain for nearly a decade of service in the CIA, and ones that ultimately would help doom his career in the agency.

As Lair questioned French diplomats and intelligence officers who came through Bangkok about the Hmong, he heard about several of the hill tribe's most powerful leaders, who came from three or four of the clans that had traditionally wielded the most influence. He also heard a great deal about a young Hmong man from a simple background. During France's war against the Viet Minh, which frequently spilled into Laos, French officers regarded most of the Hmong as tough fighters but not capable of leading—in politics or on the battlefield. Even the few Hmong who had received some French educa tion were scorned by hardened French officers when it came to their leadership skills.[36] Yet there was an exception to the French officers' disdain for Hmong leaders.

French officers had quickly taken to Vang Pao, a squat, five-foot-five-inch man with an oval face, high cheekbones, and skin pocked with blot-like birthmarks. He maintained a wisp of a mustache and, sometimes, a small, rectangular strip of a goatee right under the middle of his bottom lip; it would have looked hip to an urbanite in the 2010s, but the goatee came mostly from Vang Pao's impatience with taking the time to shave. In addition, he seemed willing to lead his men into bloody encounters. As the historian Mai Na M. Lee notes, other Hmong leaders, such as the more urbane Touby Lyfoung, the older Hmong man who originally served as Vang Pao's mentor, somehow seemed to avoid battles in the French Indochina War that involved much shooting; they stuck to politics. Vang Pao, she writes in her book *Dreams of the Hmong Kingdom: The Quest for Legitimation in French Indochina, 1850–1960*, was the right man for a bloody campaign.[37]

Vang Pao wore his black, wiry hair in a military-style cut that made it stick almost straight up, and though his moon-shaped face could break out into a wide grin, his normal look was one of fierce concentration, as if he might let out a scream at any moment. He dressed in a loose, green, army officer–style collared shirt mostly unadorned with medals or trinkets. His hands and forearms bore the scars of smacking through brush and trees on long marches. He always kept his favorite combat knife, a long dagger with the blade curved just at the tip, in a pouch on his belt. He was rarely without a gun strapped to his body in either a shoulder holster or a waist holster.

Vang Pao won a reputation with the French and the Hmong for his forceful command, his fierceness, and his boundless energy. His mentor Touby Lyfoung, a rich, Francophile Hmong leader from one of the most powerful clans, believed that the young man was a kind of military prodigy—someone who could do little other than fight but who had enormous innate skills in this area. "He is a pure military officer," Touby Lyfoung said of Vang Pao.[38] (Touby Lyfoung's and Vang Pao's relationship later would become more acrimonious, as the protégé gained more and more power.)

Vang Pao loved to walk and rarely sat even for meetings. He could not hold a conversation without interrupting and interjecting ideas nearly every sentence. One CIA officer who dealt with him, Stuart Methven, remembered that Vang Pao "had a reservoir of restless energy and was constantly shifting back and forth on the balls of his feet as he talked."[39]

Vang Pao had several other qualities that made him attractive as an ally. He was from a modest background: He hailed from one of the less powerful Hmong clans, which theoretically might make it easier to work with him. Unlike many Hmong, Vang Pao expressed his loyalty to the Laotian king, Sisavang Vong, though he did not worship Laotian royalty. Still, Vang Pao believed in Laos as a country and would fight the communists not just for the Hmong but for all of Laos.[40] "My men died for the king, I sacrificed men I loved [fighting] for the king," Vang Pao said later. "I believed we Hmong . . . could be integrated into the Laotian nation."[41] When CIA agents and aid workers came to the Hmong regions of Laos, Vang Pao advised them not to learn Hmong but instead to learn the Lao language. "Vang Pao said explicitly, 'Don't speak Hmong. This is Laos,'" recalled Win McKeithen, a former aid worker in Laos.[42]

Hmong society, which numbered about three hundred thousand in Laos by the end of Eisenhower's presidency, was not as stratified as lowland Lao or Thai societies, and Vang Pao's humble background did not stop him from gaining power within Hmong society. Groups of Hmong lived in many other Southeast Asian nations, too, at the time: Thailand, Vietnam, Cambodia, Burma (now Myanmar), and the southwestern portion of China. Although Hmong clan leaders were powerful, they were not all-powerful. Different Hmong clans alternatively clashed with one another and worked together, and leaders could emerge from less prominent clans. This was a sharp contrast from lowland Lao or Thai society, where a small group of men of royal blood dominated politics.

Although Hmong society was not as unequal as others in the region, it was not necessarily democratic in the modern way. And whether Vang Pao was ever really interested in democracy was hard to tell. From an early age, as he began to work with French officers and learn about France and other powerful countries, he appeared fascinated with the French and American systems of government. Vang Pao knew that Hmong society had always valued its freedom from the outside world and its freedom to decide its own fate; he understood that the Hmong had never allowed one ruler to dominate them. Yet to many of the Americans who met him, Vang Pao also always had in him a brutal, potentially dictatorial streak. Charlie Weitz, an American CIA contract pilot who worked with Vang Pao, remembered: "I'll never forget the first time I met [Vang Pao.] [His men] were dragging a defector down toward him. As he walked by, he just pulled out his gun, blew the guy's head off, and kept on walking."[43]

Vang Pao seemed to have been born naturally ambitious. His sister remembered him as a cheerful and jocular young boy, but before he was even ten years old, that jocularity had vanished. He had witnessed skirmishes with Japanese troops during World War II, when the Japanese had evicted a caretaker French regime in Laos and were hunting down Hmong who had worked with the French.

Vang Pao was immediately entranced by fighting. He started a formal military career at age fourteen in the waning days of World War II, serving as an aide to Touby Lyfoung, who recognized in the uneducated young man a fierceness that could be a major asset in wartime, and who knew that Vang Pao was unknown to the Japanese officers, allowing him to sneak in and out of Hmong villages without being followed or caught.[44] Vang Pao did not go back to the classroom after that. At fourteen, Vang Pao, who had only spent five years in a school of any kind, and had skipped most of his classes anyway, began decades of battle.

Touby Lyfoung and other older Hmong leaders gave Vang Pao the important job of running secret messages across Hmong country about Japanese movements in Indochina, where Japan was imprisoning hundreds of French officials. Japan had originally allowed French collaborators to maintain control of parts of Indochina. But the Japanese would eventually take direct command of the former Indochinese colonies away from a colonial government led by officials who pledged allegiance to the Vichy French regime that collaborated with Axis powers. After the Japanese were defeated in the war, and France returned to its Indochinese colonies, Vang Pao joined the military police and, ultimately, a military contingent comprised of lowland Lao and hill tribes. The newly formed Laotian army, trained and led mostly by French officers, would fight with the French against Viet Minh forces making incursions into Laos or conducting intelligence raids in Laos. It was the first phase of what would be a decades-long civil war in Laos.

Though still only in his twenties, Vang Pao repeatedly demonstrated his fighting skill and, notably, his ability to win recruits to the national army fighting the Pathet Lao and their Vietnamese backers. Although Vang Pao insisted that he had, from the beginning of his military career, chosen to fight against communism—which he viewed as opposed to the Hmong's freedom—some of his acquaintances suggested that if he had thought the communists would win, he well might have sided with them early on.[45] Still, early in his career, Vang Pao chose the anti-communist side. He toured northern Laos, convincing not only Hmong but also ethnic Lao to join him—a rarity, since many lowland Lao considered the hill tribes barely human, the result of hundreds of years of Laotian education and customs that taught that the tribes were uncultured savages, members of a lower social order. Many wealthy lowland Lao historically expected hill tribes—Hmong, Yao, Khmu, and others—to bow to the ground before them whenever they crossed paths.[46]

French officers eager to cultivate the young Hmong leader pushed him to enter France's military training program in Laos. They even arranged for a plane to air-drop him the entrance exam—and made sure he passed. When it became apparent that the French verbs, with their irregular conjugations, were too hard for the young Hmong officer to understand, the French test proctor looked over the exam and then dictated all the correct test answers.[47]

The French also gave Vang Pao small commands of guerilla teams used to infiltrate enemy encampments and spy or kill. In one engagement during his apprenticeship under the French, Vang Pao and twenty-three other army soldiers ambushed Viet Minh couriers in a small house where the couriers were resting. The Viet Minh prided themselves on their intelligence and their sentries, and on never being caught unaware, even when fighting outside their own country. But they had no warning of Vang Pao's attack. His team killed ten of the couriers on the spot and captured rubber tubes that contained Viet Minh military orders for an upcoming campaign in Laos.[48] When Vang Pao returned to meet with his French commanders, they were elated. By the late 1950s, stories of Vang Pao's fighting exploits had been passed through word of mouth to nearly every Hmong clan in north and central Laos.

The Hmong leader's history of fighting certainly helped Vang Pao's image with other Hmong. As the historian Mai Na M. Lee notes, martial prowess had historically been a critical component for any Hmong man trying to gain a following. The hill tribe had fought many wars, and during an uprising in the French colonial period, some groups of Hmong had proven themselves to be brilliant guerilla fighters. Oratorical skills, which Vang Pao also would demonstrate, mattered too.[49] Lee, like some other Hmong scholars, believes that violence has long played a central role in Hmong mythology and folk-lore, which often celebrated kidnappings, killings, and other brutality.

The encounter with the intelligence couriers displayed perfectly Vang Pao's fighting style, which could, with little warning, devolve into outright cruelty. None of the Viet Minh ambushed by Vang Pao and his men was allowed to survive the battle. When one wounded Vietnamese soldier fled the house, Vang Pao followed a trail of blood to a nearby cave and sighted the trapped man. Vang Pao then hurled grenades inside until he heard no more sounds.[50] On many occasions later in his career, when Vang Pao led the Hmong army in the long fight against communist forces, his men would capture Pathet Lao or North Vietnamese soldiers and then torture them or simply execute them. Vang Pao and other Hmong soldiers were not shy about these practices, and they rarely heeded CIA officers who cautioned them to act more humanely toward prisoners. On several occasions when US congressmen and senators were visiting Vang Pao's main base in the war, the city of Long Cheng, the Hmong leader told the visitors that his men had electrocuted, beaten, and starved enemy prisoners in hopes of getting them to provide valuable information.[51]

After the French loss of its Indochinese colonies, Laos had en-tered an uneasy peace between communists, backed by their patrons in Vietnam, and anti-communists. Skirmishes between the two sides erupted constantly, though a large-scale countrywide war did not ex-plode until 1960. Yet Vang Pao had become convinced that a larger war loomed in independent Laos. The non-communists were divided between groups of truly liberal reformers who wanted to modernize Laos, and more traditional royalists who basically wanted to keep the feudal system that had existed for centuries. Some of the Laotian re-formers despaired at how dependent the country was becoming on US aid, which they feared would do little to modernize Laos's econ-omy but instead would just fuel corruption.

Laos's system of weak kings and prime ministers would fall apart, Vang Pao told several other Hmong clan leaders. The divisions among the non-communists and the vast economic inequality in Laos could make the country easy prey for a communist movement. The hungry outside powers that had mostly let Laos be would no longer be so generous now that France was gone, and China, Vietnam, and Thailand were all eying parts of Laos. And when Hanoi launched a larger war in Laos, Vang Pao warned, communist forces would target the Hmong in particular, since the hill tribe had been among the most ardent backers of the French in the previous war.[52]

Bill Sullivan, the American ambassador in Vientiane, heard all about the losses in Sam Neua as Tony Poe evacuated the wounded and left the dead, and Hmong refugees fled out of the area, but he took the news coolly. Laos was a war, and it was a war that, by 1965, he had mostly under his control. Neither the Hmong nor Laos in general held any particular personal meaning for him, beyond what the war meant for US interests. When Poe, recovering from his wounds at the hospital in northeast Thailand, heard that one of the most capable Laotian officers had been killed at Sam Neua, he cried for several hours, and tried to get the nurses to pour him whiskey shots in his hospital bed.[53] Bill Sullivan read the casualty reports and then set them aside in his office.

Sullivan asked one of his aides at the US Embassy to find out more about the losses at Sam Neua and whether the casualties could trigger infighting among the Hmong clans. Keeping the Hmong fighting, Sullivan knew, was critical to keeping the war going, but he had no illusions about the operation being led by the Hmong or, in the end, being about serving the Hmong at all. But he certainly did not want a loss to hinder Vang Pao's recruiting men to his army or planning for new attacks.

Ambassador Sullivan's realm of power encompassed far more than the usual ambassadorial duties of filing reports on the political situation in the country, attending diplomatic receptions, conveying messages from Washington to local leaders, and handling the Americans living in the country. In many respects, he was the most powerful US ambassador in the world—in charge of a war. No other American diplomat could say the same.

When Sullivan had taken up his post in Vientiane in December 1964, he was the youngest ambassador in the Foreign Service. With his clipped and commanding voice—he had been a famed orator in college at Brown University—and patrician manner, Sullivan had risen quickly in the Foreign Service. After World War II, he had served as a young diplomat in Bangkok, where one of his jobs had been to maintain contact with Vietnamese nationalists (many of them communist) who operated in the Thai capital. This was before France fought to keep its colonial possessions, the divisions of the Cold War hardened, and Thailand became an unyielding foe of communism. Despite his age—before his wiry, ropy hair had turned grayish-white and his waist thickened—Sullivan's thick, arched eyebrows and intense glare made him seem older than he was. This proved to be a valuable asset in Asia, where aged men tended to command respect. He could, from an early age in the Foreign Service, easily dominate a room full of older men.

Before coming to Laos, Sullivan had also briefly worked at the American mission in Saigon. "He was the kind of person who seemed like he came carved in stone," said one former Sullivan aide.[54] "He was not a man who really entertained a lot of self-doubt about what he was doing . . . He assumed naturally that if he did it, it would be right."

Sullivan also, critically, had served as the number two aide to top American negotiator Averell Harriman during the Geneva talks, hammering out the 1962 accords that were supposed to make all foreign forces withdraw from Laos. In Washington, DC, where you ascended not necessarily because of your talent or ideas but because you had attached yourself to the right powerful person, Harriman was a foolproof mentor: a man who had been governor of New York and had run for president twice.[55] President John F. Kennedy trusted

Harriman, who was owed favors by nearly every Democratic politician. Many of Harriman's aides saw their professional standing soar: one of Harriman's favorite aides late in his career, the diplomat Richard Holbrooke, would go on to become a driving force in American foreign policy during the Jimmy Carter and Bill Clinton administrations. Other Harriman aides would forge similarly illustrious careers.

Sullivan was one of Harriman's favorites. Leonard Unger, who preceded Sullivan as ambassador to Laos, said that Foreign Service officers used to call Sullivan one of the "gold dust twins," along with another favored Harriman aide named Michael Forrestal, because these men had long had Harriman's ear and seemed destined for greatness.[56] In 1962, when President Kennedy chose Harriman to negotiate the Geneva accords, Harriman picked Sullivan as his deputy, reportedly over the objections of many top American officials who thought that Sullivan was too young for the job.[57] Sullivan's prominent role in the negotiations made him one of the few younger American diplomats experienced in dealing with Hanoi's leaders and diplomats. Two years later, Harriman ardently advocated for putting Sullivan in the embassy in Vientiane, one of the most important postings in the world.

Long before taking the post, Sullivan had realized that the tiny kingdom was going to be vital to US strategy in Southeast Asia. He had closely followed the demise of France's forces in Indochina, and he was close enough to the senior leaders of the Eisenhower and Kennedy State Departments to know that aid to the South Vietnamese military had turned into the insertion of American military advisors into Vietnam. In 1964, Sullivan had run a secret committee designed to provide the White House with scenarios for how to assist the South Vietnamese, and he thought that the war in Vietnam would inevitably draw in all of the countries in the region, as well as the United

States. In exercises that Sullivan had run to prepare for fighting in Indochina, Laos had played a critical role in the US strategies, serving as a buffer and also a place where the United States could attack Hanoi's divisions, which frequently moved in and out of northern Laos and used parts of Laos to move supplies. So Sullivan accepted the ambassadorship to Laos not as a second or third choice to some preferred posting in Europe or bigger Asian countries; he entered the job full of intense interest in the country, and already considered one of the leading experts on the kingdom.

Unlike many diplomats, Sullivan also had respect for the CIA. He had enjoyed excellent relationships with CIA officers at his previous State Department postings. Sullivan sometimes had chafed at how much more the agency's men were able to get done, as compared with Foreign Service officers.

From reading up on the cables that had been sent by former US ambassadors to Laos, Sullivan had gained some comprehension of how Operation Momentum worked. The agency in Laos controlled the operation, but the ambassador had a role. Previously Kennedy had directed that the ambassador must approve US military operations in Laos, but he'd also said that the CIA should manage the overall operation, creating an inherent tension in how the secret war was to be run. Previous ambassadors who had antagonized the CIA station in Vientiane had wound up frozen out of policy making. Sullivan was not a man who ever wanted to be on the outside.

The CIA just had more bodies on Laos policy, which gave it a natural advantage over the embassy and the State Department. "Where the State Department . . . had three people on the Laos desk, the CIA had six," remembered Roger Hilsman, an Asia expert who served in several positions at the State Department under Kennedy. "This meant that the CIA could always afford to be represented at an interdepartmental meeting, that it could spare the manpower to prepare papers that would dominate the meeting."[58]

Sullivan had cultivated a close relationship with the CIA station in Laos immediately, and shortly upon his arrival, he assumed joint command of the war. He was not going to simply let the agency run the secret war, no matter how many men it had. Indeed, Sullivan soon earned the nickname Field Marshal from William Westmoreland, the head of Military Assistance Command in Vietnam between 1964 and 1968. The nickname circulated widely among US officers in Vietnam, many of whom were distraught over the idea that a diplomat was running a war.[59]

Although Sullivan had been a gunnery officer during World War II, he had no experience directing a war. But he had come to the kingdom convinced of his knowledge of the country, and if he had doubts about his abilities to oversee military operations, he did not betray them. Even at a time when diplomatic protocol remained important and ambassadors wielded far more power than they do in today's technologically interconnected world, where leaders can just call one another, Sullivan came across to other ambassadors as arrogant.

But to his credit, his colleagues generally remembered Sullivan as brilliant as well. As part of the Indochina war study group, which he ran for the White House before he became ambassador to Laos, he had already proposed greater US involvement in the Vietnam War. In the study group, Sullivan suggested that "American personnel, who have hitherto served only as advisors should be integrated into the Vietnamese chain of command"—that Washington should essentially take over the war from the South Vietnamese.[60]

Anyone who questioned Sullivan's command in Laos was quickly dismissed by the ambassador. "Sullivan had marching orders from the White House [to run the war with the CIA], and he made no secret of his clout," Westmoreland said.[61] Sullivan was not shy about dropping the names of all the people he had worked with in Washington or mentioning that he could call upon his Washington contacts to back him up in case the agency, other State Department officials, or military men tried to cut him out of command in Laos. "By the

time I went to Laos as ambassador, I had been working very closely
with [National Security Advisor] McGeorge Bundy, [Secretary of De-
fense] Robert McNamara . . . [Director of Central Intelligence] John
McCone . . . all of whom I could get in touch with directly," Sullivan
told one CIA historian.[62] In his memoir, Sullivan wrote, "Washington gave me a free hand to run [the Laos war] as best I could without
interference."[63]

Sullivan had even come to know President Lyndon Johnson personally, from Sullivan's time planning scenarios for the Vietnam War.
He told one historian that Johnson often pressed him to take more
money for managing the Laos operation.[64] The president also used to
call Sullivan personally every six months or so.

Even Westmoreland, who would come to command nearly five
hundred thousand US troops by 1968, could not trump Sullivan's authority in Laos. Once, after the general sent him a plan that would
have expanded the US military's role in Laos, Sullivan noted mock-
ingly in a memo that the strategy seemed like it came "out of the
opium pipe."[65] And sure enough, the Westmoreland plan was quashed.

Chapter 4

Laos Before the CIA, and the CIA Before Laos

WHEN THE CIA WAS CREATED AFTER WORLD WAR II, EVEN the most ambitious CIA leaders would not have predicted that agency operatives in Laos would eventually be training tens of thousands of local fighters, calling in air strikes, and leading engagements against the North Vietnamese and Laotian communist forces. Before the Second World War, the United States did not even possess a real global intelligence agency. White Houses relied upon mishmashes of army intelligence sources, friends of the president who traveled to foreign countries, diplomats, and other unofficial intelligence channels to gather information. Early in WWII, President Franklin Roosevelt realized that the United States needed a permanent global intelligence agency. But even then, the organization he created, the Office of Strategic Services, had more in common with the genteel intelligence-gathering operations of Britain at that time than with the CIA today. The OSS, whose enemies nicknamed it "Oh So Social" for its love of parties and other events as a means of gathering information in Europe, had an almost amateurish quality, its wartime station chiefs hatching plans that seemed to top each other in preposterousness. "Woe to the officer who turned down a project because on its face it seemed ridiculous or at least unusual," remembered one former OSS officer.[1]

The organization's founder, William "Wild Bill" Donovan, a former officer in World War I and a prominent New York politician, had an enormous regard—even envy—for US elites, probably because Donovan himself had come from a modest background but had developed extensive connections among the upper classes through politics and through his wife, a wealthy heiress. Tasked with forming the OSS, Donovan and other OSS leaders seemed to prefer smart and gregarious men from the right families and right Ivy League clubs; when the organization looked for female employees, its commanders hunted through the Social Register.[2] This old-boys' network persisted into the early days of the CIA, when the agency's recruiters scoured Ivy League schools to pinpoint men—usually from wealthy backgrounds—in the junior and senior classes who could be hired.

The OSS retained a freewheeling feel. A high percentage of OSSers were also political liberals, hardly resembling the more hawkish professional analysts and operatives who would give their entire working lives to the CIA and would come to dominate the agency between the 1960s and late 1980s. OSS operatives took cues from Franklin D. Roosevelt, who had openly voiced his desire for the end of colonial rule in Asia as the United States became involved in World War II. Roosevelt told a group of White House reporters at the March 1941 White House Correspondents' dinner: "There never was, there isn't now, and there never will be, any race of people on the earth fit to serve as masters over their fellow men . . . We believe that any nationality, no matter how small, has the inherent right to its own nationhood."[3] These ideas formed the core of Roosevelt's Atlantic Charter in August 1941, issued at a conference with British prime minister Winston Churchill in Newfoundland. It called on "the right of all peoples to choose the form of government under which they will live."[4] This idealized vision of the United States helping to bring democracy to people in countries around the world would later be contradicted by US actions in Asia, but the vision remained a powerful part of American thinking in the US foreign policy establishment, including among OSSers and, later, many CIA operatives.

After World War II ended, most of the OSS men and women went back to their lives in business and finance and law and academia and other professions. Still, the idea of a national intelligence agency did not vanish, and the leaders of the administration inherited by President Harry S. Truman after Roosevelt's death realized that the United States, now a global power, could not simply return to the isolationism and amateur intelligence gathering of the 1930s.[5] Truman did not take steps immediately after World War II ended, but as the world changed around him, it left him with virtually no choice. Sovietologist George F. Kennan, who had served in the US Embassy in Moscow during and immediately after World War II, wrote a now-famous article in the journal *Foreign Affairs* in 1947. Kennan argued that the Soviet Union, the inheritor of tsarist Russia, saw itself at war against capitalism around the globe but that the United States and other Western nations must prepare to use force around the world to counter the Soviet threat to Europe and the rest of the world.[6] The article became a sensation in Washington, influencing the policy debate like almost no other work before or since. Kennan's theory was adopted quickly by many senior policy makers around Truman. The Soviets, they became convinced, possessed a massive worldwide spying network that had leapt ahead of the piecemeal US spying operation, just as communism seemed poised to sweep through Western Europe into Italy and France.[7] Therefore the United States needed a global clandestine intelligence service far more sophisticated than the OSS to counter and contain the menace of communism.

By the late 1940s, the division of Europe into clear communist and pro-Western blocs seemed to be confirming Kennan's nightmares. In 1947 Truman signed a new National Security Act focusing American policy on stopping communism's advance. As part of this broader mission, the act also created the Central Intelligence Agency.[8]

The CIA remained smaller and weaker, within the bureaucracy, than many other government agencies. One of its first heads, a navy man named Roscoe Hillenkoetter, had managed intelligence for the Pacific Fleet during World War II. But he had no deep Washington connections and little appetite for the intrabureaucracy blood sport critical to getting anything done in the capital.[9] Hillenkoetter did not even want the job; before accepting, reluctantly, he had tried furiously to persuade Truman to name someone else.

The agency's leader sat atop an organization that had to make its own connections and develop its own reservoir of power in Washington, where the Pentagon and the State Department each had more than one hundred years of experience in foreign affairs. "From the outset, it [the CIA] faced fierce and relentless opponents within the Pentagon and the State Department," wrote Tim Weiner in his account of the birth of the CIA, *Legacy of Ashes*.[10]

The CIA did not even have a decent place to work. When the intelligence organization was launched, before a headquarters was built for it in Langley, Virginia, it operated out of a jumble of Victorian-era brick buildings in Washington's West End, dwarfed by the giant, fortresslike State Department located directly across the street.[11]

Allen Dulles, the director of central intelligence for most of the Eisenhower administration, and the most powerful early head of the CIA, was not Hillenkoetter. For much of World War II, he had worked for the OSS in Switzerland, and he wanted the job. Dulles came from the same patrician background as most other OSSers—he had attended Princeton University, and his grandfather had been secretary of state in the nineteenth century—but he had clashed repeatedly with other men in the OSS. Dulles normally had a smiling, almost grandfatherly, look, with "twinkling eyes, a belly laugh, and an almost impish deviousness," according to Weiner. But those who knew him recognized well the deviousness behind the mask. Dulles "was a duplicitous man . . . ruthlessly ambitious. He was not above misleading Congress or his colleagues or even his commander in chief," wrote Weiner.[12] Near the end of World War II, Dulles worked secretly with Karl Wolff, a top Nazi SS leader in Italy, to broker a surrender of German forces in northern Italy. In exchange, Wolff and his lieutenants were promised legal immunity despite the massive atrocities they had committed during the Nazi occupation of Italy—atrocities that Dulles knew all about.[13] President Franklin D. Roosevelt had expressly prohibited these kinds of conditional surrenders that assured top Nazi leaders of safe harbor in Europe. After the war, Dulles went to great lengths to protect Wolff from prosecution.[14]

When Dwight D. Eisenhower won the 1952 presidential election, Dulles, with his sterling Republican Party credentials and intelligence background, seemed a natural choice to head the CIA. And Eisenhower, a career soldier with a soldier's reticence for large ground wars, enthusiastically supported the growth of the CIA. Eisenhower believed covert action to be a potentially less costly means of fighting communism, in terms of lives, than a traditional war. The president encouraged Dulles to make the agency more aggressive: to proactively topple potentially communist foreign leaders and suffocate anti-Western revolutions.[15] Agency men helped oust left-leaning nationalist leaders in Iran and Guatemala and eliminate potential anti-American revolutionaries in countries such as the Congo and Indonesia.

Yet while Dulles demanded fealty to the CIA as a profession and to the ideological basis of the Cold War (and to himself), he also delegated a great deal of authority to local operatives out in the field. Perhaps this was necessary at a time when global communications remained limited, and no one in Washington could manage an operation around the globe in real time.[16] But the director's willingness to delegate meant that local operatives in Southeast Asia would play a central role in launching the secret war in Laos.

Though Dulles began building a disciplined and larger agency out of the chaos he had inherited from the disbanded OSS and the Hillenkoetter years, Dulles's writ, at least when Eisenhower took office, did not include running a whole war. The president's concept of more aggressive, expanded covert action did not include the agency leading full-on proxy wars or serving as an alternative to the armed forces. A handful of CIA operatives such as Tony Poe could train foreign fighters and spies like the Chinese Muslims and Tibetans, but the CIA operatives would not actually lead their students into battle. (Many of Poe's trainees learned from him at sites in the United States and then were flown back to Asia to infiltrate China. Poe claimed sometimes that he had accompanied the trainees into China and also helped the Dalai Lama flee, but Tibetan historians have concluded that this was not true.)[17] Poe and other CIA trainers usually could not rescue their charges once they sent them into battle, and could not even provide them with modern weaponry.

Tony Poe saw firsthand the limitations of working in the agency's small paramilitary branch before the 1960s. "It was made very clear to me that the agency was training people, that we weren't supposed to be actually fighting, or making decisions for them . . . A lot of my bosses didn't even think we should be training guerillas, that it wasn't real CIA work," Poe said. "We [paramilitary trainers] were looked at by a lot of clandestine officers in CIA—particularly the more old boys—like thugs, not intelligence agents." And even when the US military piled surplus weapons in dumps in Okinawa and Hawaii, Poe could procure for his men only vintage rifles from the First World War—which he joked would have been perfect for Civil War-era Gettysburg.[18] Even at the beginning of Operation Momentum, the Hmong often fought with outdated, World War II equipment. "I remember numerous times where my gun jammed," said Jer Xiong Yang, a Hmong fighter.[19]

Poe chafed at his limitations, but he had little idea, when the agency sent him to Laos, how much the power dynamic between the CIA and the uniformed military would change, and how much he would benefit from the change.

———

CIA head Dulles understood that if the agency could develop expertise in training small groups of fighters, it would be one more reason the CIA could ask for more money, more power, and more men. But well into the 1950s, even some of Dulles's closest aides worried that any CIA paramilitary programs would have serious unintended consequences. Even the smaller training programs CIA had conducted in the 1950s, whether for Guatemalan mercenaries or Tibetan guerillas, were controversial within agency headquarters—not to mention in the US military and the State Department, where agency paramilitary operations were seen as intrusions on turf. For the Foreign Service, having CIA military trainers operate in the same countries where Foreign Service officers served could undermine State's authority, since Foreign Service officers rarely were briefed on what the agency's trainers were doing. Diplomats often learned about these paramilitary operations from their counterparts from other Western countries rather than from the CIA itself.

The Central Intelligence Agency was divided on whether to expand its paramilitary operations—and on how much CIA officers should actually be allowed to fight and kill in the field. "There were quite a few station chiefs in CIA, and back at Langley, who thought that you couldn't do military work and intelligence work very well together; that's why they were separated," said Bill Lair. "They thought that training an army just wasn't what CIA did. It wasn't spy work. Let the military do that if they wanted."[20]

This ambivalence about what the CIA should be doing was reflected in how it prepared its recruits. When the agency set up its first training programs at "the Farm," a sprawling complex near Williamsburg, Virginia, on over nine thousand acres of land, it had modeled some aspects of training for clandestine CIA operatives on army and marine programs. The facility had been set up during World War II, and when the agency took over much of the property in 1951, it kept some of the squat, military-style barracks for housing trainees. Some days, the men preparing to become clandestine operatives took long runs through the woods dotting the property, in groups that made them look, at first glance, like army grunts. A few new recruits who would be sent to remote locations such as the Congo, were separated out and sent out on multiday survival programs in another part of the Farm, where they had to eat whatever they could strip from trees or kill in the woods, remembered Joseph Lazarsky, a former clandestine officer who served in Southeast Asia in the 1940s and 1950s and attended the survival training at the Farm.

But if the Farm bore some superficial resemblance to marine and army programs, training at the Farm and other sites wasn't exactly boot camp. Most CIA hires in the 1950s did not learn how to use handguns, let alone how to teach other people to use artillery, machine guns, and other weapons of war. Some nights, recruits would don jackets and ties and drive to Richmond, Virginia, or Washington, DC, to drink cocktails, eat steak dinners, and search for women—latitude that was not usually available at marines training. No drill sergeants got up in the faces of recruits at the Farm, and even on group runs, no one punished the men for not running at a certain pace. One CIA operative who spent much of his career in Southeast Asia, Campbell James, remembered that he often stopped in the middle of group physical activities at the Farm for extended smoke breaks—and was never punished.[21] In fact, some of the instructors sat down with him for a few cigarettes. Most days during a three- or four-week Farm course resembled a school cram session, with daytime classes rather than push-ups, and nights devoted to more classes or skipping off campus. "Some of the World War II or Korea veterans knew how to handle military weapons . . . but there were also plenty of just fancy college boys who had never shot a gun, and they didn't go to training to do military stuff . . . that wasn't considered spy work," said Lazarsky. "Spy work was turning communists, pretending to be a diplomat or a businessman, urban life . . . not some kind of guerilla fighting."[22]

Once they left the Farm, CIA men mostly stuck to this traditional kind of intelligence work. CIA station chiefs and other clandestine operatives in major intelligence hubs in Europe and Asia often did not carry guns. "It was considered part of spy work to influence politicians; even maybe be involved in a coup," said Lazarsky. "But it wasn't like the station chief in Berlin was going to get out a revolver and shoot someone."

Of course, killing people, although not the main part of the job, had always been an element of spy work. The agency would attempt to assassinate foreign leaders, including, most notoriously, Fidel Castro. In fomenting coups during Dulles's tenure as director in places such as Guatemala and Iran, the agency played a role in deaths resulting from the putsches and from wars that followed the coups.

But until the Laos operation, there was a natural limit on the number of people that the agency could kill. The agency had no army, no warplanes, no nuclear weapons, and no missiles. It had only a handful of military trainers. Assassinations could, by definition, lead to only a minimal number of deaths. The agency's Asian airline, Civil Air Transport, like other CIA-backed airlines in other parts of the world, moved money and supplies and sometimes agency operatives, but it didn't drop bombs.

However, the agency also had few people watching it—far fewer than the State Department or the uniformed US military, who had to provide much more public documentation on their employees and their activities. Technically, the CIA had to report regularly to Congress's intelligence committees about all of its activities, but as the agency's own classified internal history of its interactions with Congress makes clear, it rarely did. "No documentary evidence has thus far been found that . . . CIA subcommittees [in Congress] were formally briefed on specific operations, either in advance or after the fact" before the 1960s, the agency's internal history reported.[23] In other words, when it came to the agency's covert actions, directors usually said nothing.[24] Still, while the CIA divulged as little as possible to Congress in the 1940s and 1950s, it had never tried to hide an entire war from Congress.

While the CIA remained a relatively small organization in the 1950s, Laos seemed as tranquil as it had been—at least superficially—for decades. For seventy years of French rule, between France's scramble for Southeast Asian colonies in the late nineteenth century and the end of French rule over colonial Indochina, Paris had mostly left the territory of modern-day Laos alone.[25] In 1960 the capital city of Vientiane, home to around sixty-eight thousand people, hardly looked large enough to call itself the capital of anything. Occasionally, buffalo wandered through the grounds of the major ministry buildings, which were rarely higher than two stories and constructed of cheap concrete blocks that sometimes washed away during rainy season. Above the muddy banks of the Mekong River, which separated Vientiane from Thailand, unpaved and rutted roads in the capital wound around Buddhist temples, jacaranda and coconut trees, and cheap restaurants, made of corrugated metal, selling Chinese food and traditional Laotian staples such as sticky rice, pounded raw meat *laap* salad tossed with mint and fish sauce, and grilled chicken dipped in finger bowls of sweet-hot dipping sauce flavored with palm sugar. Occasionally, Vientiane's narrow side streets concealed small French cafes, often run by Frenchmen who couldn't stand the idea of going back to France, even after the end of the colonial era. The cafes would serve intriguing mixes of colonial and local foods: Vietnamese-style drip coffee and crusty white French bread, baked in loaves every morning by Lao women dressed in black *pasins*, the Laotian version of Southeast Asian sarongs. (France had left little in Laos, but many

Laotians had made the bread a morning staple of their diets.) As the sun set in the late afternoon, makeshift bars would open up along the Mekong, with strings of Christmas-style lights erected and plastic chairs set out for patrons sharing oversized bottles of beer poured over glasses of ice.

Though they claimed to be civilizing Laos after centuries of Laotian royal rule, the French had done little to upgrade Vientiane's roads, create any kind of lasting modern political system, or build any schools. The historian Lee notes that in the beginning of the twentieth century, France had fewer colonial officials in Laos than anywhere else in its empire.[26] Most French officials seemed to regard Laos as the least promising Indochinese colony, and most Laotians as lazy and uninterested in progress. Vietnam, with its abundant rice deltas and large population of potential consumers and essential rubber crops, was the Indochinese jewel. The French made virtually no preparations for a future independent Laos. After World War II, Charles de Gaulle and other Gaullist French leaders considered reclaiming Vietnam essential to France's status as a world power. They had less interest in Laos, though they wanted to retain it as some kind of protectorate as well.

As one French colonial official explained in an article in a prestigious Parisian journal on Asia, "[The Laotians] will be of no use for our civilizing actions, for which they will create nothing but obstacles."[27] French colonial officials considered the highland-dwelling hill tribes hardier and less indolent than the lowland Lao, and advocated breeding the two together to create a new Laotian mestizo race.[28] The French often compared the Hmong to the tough maquis, the anti-Nazi French guerillas who operated in Europe during World War II.[29] Like the maquis, the Hmong could live off the land and were adept at utilizing brush, mountains, rivers, and other local features to ambush much larger armies. Still, the French did not put schools in the highlands, the home of the Hmong, and most of the highlands had no radio or phone connection to the outside world, either.

The small community of foreigners residing in Vientiane in 1960 numbered around a thousand and consisted mostly of diplomats and their spouses, a small group of Chinese and Vietnamese businesspeople, a few aid workers, and the occasional freelance journalist.[30] The looming war next door in Vietnam, and even the uneasy peace between communists and non-communists in Laos itself, had not completely penetrated Vientiane's sense of otherworldly quiet. Foreign diplomats and their wives felt so safe in the capital that they often would water-ski on flat stretches of the Mekong, exposing themselves in a way few would have done in Saigon, where assassinations of foreign officials and foreign businesspeople had become common.[31] Even as the war spread in Laos, later in the 1960s, Vientiane's foreigner community would try to ignore it, attending black-tie balls at embassies and drinking and smoking pot at restaurants and nightclubs. The city would even attract tourists: mostly American hippies carrying backpacks, who followed an overland path from Kabul, to Kathmandu, to Delhi, to Bangkok, to Vientiane, all places with relatively little law and order, cheap and plentiful drugs, and auras of Eastern mysticism.

In part because of this general outside ignorance about the country, the few foreigners who did come to Laos—whether diplomats or backpackers—tended to fall into the trap of viewing it romantically as a land that time forgot. One apocryphal French saying about Indochina and the supposed Laotian indolence declared, "The Vietnamese plant the rice, the Cambodians watch it grow, and the Laotians listen to it grow."[32]

———

Laos, however, had not been completely ignored by the world. During the war between Vietnam and France that ended in 1954, fighting frequently spilled over into the kingdom. Although Laos's independence movement had been smaller than that of some other French and British colonies, a group of Laotian nationalists had emerged at the end of World War II, committed to Laotian independence. This group had included some communists, as well as Laotians committed to some kind of social democratic future government. The Japanese had allowed Laos to obtain de jure independence near the end of World War II, though the country was never truly self-governing; after the end of the war, Laos's king, who'd had little political authority under French rule but remained a popular symbol, wanted the French to retake control of the country. Some of the small group of nationalists continued to battle the French, inside Laos or from exile; a contingent of the nationalists tried to dismiss the king and set up its own government in Vientiane. Other groups of Laotian independence fighters, sometimes aided by the Vietnamese, tried to stop Paris's reconquest by confronting French forces in southern Laos as early as 1946. The proindependence government lasted about six months before collapsing due to lack of support from many rural Laotians, who still worshipped the king and were fearful of life without the French and, possibly, the royal family. French forces quashed the proindependence fighters easily. In August 1946 the king blessed an agreement between France and Laos under which Laos again became essentially a colony, although it gained a high degree of self-rule within the French Union in 1949. Laos held elections in 1947 and again in 1951 for a Laotian constituent assembly and then a parliament that had powers of self-rule but not complete independence from Paris. The 1947 election was nonpartisan, and though the 1951 election saw the formation of political parties, they had little support in many rural areas, where national politics was often ignored.

But as the Viet Minh held out longer and longer against the French in Vietnam, Paris became increasingly willing to grant Laos real independence. France began to accommodate Laotians' desire for real independence in order to rally the country against the Viet Minh, maintain some kind of British Commonwealth–style ties with Laos that could perpetuate French influence in Southeast Asia, and focus its political resources on Vietnam.

In April 1953 the Viet Minh invaded Laos, trying to bloody the French expeditionary army. During the invasion, Pathet Lao guerillas came into Laos, set up bases, and established a temporary government in a provincial town in the northeast. The Laotian communist movement had started in the 1930s, when a handful of Laotians joined the Indochinese Communist Party founded by Ho Chi Minh and dedicated to independence from France. The number of Laotians in the organization remained very small, but in the mid-1940s, the party recruited more Laotians, including some from the ranks of the nationalists who had tried to prevent the French from returning after World War II. The inequality in Laotian society, with a tiny elite dominating the cities of Vientiane and Luang Prabang, theoretically could have been an asset for the organization's recruiting. But the fact that Laos had so few urban centers, and so many rural men and women who barely interacted with modern politics or economics, limited the numbers of Laotians whom communists could recruit. Several of the men who would go on to lead the Pathet Lao, however, joined in the mid-1940s, living in exile in Vietnam after France reclaimed its authority over Laos. The Laotian communists' links to Vietnam would be extremely close from the mid-1940s on.

At a meeting in 1951, Vietnamese leaders and communists from other parts of Southeast Asia formally disbanded the Indochinese Communist Party, to replace it with national communist parties that could pursue revolutions against the French—and eventually against non-communist local leaders—more effectively on a country-by-country basis. The party in Cambodia became the Kampuchean People's Revolutionary Party (KPRP), though Hanoi wielded significant influence over the Cambodian communists too. The Laotian communists formed the Pathet Lao.

The Pathet Lao declared that it was going to work with Hanoi to fight French control of Indochina, though few Pathet Lao leaders actually fought against French forces between 1951 and 1954; they would spend their time setting up strongholds in Laos for a future conflict. The identities of many of the Pathet Lao leaders were kept secret from the public, and at the beginning, the organization was a bare-bones structure. Its first Congress, in 1955, was attended by about twenty-five members and essentially managed by members of the Communist Party of Vietnam. Meanwhile, the Pathet Lao was still largely unknown, as an organization, in most parts of Laos. That would change quickly, though, as it developed an effective propaganda apparatus and as the organization's public leaders—those who did not remain in hiding during the long Laotian civil war—proved adept at wooing the public.

For Hanoi's leaders, the 1953 incursion into Laos was initially a means to stretch the French military and reduce French pressure on Viet Minh strongholds in northern Vietnam. But once the bases inside were established, the Pathet Lao had an operational headquarters, giving Hanoi a stronger foothold to expand its operations in Laos and, in the future, win more recruits from Laotian society. The Pathet Lao began striking farther into the country and frequently confronted the new national army, leading to bigger and bigger battles in Laos. After 1953, there would be moments of relative peace, but, in general, a civil war would continue in Laos for more than two decades.

The White House had taken notice of the fighting. According to Fredrik Logevall, a historian of the French Indochina War, "In Eisenhower's judgment [in April 1953], the fall of Laos would be no less disastrous than the fall of Vietnam, and probably more so, for communist control of Laos would permit a hostile drive west as well as south" toward Thailand.[33] France had to quickly shuttle troops that April to defend the towns of central Laos, including the royal city of Luang Prabang, which was nearly surrounded by the end of April.[34] (The Viet Minh troops withdrew before making it to Luang Prabang, in order to launch offensives elsewhere in Vietnam itself.)

The Viet Minh's advances into Laos in 1953 were partly responsible for France's decision to establish a jungle base at Dien Bien Phu in northwestern Vietnam, near the Laos border and also close to the Viet Minh rear supply lines—close enough that Viet Minh commanders would probably have to attack Dien Bien Phu.[35] The base was supposed to replicate a previous French triumph in the war, in Na San, where French troops had created a remote base, lured Viet Minh troops toward it, and then used French command of artillery to annihilate them. But the strategy did not work as it had at Na San, where the Viet Minh had been poorly prepared, had not occupied the high ground, and had launched suicidal frontal attacks against French soldiers poised atop hills. Instead, Dien Bien Phu was a disastrous decision that allowed the Viet Minh to surround the defenders and shell them mercilessly.

At the 1954 Geneva accords, Laos was granted full independence. And after the end of French colonialism in Southeast Asia, the country still had a strategic position. It was surrounded by powerful neighbors aligned on different sides of the Cold War: North Vietnam and China, with the communist bloc; and Thailand, Malaya (later Malaysia and Singapore), South Vietnam, and other countries in Southeast Asia, with the West. Laos stood between communist North Vietnam and the rest of Asia.[36] The close proximity of Southeast Asia to Mao's China, which had fought the United States to a standstill in Korea and publicly declared itself to be in the business of fostering revolutionary movements—Beijing would develop links to communist parties in Indonesia, Burma, and Thailand, among other places in the region— also made Laos a plausible place for China to exert significant influence. China offered newly independent Laos money to build roads and other infrastructure. Some US officials believed that Chinese officials were cultivating close relations not only with communist Laotian leaders but also with the non-communist royalist leaders who had taken over the government.

Laos also clearly was important to Ho Chi Minh's party, the dominant force in the Viet Minh. Though not as large as China or the Soviet Union, and still very poor, Vietnam had the potential to be

a regional power. The country contained nearly thirty million people, had a charismatic and genuinely popular nationalist leader in Ho
Chi Minh, and now had a battle-toughened army that had defeated a
major Western power. For Hanoi's leaders, Laos was as important as a
buffer state as the kingdom was for the conservative Thai generals—
probably more so, since the Vietnamese leaders had far fewer close
friends than foreign analysts, who saw communism as monolithic,
had imagined. Although Ho Chi Minh's party had built ties with
Moscow and Beijing, Vietnam and China had been natural enemies
for centuries, and within Ho Chi Minh's party, suspicion of China remained common. In addition, before the late 1940s the Soviet Union
had barely provided Ho Chi Minh and his men any aid at all, and
Chinese leaders had remained consumed by their own civil war until
1949. (In the late 1950s, China would increase shipments of military
aid to the Vietnamese communists, and eventually, in the late 1960s,
it would send more than a hundred thousand advisors, mechanics,
engineers, and other support troops to help the North Vietnamese.)[37]

Fearing international isolation, and worried that Western countries and the conservative Thai regime would never allow a unified
communist-led Vietnam to exist, leaders of the Communist Party of
Vietnam looked for ways to expand Hanoi's influence in the region, create more allies, and protect itself from invasion. Laos could be critical for
moving men and weapons toward the south of Vietnam if the reunification of Vietnam promised after France's defeat did not occur peacefully.

The French had not prepared Laos for the transition to independence. Laotians had no experience with elections or parliamentary
government. Still, an election was held in 1955, and the party that had
won the elections under self-rule won again. After independence, the
Laotian monarchy, the head of state, was maintained in the city of
Luang Prabang as a unifying and a constitutional symbol; at times in
the 1950s and 1960s, American officials, frustrated with poor leadership by Laotian politicians, appealed to the king to essentially take
control of government.

But the kings of Laos at the time were restrained by the constitutional monarchy and vested with relatively little power. Sisavang Vong, who was the king from 1904 until his death in 1959, was at least relatively charismatic: a man with extensive experience from his reign and with an astute knowledge of power and regional politics, even if he was limited in what he could actually do. He was, however, a supporter of France's rule in Laos and wary of the idea of independence. But when he died, the monarchy was inherited by his son, King Savang Vatthana, a man with less interest in Laotian politics at all and with limited skills as a public speaker or a politician. The new king preferred to spend his time on his hobbies, such as antique cars, rather than help manage the affairs of state and government.

Meanwhile, the country's few French-trained civilian politicians had little of the common touch, and Laos's inexperience with democracy made them unsure of how much legitimacy they could derive from elections. In comparison with Cambodia, where the wily and (in the 1950s and early 1960s) popular King Sihanouk, who loved politics and certainly did not doubt his own legitimacy, would not allow the country to be dominated by any outside power, Laos was a potential client state. The most charismatic Laotian politician, Prince Souphanouvong, had lived in Vietnam for more than fifteen years, was close with Hanoi's leaders, and had helped found the Pathet Lao while its other leaders were in exile. Although the prince did not wield as much power as some of the other Pathet Lao leaders, whose identities remained concealed, the prince's magnetism and the prestige conferred by his royal background helped win over rural peasant support for the communists. Two of the other leading politicians at the time of independence were princely half brothers of Souphanouvong; the oldest, Prince Souvanna Phouma, became prime minister in 1954 and would be at the center of Laos's civil war. Souvanna hoped to keep Laos neutral in Southeast Asian politics, as well as in the Cold War—a strategy sought by some other leaders in the regions, such as Cambodia's Sihanouk. Sihanouk was able to maintain neutrality far longer; Souvanna's attempts to make Laos neutral would not be successful.

Hanoi's leaders would make every effort to dominate the Pathet Lao, an organization that, after all, had been formed at Viet Minh headquarters outside Hanoi during the war against France, and which would be dependent on Vietnamese aid, arms, and troop support in the Laotian war. Once the Pathet Lao was established in Laos's northeast, and the Laotian national army proved so weak, Hanoi's leaders sensed that a joint Laotian-Vietnamese force could win a larger war in Laos. However, after the 1954 accords, they held off on backing an armed, revolutionary fight in South Vietnam. That changed in 1959, when Hanoi's politburo decided to support armed attacks in South Vietnam against the regime of South Vietnam's president, Ngo Dinh Diem. North Vietnam's leaders needed Laos's territory to move supplies and men into South Vietnam.[38]

Laos continued holding parliamentary elections after independence, but electoral politics did little to change the lives of impoverished rural people in Laos, who comprised more than 90 percent of the population in the late 1950s.

In addition, the elected Laotian politicians proved incapable of holding together a coalition government involving the Pathet Lao and conservative royalist forces, despite the fact that the Laotian political elite was tiny and the major players knew one another well and often were related by blood. Souvanna led an attempt at a coalition government formed in 1956, but he could not effectively quell the suspicions of both rightist Laotian leaders and the Pathet Lao, and the skirmishing between government troops and Pathet Lao forces in areas in the northeast. He could not convince the Pathet Lao to join the national army, and his position as prime minister became weaker and weaker. In 1958 a group of conservative Laotian politicians forced him to resign.

It certainly did not help Souvanna that the United States threatened to withdraw its aid to the government, or that the Eisenhower administration began openly cultivating and funding more conservative politicians as well as a group of younger army officers who wanted to get rid of Souvanna.[39] Rothwell Brown, the head of the de facto US military mission in Laos, wrote in an unpublished memoir that the Eisenhower administration had "used every means available to overthrow [Souvanna's] government" in 1958.[40] A right-wing and more openly pro-US government came into office and repudiated any efforts at conciliation with the Pathet Lao, leading many of the Pathet Lao fighters to flee to Vietnam for a brief period. By the end of 1959, that government also would be deposed, in a bloodless coup, replaced by an even more conservative military regime backed by the United States. However, the military regime would prove even more ineffective at running the country—and even more avaricious—than the civilian governments that preceded it.

Hmong society was not static, either. In the 1950s, the Hmong still lived much as they had for centuries, but they had gained battle experience with the French and feared the change that might come from communist rule. The Hmong shared some traits with other ethnic groups that roamed northern Southeast Asia. For one thing, they tended to migrate from location to location: cutting down forest to farm opium or rice or maize and raise a few pigs, and then moving on to the next forestlands after having exhausted the soil in their current site. They were poor, and few Hmong attended school—life expectancy for Hmong in Laos hovered around forty-five at the end of the 1950s. Laos was one of the poorest countries in the world, with an average income per person of about $75 per year, and the Hmong were generally poorer than lowland Laotians in the south of the country. By several estimates, there were less than thirty university graduates in the whole country in 1955. (All had trained outside Laos, as it did not have its own university then.)[41] Death in childbirth was common, and children who survived often suffered from debilitating diseases such as beriberi, because their mothers ate such unvaried diets during the first months of their babies' lives. Modern health care was almost totally absent from the highlands of northern Laos, and there were no French-trained Hmong doctors. Aside from a handful of clan leaders who had the political contacts to travel regularly to Vientiane and Thailand, most sick or dying Hmong made do with traditional herbal remedies and the prayers of Hmong shamans. The economic situation was similar or worse for most of the other hill tribes living in northern Laos: the Akha, the Lahu, and others.

But the Hmong also were basically free. The Hmong had originally migrated from China, spreading throughout Southeast Asia while also remaining in parts of southern China. Like most of the groups that lived in the mountains and hills in Southeast Asia and China, they valued distance from any powerful authority. James Scott, an anthropologist who has studied the hill tribes for years, writes that groups like the Hmong were the original anarchists, escaping state societies by fleeing for the most rugged terrain possible—places where government could not follow them. When confronted by authority, the Hmong would attempt to crush it or to relocate elsewhere. Still, the Hmong did have their own type of local government, with each clan running its own affairs—a kind of local democracy in the Southeast Asian uplands. The clans would come together at important times, and some Hmong historians believed that they would hold discussions until all the clan leaders could reach a consensus on a decision. "In a most democratic way, all clans had equal voice in the discussions, which continued until all points of view had been heard, reviewed, and contemplated," wrote Jane Hamilton-Merritt, an expert on the Hmong.[42] Other Hmong historians note that, while the group sometimes reached consensus, it often was bitterly divided by clan rivalries and small-scale clan warfare.

The Hmong protected their culture, their mobility, and their kind of anarchic democracy. They spoke their own language, though it was not written; worshipped their own set of non-Buddhist gods; and had their own shamans who interpreted the ways of the world, communicating between Hmong people and the spirit world. They rarely attempted to raise large herds of cattle or litters of pigs, like some Lao people did in the flatter and lusher south of the country, where there was more food for animals to eat and rice could be grown in wide, flooded paddies. Hmong wore their own traditional attire such as thick silver neck rings; long, baggy trousers for men; jackets embroidered with delicate and ornate geometric designs; and stringy, long necklaces jangling with silver circles that looked like vertical rows of quarters.[43] "Silver rings dangle from earlobes; numerous silver necklaces, which may total more than ten pounds in weight, adorn the neck. These are the [Hmong] woman's bank account," wrote *National Geographic* upon "discovering" Hmong villages in remote northern Laos in 1952.[44] Many Hmong families did not use cash, bartering for goods at village markets. Some Hmong who grew opium used small bundles of the slightly sticky dried gum from opium plants, wrapped in paper or plastic or dried leaves, as a kind of cash.

The Hmong had, generally, managed to maintain their independence even when some of the other ethnic minority hill tribes, who were even less organized and smaller in number, had been forced to move into more traditional villages and urban areas. Since the late nineteenth century, many Hmong clans, residing in small villages of ten or twenty families, had lived in areas of northern and north-central Laos regarded by the French, and the Laotian king, as essentially self-governing. When the French had tried to subdue large swaths of the Hmong's traditional land and collect high taxes from the Hmong, they faced ferocious guerilla uprisings that slowly bled French forces and took years to put down, even though the Hmong were often armed only with homemade flintlocks and other basic weapons.[45] Allowing the Hmong a degree of self-governance was easier for Paris than trying to combat the Hmong with a counterinsurgency. Few royal or French officials came to areas around the Plain of

Jars to tell local Hmong leaders anything. When the French withdrew in 1954, most of the Hmong clans—at least, the clan leaders who played a role in national politics—preferred to side with the weak Laotian government in the capital rather than with the Vietnamese and Laotian communists. Although the communists' ideology might have seemed attractive to a hilltribe group that was poorer than the lowland Lao and that had been on the margins of politics in Laos, many Hmong clan leaders were more concerned that the communists posed the possibility of a stronger national government if they ever came to power.

In addition, despite their professed belief in the equality of all men, many of the communist Laotian leaders, just like the traditional royalist Laotians, regarded the hill tribes as lesser people. By the end of the 1950s, many Hmong clan leaders had seen that already: in areas controlled by the Pathet Lao communists in the northeast of Laos, revolutionaries had established local governments with massive powers over citizens' personal lives. The Hmong also had, over the years, spent much of their time living at higher altitudes and hiking through the hills of central and northern Laos, much of which was covered by forest and rocky slides and sharp cliffs with narrow river valleys; there were few paved roads or tracks. Intense physical exercise had given many Hmong broad shoulders and chests and squat, highly muscular legs; Southeast Asia historian and analyst Kenneth Conboy wrote that "mountain life had also left them with considerable stamina, the average Hmong male being capable of carrying a 110-pound backpack at a rapid pace in high altitudes."[46] The deep-seated antipathy among some Hmong leaders for the Pathet Lao, along with the Hmong's natural abilities and their fear that they would have nowhere to run if the communists took over, would make the Hmong a perfect proxy army.

Chapter 5

The CIA Meets Laos

CIA HEAD ALLEN DULLES HAD BEEN AN ENTHUSIASTIC
supporter of the Eisenhower administration's economic aid to France
in the Indochina War. Even after France withdrew, Dulles remained
convinced that Indochina was one of the best places in the world for
the West to confront communism. Senior US officials, deeply concerned with ensuring that Japan rebuilt itself and developed a close alliance with the United States after World War II, also saw Indochina,
which was rich in rubber, tin, and other minerals, as an important
market for Japanese goods and investment.[1] Inside the agency, not
only Dulles but also senior leaders of the Far East division further believed the CIA could take a more central role in managing the Indochina War.

Despite Dulles's interest in Laos, the country might have remained
in relative obscurity if not for a series of events that occurred in 1960
and 1961, and a rapid sequence of decisions made by a small group
of US policy makers. The speed at which these decisions were made,
the ability of a handful of policy makers to dominate decision making, and then the United States' baffling inability, for years, to rethink
the basis of these decisions and shift policy—all of these characteris-
tics were true of US policy on Laos. For a decade after 1960, American leaders barely stopped to reassess the United States' commitment
to such "an improbable place for the United States—or anybody, for
that matter—to become involved," in the words of one Laos historian.

This would become a common feature of US policy as the country's global presence expanded.

———

Though the Royal Lao Army contained only around thirty thousand men in 1960, twenty-six-year-old Captain Kong Le was not among the army leaders known well by Western diplomats. Before the summer of 1960, his name barely appeared in diplomatic cables from Vientiane. Barely five feet tall, with a birdlike body, he was shy and looked almost emaciated. Only a captain in an army heavy with generals, Kong Le had an instinctual feel for battle but little formal education. He hailed from another ethnic minority, the Lao Theung, rather than from the majority lowland Lao ethnic group, which provided most of the officers of the national army.[2] Kong Le had not involved himself in Laos's political struggles, though he had on several occasions told men serving under him that he was tired of Laos's corruption and wanted to free the country from foreign patrons.

But in August 1960 Kong Le ignited a wave of conflict in Laos that terrified the White House and led to the secret war. While most of Laos's government ministers were away in Luang Prabang, residence of the king, Kong Le struck. Leading a battalion of roughly three hundred loyal men, the captain launched a coup, strutting down the river road past the clutch of French shops in the town center that sold imported goods such as foie gras and Camembert cheese.[3] Apparently the young captain had long wanted to stage a coup to remove much of Laos's corrupt political class. It was an idealistic, albeit poorly formed, scheme—even Kong Le's enemies admitted the captain was sincere in his ideas, if naïve in politics.

Kong Le broadcast the putsch on the national radio station, seized the Defense Ministry, and commandeered most other government buildings. With much of the army also away from the capital, he met little resistance at first. The captain's demand for cleaning out the political class seemed to go down well with the population in Vientiane, which hoped that someone could put an end to the constant skirmishing between political factions. (The Pathet Lao had launched new guerilla attacks in the summer of 1959 against government positions.) Also, the greed and venality of many national army leaders were well known, and many residents could tell stories, apocryphal or not, of large villas built with money and concrete meant to be used for infrastructure projects. A *Wall Street Journal* reporter visiting Vientiane in 1958 found an elite class in the capital "ecstatically drowning in American aid" and spending frantically on imported perfumes, European cars, and luxurious musical instruments, in a country with an average income of around $150.[4]

Crowds cheered as Kong Le and his men strode into the capital's soccer stadium.[5] The captain announced that he personally had no interest in running Laos. He called on eminent Laotian statesman Souvanna Phouma to form a government again.

Although Kong Le's coup went peacefully at first, Western countries soon became nervous. The previous government in Laos had been unabashedly pro-American. In the fall of 1960, Souvanna Phouma, who had attempted to form a coalition government in the mid-1950s, again invited both Pathet Lao and right-wing leaders to Vientiane to negotiate the country's future and, he hoped, form a government that would be neutral in the Cold War. Though Souvanna was a skillful politician, he was perceived by many Laotians as "naïve and weak toward the communists, partly because of his [incorrect] belief that his half brother [Prince] Souphanouvong was not a communist," wrote historian Sutayut Osornprasop.[6] Soviet leaders seemed to sense that they could influence the war in Laos and possibly even win the government as a partner. Four months after the coup, Moscow airdropped howitzers, heavy mortars, rifles, and ammunition to Kong Le and his men.[7] The drop was relatively small, compared with US assistance given to the national army, but it was enough to spark fear in Washington and Bangkok.

Asking communists to join a government—that was a precedent

Washington did not want set in any country, and particularly not in one right next to Vietnam and China. US officials in Washington suddenly barraged American diplomats in Vientiane with orders and requests for information. Souvanna's plan was not acceptable to the Eisenhower administration. "The United States considered Souvanna Phouma's return to office bad news. A Department of State cable said that the United States sought "to bring about an acceptable power balance of non-communist elements which [also] would eliminate Kong Le," according to one US government history of the 1960 Laos crisis.[8]

In the middle of December 1960, civil war erupted. Kong Le and his forces, which had now expanded beyond the original group of three hundred, as sympathizers flocked to his side, fought a pitched battle for Vientiane with troops under right-wing general Phoumi Nosavan. (By 1961, Kong Le would have some 8,000 men under his control, and Kong Le's coup had split the army, with most of the soldiers from the national army allying with Phoumi.)[9] Phoumi enjoyed the backing of neighboring Thailand's conservative ruling generals, and, increasingly, a US government that at the highest levels had become almost obsessed with Laos. Bangkok and the panicked Eisenhower administration provided Phoumi, a mediocre military leader with little popular support, with money, advisors, and arms; the Thai government, run by a military regime that had revived the monarchy and did not want to see other kings in the region toppled, sent many of its most experienced commandos. During the battle, the Thais would all but command Phoumi's units for him.[10]

Vientiane had not witnessed much actual fighting before, even during France's Indochina War and the years of intermittent skirmishes in Laos between communist and non-communist forces. But beginning on December 13, 1960, the city became a battleground. The streets emptied of people and shopkeepers rolled down their metal doors as Phoumi's armored cars rolled into the city, firing indiscriminately with machine guns and mortars. Shells from both sides rained from the sky, and tracers lit up the night. Much of the city's small downtown area of wood shops and cafes burned to the ground, sometimes with store owners and their children inside.[11] Wayward artillery strikes hit the upswept rooftops of Buddhist temples—their white paint looking luminescent in the harsh tropical sun—and fell onto people's homes and the few government buildings in the city. Kong Le and Phoumi's men fought back and forth for days in close quarters, shelling the airport, the foreign embassies, and much of the population.[12]

"Throughout much of the battle, the combatant forces were separated by a no-man's-land . . . four city blocks wide," wrote one observer of the battle. "Both sides poured out a deafening volume of fire across this area."[13] When fighters on either side passed any building where they thought enemy troops could be hiding, they raked it with machine gun fire until everyone inside was dead, whether or not the structure actually contained any fighting men.

On December 16, after four days of hard fighting, Kong Le and his men retreated. By then, more than half the city had been destroyed, and a large percentage of its population had fled, carrying sacks of rice and bags of clothes as they trudged along the dirt roads out of the capital.

Back in Washington, Phoumi's triumph provided only minimal reassurance in what had become a full-blown crisis. American leaders had become even more worried about whether Laos could hold off a communist takeover, even after Kong Le and his men retreated from Vientiane. General Phoumi and the king soon appointed an interim caretaker government, but Kong Le and his men rebuilt their force and made an alliance with communist forces, together threatening Vientiane and other cities. Meanwhile, Souvanna, whom the CIA, the US military, Thai leaders, and many senior Eisenhower administration officials worried was a closeted communist, remained the most influential politician in the country—and would soon become prime minister again.

Director of Central Intelligence Dulles had for several years warned Eisenhower's National Security Council that "a possible Communist takeover of Laos" was in the cards, and that this invasion would help spread communism throughout the region. The success of Ho Chi Minh's forces against the French, the growing popularity of communists in Indonesia, the roiling communist insurgency in Malaysia, and the reports that Beijing was funding insurgencies in Burma, Thailand, and other countries in the region exacerbated the administration's fear of losing Southeast Asia.

The CIA head's deputies pigeonholed their contacts at the White House with the same all-or-nothing message, warning that Kong Le's men and the communists, supported by Moscow, Beijing, and Hanoi, could strike back at any time. They also cautioned that the effete Francophile Souvanna Phouma, who loved to play tennis and had great respect for French democracy, would not stand up to the Pathet Lao and its allies.[14] "The Americans say I am a communist," Souvanna lamented. "All this is heartbreaking. How can they think I am a communist? I am looking for a way to keep Laos non-communist."[15]

While Dulles warned of the communist threat in Laos, the US Embassy in Vientiane, which was supposed to provide the most knowledgeable counsel about the country, had been headed by ineffectual and uninterested ambassadors. The United States had no depth of knowledge about Indochina overall; before World War II, fewer than a hundred Americans lived in Indochina, and the US consul in Saigon had little to do.[16] Although the US diplomatic establishment had worked to quickly amass contacts and information about Vietnam as the Truman and Eisenhower administrations aided the French war effort, few US diplomats came to know Laos well until the 1960s. The first US ambassador to Laos, Charles Yost, said that upon arriving in Vientiane in 1954, he found the villa where US diplomats conducted business "the most primitive and ill-equipped diplomatic post I have ever encountered": two rooms, with vultures outside devouring random animal parts that had been tossed out of a nearby slaughterhouse.[17]

Graham Parsons, ambassador to Laos from 1956 to 1958, had never served in Southeast Asia before coming to Vientiane. There he spent much of his time focusing on maintaining rigid diplomatic protocol within the American community in Laos.[18] As ambassador, Parsons offered Americans arriving in Laos a welcome brochure that featured a lengthy discourse on "the proper honorific when greeting a fellow American," how to make a formal business call on the ambassador, and exactly how far in advance, by the minute, to arrive at American functions.[19] Parsons dictated exactly how many business cards Americans should leave for the ambassador when they announced their arrival in Laos, and how many—and what type of—business cards *wives* should leave when they paid a formal call on the ambassador's wife.[20] The ambassador spent a great deal of his remaining time lecturing Laotian politicians about their own country and seemed to be thoroughly reviled by them. Parsons was then succeeded by Horace Smith, who served from the spring of 1958 until the spring of 1960 and made little impact. "Laos was a mess . . . when Smith was ambassador there," said Bill Sullivan.[21]

Smith's successor, Winthrop Brown, had arrived in Laos less than a month before the Kong Le coup in August 1960. Brown knew little about the Southeast Asian country before he took the reins, and had little time to develop contacts among local officials and intelligence sources before the battle of Vientiane.[22] He was not as obsessed with protocol as Parsons, but he was not prepared to rebut the theories and proposals of the CIA.

An embassy that had little knowledge of actual political conditions in Laos had little ability to determine whether the country actually was going to go communist, who in Laos truly was a communist, or whether Laos even mattered to the broader Cold War ideological battle. Many US military advisors knew just as little about the coun-

try as Parsons and Brown. And Laos had few resident foreign journalists to provide informed analysis. A weak and poorly informed
embassy that disdained Laotians; a lack of broader knowledge about
Laos among American elites; and a handful of people in Washington,
Bangkok, and Vientiane, mostly from the CIA, with strong opinions
about what the United States should do—the conditions were ideal
for those in the agency who believed Laos would be "a great place to
have a war."[23]

The agency's station chief in Vientiane in 1960, Gordon Jor-
gensen, had already established a direct channel to the White House,
one separate from normal diplomatic cables. Though theoretically undercover as a political officer at the embassy, he lived in his
own vast residence outside the US Embassy compound, suggesting
strongly that he was not a low-paid, low-level Foreign Service officer.[24] As Kong Le's coup unleashed fighting in Vientiane and panic
in Washington, the CIA station stopped even informing the embassy
of what it was doing in the kingdom.[25] Brown recommended that the
White House support a neutral government in Laos, and noted that
Kong Le and Souvanna were not communists. But the State Department's top leaders "gave [Brown] little support." Christian Chapman,
who served on the Laos desk in the State Department, said "the Pentagon considered Winthrop Brown virtually a traitor, gone-soft kind
of thing."[26]

Cable traffic among the CIA station in Vientiane, Eisenhower's senior advisors, and the Pentagon's top Asia experts flowed back and
forth frequently during the last days of Eisenhower's presidency.
Brown remained mostly oblivious to the fact that the agency and several senior military leaders were proposing either a US army invasion
of Laos or a covert paramilitary operation that would marshal local
anti-communist forces against the communist threat. On the National
Security Council staff, several East Asia specialists, together with the
Joint Chiefs of Staff, offered the president a memorandum outlining

steps for inserting US ground troops into Laos if the political situation continued to deteriorate. It included possibly airlifting nearly a quarter million American troops into the kingdom. The Joint Chiefs and the Cabinet even discussed launching tactical nuclear weapons if the political situation in Laos continued to deteriorate.[27]

Chapter 6

Operation Momentum Begins

AFTER PHOUMI HAD DRIVEN KONG LE OUT OF VIENTIANE, the Eisenhower administration had no clear idea what to do next. With the actual ambassador to Laos written off by Washington as useless, Bill Lair suggested to his bosses in the Far East division that he meet with Vang Pao.

By the end of 1960, Lair had been watching the Hmong for over a decade as they fought the Lao and Vietnamese communists on and off. He had also established a name for himself as a CIA operative who understood Laos's complex yet intimate politics; for example, anti-communist Souvanna's half brother was Prince Souphanouvong, the figurehead leader of the Pathet Lao. (The Pathet Lao's most powerful leaders chose mostly to stay in hiding.) Amidst the Eisenhower administration's panic, Lair had been tasked by CIA headquarters to enter Laos, build up more intelligence sources about the mostly unknown Kong Le, and devise a plan to foment opposition to the captain's coup. Lair brought several groups of his Thai paratroopers into Laos and then established a base for himself in the southern city of Savanakhet in November 1960, a few months after the coup. Through the radio dispatch he set up in Savanakhet—and with bricks of currency provided by the CIA—Lair soon was playing a central role in whipping up support for the anti–Kong Le forces that would attack Vientiane in December. With the radio dispatch, Lair directed teams of the Thai paratroopers as they trained Phoumi's ragtag army and helped lay plans for the assault on the Laotian capital.[1]

Lair had heard from French and Laotian officials that Vang Pao was the only Hmong who could deliver a significant force of men. Thai paratroopers who had met the Hmong leader told Lair that Vang Pao already had around five thousand men loyal to him.

Lair's advice, delivered to the station chief in Vientiane and the leaders of the Far East division, carried weight; the previous Southeast Asian force Lair had trained, the Thai paratroopers, had played a critical role in aiding Phoumi's battle for Vientiane. The Thais, who had learned about modern communications, light weapons, attack techniques, unconventional warfare, and armor, helped command the attack, and taught Phoumi and his men how to utilize code to protect their messages to one another, a major step forward in Laos's rudimentary warfare.[2]

Desmond Fitzgerald, the head of the Far East division, who was visiting Vientiane in December 1960, shortly after the battle for the city ended, wondered if the Hmong could become just as skilled.[3] Fitzgerald had traveled to Vientiane after visiting Vietnam, and had arranged a private dinner in the Laotian capital with Lair. Fitzgerald had been a proponent of the Thai paratrooper training program, protecting it from budget cuts, but he had many questions.[4] How many Hmong could be molded into an army? How would they be used? What do the Hmong want? How would Vang Pao be managed? What would the CIA's role be? Fitzgerald was already inclined to support a CIA training program for the Hmong, but he encouraged Lair to think much bigger. A Hmong training program could encompass thousands of men, Fitzgerald suggested.

Lair thought about these questions. With a potent guerilla force in the north, the United States could possibly reduce the area held by the Pathet Lao and its North Vietnamese backers to a minimum, he told Fitzgerald.[5] At the least, America could help the Hmong protect their area of Laos from communist incursion. He sketched out an off-the-cuff plan for Fitzgerald for a Hmong training program, one that eventually could be built into the large-scale operation Fitzgerald had described.[6] The Far East division chief was enthusiastic, and encouraged Lair to get a sense of Vang Pao's demeanor and military skill. The operation could succeed only with a Hmong at its head who could unite rival clans and become a leader, Fitzgerald cautioned Lair. Was Vang Pao that man?[7]

In January 1961, near the end of Eisenhower's presidency, Bill Lair met Vang Pao at a site where Vang Pao had previously met Stuart Methven, another CIA operative. Although Lair had lived in Southeast Asia for a decade and worked closely with some of Thailand's most elite soldiers, he returned from his first meeting with the Hmong leader impressed. Lair had expected to encounter the kind of verbal misdirection and obscurity he had seen from most Laotian and Thai leaders. Yet the Hmong leader was blunt from the start.

Lair returned quickly and met Vang Pao again, and Vang Pao promised that he could produce an army of ten thousand Hmong who could be trained by the United States.[8] A US-trained force could do much more than hold its ground—it could push the North Vietnamese out of northern and central Laos, Vang Pao claimed. The Hmong leader took Lair to his makeshift camp and gave him an impromptu tour of his army's ranks.[9] Lair was less impressed with Vang Pao's men than he was with the Hmong leader—the group of fighters milled about in dirty, fraying clothes. But Lair believed that with aid, guidance, and better recruiting, the Hmong could winnow out their worst fighters and shape up their army.

Lair had heard from French intelligence officers that Vang Pao's sharp mind too often was undermined by the man's rage, sadness, or manic energy—that Vang Pao's passion sometimes overtook his abilities and knowledge. Lair also saw the fury and the frenzy: the Hmong leader made Lair walk most of the time they talked.

Lair drafted a cable that outlined a plan to begin transforming the

Hmong into a kind of Southeast Asian maquis.[10] The plan noted that the United States could work with the Hmong for a minimal amount of money, and that the Hmong could be more effective than the national Laotian army, which was unwieldy and hard to control. The United States did not have to spend money buying the Hmong rations of beef and eggs and ice cream, as it did for US troops stationed in Southeast Asia, since the Hmong could subsist on rice and local food; what's more, Hmong soldiers would get about $3 per month in pay, compared with as much as $339 per month for US Army privates serving in Vietnam. The program could start with five hundred or a thousand Hmong, but could be scaled up, just as Fitzgerald had wanted.

The Hmong and the CIA could create a base of operations somewhere in northern Laos, Lair proposed. The Hmong army could use the base, as well as the high mountains ringing communist-controlled territory, to venture out into the northeast and east, where communist forces were strongest. They could lure communist forces into skirmishes, kill or capture a few men in each communist platoon, and then escape through jungles and mountains back to the Hmong base. This guerilla style would fit the Hmong way of fighting. But Lair warned his bosses that if they tried to use the Hmong as a traditional infantry, the army could disintegrate.[11] Lair would repeatedly caution Vang Pao, too, to stick to the attack-and-retreat style that suited the Hmong. "In the very beginning, I always tried to indoctrinate VP . . . we don't try to hold anything," Lair said. "If you are being attacked heavily, just leave. We just go somewhere else."[12]

Since the agency had never worked closely with the Hmong or Vang Pao before, Lair did not expect his memo to be approved immediately, despite Fitzgerald's enthusiasm. Yet with few other decent options available for fighting in Laos, and with Lair's record of success with the Thai paratroopers, the answer came back "surprisingly soon," Lair recalled. "It was almost like it came back overnight."[13]

If Lair was surprised to get such a quick yes, the always outwardly confident Vang Pao seemed wholly unsurprised that the most powerful country in the world had signed on with his ragged guerilla army. The United States had signed on to back the Hmong, he told other Laotian leaders, because Vang Pao and his men were the only ones who could save Laos. And they would, he promised.[14]

Chapter 7

Kennedy Expands Momentum

WHEN HE BECAME THE THIRTY-FIFTH PRESIDENT OF THE United States on January 20, 1961, John F. Kennedy was surprised to learn from Eisenhower that the United States had as many as 700 CIA trainers and operatives in Laos.[1] He listened to the war contingency plans of his Joint Chiefs of Staff, who had backed down from their earlier plans of sending in 250,000 troops but wanted a firm commitment from the president that, if the situation in Laos remained chaotic, he would send some 60,000 US troops into the kingdom.[2] Kennedy followed closely the battle for Nam Tha, a major town in the north that a joint communist force attacked throughout the first half of 1962. By May 1962, the national army's defenses at Nam Tha would collapse.

The Laotian and Vietnamese communists' attack on Nam Tha, warned the Joint Chiefs, signified that Hanoi and the Pathet Lao were abandoning a strategy of quick strikes—of what the generals called "limited but constant encroachment"—into Laos.[3] Instead, the Joint Chiefs cautioned, the enemy might launch a large nationwide attack.[4] Kennedy had heeded the grim warnings from Eisenhower and his aides about Laos, and he shared Eisenhower's view that Indochina had essential resources and was critical to US ally Japan. Washington had already committed itself significantly to Vientiane, funding much of the Laotian government's budget and national army, and it was always hard to make a sharp break in policy. The young president also believed—at least to an extent—in the domino principle that Eisenhower had enunciated, even if he was shocked when Eisenhower told him "extreme measures" must be taken to save Laos, since the kingdom was critical to stopping communism. (Eisenhower also told the president elect that these measures should include tactical nuclear weapons, if necessary.)[5] At a press conference, Kennedy told reporters: "If Laos fell into Communist hands, it would increase the danger along the northern frontiers of Thailand. It would put additional pressure on Cambodia and would put additional pressure on South Vietnam, which in itself would put additional pressure on Malaya [modern day Malaysia]. So I do accept the view that there is an interrelationship in these countries."[6]

But Kennedy had grave doubts about committing US forces to Laos. Several of his aides recommended that the president try to move Laos to the policy back burner—especially since the Soviets did not seem to consider Laos a high priority. As Kennedy's advisors reminded him, even Soviet leader Nikita Khrushchev, who had spent much of the June 1961 Vienna Summit between the two men haranguing Kennedy, suddenly seemed agreeable when the conversation turned to Laos. Khrushchev had told Kennedy that the two powers should find some acceptable compromise that resulted in a "neutral and independent Laos."[7]

Kennedy had a number of reasons, in fact, why he did not want American ground troops in Laos. He retained a skepticism that any Western forces could prevail in Indochina, be it Laos, Vietnam, or Cambodia. As a Massachusetts congressman in 1951, Kennedy had visited France's Indochinese colonies during the height of the French Indochina War. Kennedy had seen the extent of US support for France's war and witnessed the antipathy of the Vietnamese population toward foreign powers, including the United States. Many locals whom Kennedy met did not see the United States as a different kind of power from France—the beneficent United States envisioned by Lansdale and, to some extent, Bill Lair. "We [the United States] are more and more becoming colonists in the minds of the local people," Kennedy wrote in his diary during his 1951 trip to Saigon.[8]

Now the president worried that inserting US ground troops into Indochina would spark far more local hatred toward the United States, so that America would, like France, be caught fighting against an enemy that enjoyed the majority of popular support. The president had limited background knowledge of Laos, and he did not seem to realize that the Pathet Lao did not have the level of popular legitimacy that Vietnam's communists enjoyed. The Pathet Lao was dominated by Hanoi and could not exist without North Vietnamese support. The Pathet Lao also lacked the popular credentials that Ho Chi Minh and his allies had gained by fighting successfully for independence. (The Laotian communists had played a relatively small role in the Laotian independence movement that had emerged after World War II, but France had granted Laos independence, and so France was still viewed relatively warmly in Laos.) Still, Kennedy worried that Laotian politicians with whom the United States allied would be seen as foreign puppets, and anti-US-intervention sentiment would bolster the communist side.

The White House was also consumed by other issues in the world; repeated foreign policy failures elsewhere made Kennedy seek a negotiated solution in Laos. In Cuba, a major policy focus, the White House had committed itself to a disastrous invasion by exiles in April 1961 at the Bay of Pigs, where Cuban exiles were routed by Cuban government forces in three days. The ferocious Vienna Summit in June 1961, during which Kennedy and Khrushchev spent much of the time verbally battering each other, further inflamed superpower tensions. In Berlin, Cold War rivalry was reaching its peak as well; in August 1961 the Soviets and East Germans had begun building the Berlin Wall, and in October 1961 US and Soviet tanks faced each other in Berlin, only about a hundred yards apart. The White House did not need to get involved in a hot war in another part of the globe while it faced crises on other fronts.

So Kennedy squashed any talk of a US ground war in Laos. He moved part of the US Navy's Seventh Fleet to the Gulf of Thailand, south of Laos, as a warning to Hanoi, Moscow, and the Pathet Lao that if Laos were overrun, the US military might intervene directly.[9] But the president wrote on a May 1961 memo sent by top aides that "Laos . . . is a most inhospitable area in which to wage a [military] campaign. Its geography, topography, and climate are built-in liabilities . . . The chances of [totally] eradicating the Communist position in Laos . . . are practically nil."[10]

Though Kennedy did not want to launch a full-scale military intervention in Laos, the president did not have a clear idea of what to do instead. He was overwhelmed with foreign policy crises, yet he was not going to abandon Laos. Kennedy still believed Laos was important to some kind of victory in Vietnam; Kennedy also shared Eisenhower's enthusiasm for covert action, even after the fiasco at the Bay of Pigs. When Winthrop Brown, the ambassador in Vientiane, met with Kennedy in Washington in February 1961, he told the president, "Laos is hopeless . . . a classic example of a political and economic vacuum."[11] Although Brown's assessment might have helped convince Kennedy not to send ground troops, Brown offered the president no alternative plan for dealing with the kingdom.

The president spiked the war contingency plans of his Joint Chiefs of Staff. Instead, Kennedy sent trusted aides to Geneva to get an agreement with communist countries declaring Laos neutral.[12] Just as he had the year before by sending the Seventh Fleet to the Gulf of Thailand, Kennedy also sent Hanoi and the Pathet Lao an implicit warning that the United States could bring more force to bear: in May 1962 the president dispatched part of an army battle group, an air force squadron, and a part of a marine battalion to Thailand for what he described as defensive measures.[13]

Supremely skilled Geneva negotiator Averell Harriman and his deputy, Bill Sullivan, hammered out the Geneva agreement in July 1962 with the Soviets, North Vietnam, China, and other countries, supposedly guaranteeing Laos's neutrality. Souvanna Phouma, who had become prime minister a fourth time in 1962 during a truce in the fighting, stayed on in the position. He would remain prime minister until the last days of the Laotian civil war, and over time, Souvanna's neutralism would veer far closer to a simple alliance with the United States.

The White House proclaimed success, and toasted Harriman and Sullivan. The regiments of marines from Okinawa, who had been put on alert shortly after the fighting began in Laos in late 1960, were told to stand down.[14]

But Kennedy did not fully trust the agreement, and, indeed, the Geneva deal fell apart quickly, though all the parties would continue for years to maintain the fiction of Laos's neutrality. Kennedy was relatively skeptical that Hanoi would withdraw from Laos. Still, like his predecessor—and his successor, Lyndon Johnson—the president also underestimated the North Vietnamese leadership: he and his advisors believed that it could eventually be made to do what the United States wanted, if the president just came up with the right combination of carrots and sticks. They would "find Ho [Chi Minh's] price . . . whether it was through bombing [the North Vietnamese] or through threatening to use [US] troops and then offering Ho a lollipop," wrote David Halberstam in *The Best and the Brightest*, his seminal account of the Kennedy and Johnson administrations' Indochina policies.[15]

Kennedy's skepticism proved correct. Few North Vietnamese actually left northern and eastern Laos. Unlike the Soviet Union, Hanoi considered Laos a top priority and was not going to abandon the commitments it had made to the Pathet Lao. Hanoi's leaders would use the accords to buy time, bolster their forces in Laos, equip the Pathet Lao, and train more Laotian fighters. The CIA reported that at least eight thousand hardened North Vietnamese troops remained in Laos after the accord was signed, and even neutral observers estimated that there were at least five thousand North Vietnamese soldiers. The Kennedy administration worried that the Soviets were continuing to drop arms into Laos to support communist forces, though it could not find clear evidence of large-scale aid from Moscow. (Even the CIA was unsure whether Moscow was really coordinating regular arms drops.) China also appeared to be staking out a larger role in Laos; after 1964, and Hanoi's acceptance that Chinese aid was necessary to the Laos war, Beijing began providing more engineers, funds, weapons, and training to Laos.[16] Washington's allies in Asia, and particularly the generals who ran the Thai government, were becoming increasingly frantic that the North Vietnamese could overrun Laos at any time they wanted.[17] A Pathet Lao–North Vietnamese takeover would potentially put communist troops along the border with Thailand, which was protected in many places only by isolated Thai military outposts on Bangkok's side of the Mekong River.

The Kennedy administration had also committed military advisors to help the government in South Vietnam. Any threat that North Vietnam and its allies could overrun Laos would be a catastrophe for US commitments to Saigon. If the Pathet Lao and Hanoi had more control over Laos, it would be almost impossible to stop their routes of men and arms through Laos and into South Vietnam. A Pathet Lao–North Vietnamese invasion of Laos also might force the Kennedy administration, confronting multiple other foreign policy crises, to send a significant contingent of US ground troops to defend Thailand.

In a memorandum for the president in June 1963, Kennedy's National Security Council staff sounded much like Eisenhower's, placing Laos at the center of their fears of communist expansion throughout Asia. "The root of the problem in Southeast Asia is the aggressive effort . . . to establish Communist control in Laos and South Vietnam as a stepping stone to control all Southeast Asia," they wrote.[18] In private, Kennedy worried increasingly that although he did not want US ground troops in the kingdom, Laos was too important to protecting the growing war effort in Indochina and saving US partner Thailand to do nothing.

Kennedy also clearly believed that, whatever his hopes for the 1962 Geneva deal, no one was pulling forces from Laos. Yet the president remained convinced that the United States had to keep any intervention in lowland Laos secret, to appear to be upholding the 1962 deal. In addition, US ground forces could eventually have to go into Vietnam, he was now convinced, and the public was unlikely to tolerate an open two-front war. The president gave the CIA authorization to expand Operation Momentum.

Lair used Kennedy's directive to get his CIA bosses to approve new weapons shipments to the Hmong. Weapons drops had been halted briefly after the Geneva deal was signed, but now they would continue for nearly a decade.[19] Vang Pao also was eventually allowed to start sending Hmong to bases in Thailand to learn to become pilots, so the Hmong could fly helicopters and small planes in Laos themselves.[20]

When Bill Lair had gotten the okay from Washington to start the Hmong operation in 1961, he had not expected results so soon. But by the summer of 1963, he already considered Momentum a success. Vang Pao's men had repeatedly ambushed communist forces in north and central Laos exactly the way the Hmong leader had promised. The Hmong would appear out of the jungle when communist troops were on a patrol, ambush three or four enemy soldiers, killing them and capturing their weapons, and vanish back into the mountains.

Unlike some of his bosses in the CIA, Lair did not view the hill tribes as uneducated, even if they did not possess formal Western-style schooling. He enthusiastically promoted the idea of training the Hmong to become pilots, an idea his bosses would approve only reluctantly. "Most people [in the US government] thought you couldn't make an effective soldier with a lot of the ethnic people. But I believed they would be better than the average American soldier sent overseas," Lair said. "In the mountains, the Hmong could walk faster than anybody because they'd never taken a step that wasn't up or down. They were uneducated, so they couldn't read or write, but they were very bright and easy to train. That's what impressed me. And they were fighting for Laos, not for the US."[21]

But Lair also had a basic understanding of the rivalries that divided Hmong clans and might hinder Vang Pao's recruiting. The Hmong leader had charisma, but Lair understood that it would take time for him to get men from all the different clans to take orders and fight together. Lair had expected the program to grow slowly, until there was more of a consensus among clan leaders behind Vang Pao's war effort.

Yet surprisingly, recruiting had not been a problem. Vang Pao's hilltribe army had grown rapidly to over twenty thousand by the spring of 1963. Lair had underestimated Vang Pao's renown from his days fighting with the French, the fear that many Hmong had of communism, their hatred of the Vietnamese, and the simple attraction of guns, money, and fighting for young men in a land where ordinary life could, even without war, be short and brutal. Vang Pao's fierce charisma helped win recruits, too. "VP, when I first met him, I think he was probably the greatest guerrilla leader in the world," Lair observed.[22] Though Lair had seen the poverty among the Hmong, he had also underestimated the drastic situation facing Hmong families. With the civil war tearing up land, many Hmong had become so desperate for anything to eat that sending sons to the secret war's army seemed a reasonable trade for the rice and salt that the United States gave in aid to hungry followers of Vang Pao.[23] And unlike the national Laotian army, Vang Pao's force also had gained a reputation for dealing with its men fairly, and for actually taking charge of the fighting, instead of hanging back and running like some of the national army generals. Vang Pao had not built a massive house with money siphoned from his military operation, like some of the national generals had, and he typically ate and drank the same things as other Hmong officers. The Hmong force paid death benefits to the families of fallen troops.[24]

Vang Pao was hardly an ascetic, and the home he would build in Long Cheng was large by Hmong standards, if not the size of generals' villas in Vientiane. As the war grew in size, and more Hmong became involved, and more soldiers got pay that they could spend, Vang Pao would enter into a variety of businesses: banking, a partial share of a Laotian airline, consumer goods, and others.[25] These businesses would make him wealthy, by Hmong standards, but they were still far from the outright theft of the state budget that had become common in Vientiane. Vang Pao made "an entirely unusual military figure" in Laos because of his relative integrity, reported a classified analysis of the war by the CIA station chief in Laos in the early 1960s.[26] According to some accounts, Vang Pao also profited from the opium trade in his country, which increased dramatically during the course of the war. Opium poppies had always been a traditional crop in parts of the hills of Laos, Thailand, southwestern China, and Burma. Many hill tribes took opium as a kind of medicine—to dull pain and to help with insomnia, among other reasons.[27] Some farmers cultivated the opium, made the sticky poppy crop into bricks, and then traveled to markets in other parts of the Southeast Asian highlands to trade it for other goods or, later on, for Laotian cash. When the Laotian war expanded, drawing in the United States and increasing the size of Vang Pao's army, the potential for growing the drug trade appeared as well.

Many former pilots for the CIA's airline in Laos, known as Air

America, remembered Hmong flying across the kingdom on Air America planes and carrying opium to sell. Other former US officials had similar recollections. Ron Rickenbach, a longtime official in Laos for the United States Agency for International Development (USAID), which disburses and manages US assistance programs, said that the introduction of regular flights in Laos by the CIA's airline helped enable drug traffickers. The CIA, he said, was not trying to get into drug smuggling, but pilots weren't asking any questions of Hmong and Lao officials who carried aboard bricks of opium. "It was then the presence of these air support services in and out of the areas in question where . . . the opium was grown that greatly facilitated an increase in production," Rickenbach said.[28] Neil Hansen, a former pilot for the CIA's airline in Laos, agreed, saying, "I've seen the sticky bricks come on board, and no one was challenging their right to carry it. It was their own property."[29]

Others in Laos, and some scholars of the CIA, suggested that the agency and Vang Pao did more than facilitate the opium trade. They argued that, for the Hmong leader and the CIA, selling opium and heroin was a way to help finance the fight. Alfred McCoy, a specialist on Southeast Asia who reported on the drug trade in Laos in the late 1960s and early 1970s, argued that selling and moving opium was, from the start of the war, central to Vang Pao's life—that he was in business as much as in war. McCoy maintained further, with some compelling detail, that CIA agents in Laos not only knew about Vang Pao's drug businesses but also encouraged the Hmong officer's control of the trade. The heroin, McCoy contended, also flowed into the hands of corrupt officials in South Vietnam, as the percentage of US soldiers in South Vietnam using drugs increased. McCoy concluded that the CIA had taken over old links among French intelligence, narcotics traffickers, and Laotian leaders. For McCoy and some other historians, this CIA involvement in narcotics in Southeast Asia fit a pattern in which agency operatives became involved in narcotics trafficking around the world, in part to fund covert operations.[30]

Without a doubt some Hmong and Laotian military men and politicians were involved in the drug trade, but Vang Pao and his supporters disputed that the Hmong leader was in the opium business, and it remains unclear whether Vang Pao was involved personally or whether he mostly looked the other way as subordinates and other tribal leaders dealt heroin and opium. Richard Secord, Bill Lair, and many other CIA operatives who worked with Vang Pao denied that they encouraged the drug trade in Southeast Asia or that the CIA profited from it. "Opium was always there [in hilltribe areas], but it wasn't [US] government policy to push it, or make money off it," said Lair.[31] "There was no commercial trade in opium going on [on US planes in Laos]," Richard Secord, the former CIA air liaison in Laos, said.[32] It remains difficult to confirm the agency's and Vang Pao's exact roles in the Southeast Asian drug trade, for despite all the CIA material that has been declassified on Laos since the mid-2000s, there is little that discusses narcotics. Paul Hillmer, a historian who has compiled the most complete group of Hmong oral histories, suggests that opium was never as central to the war effort as some like McCoy have suggested, and that there was only weak evidence, at best, that Vang Pao was involved in drugs at all.[33]

Still, even if Vang Pao derived part of his power from control over the opium trade, it was undeniable that Hmong men were walking across northern Laos to join his army. They might have come in part because of the promise of money, which might have been either money directly from the CIA or from the opium trade, but the allure of cash was only part of the reason. "The volunteers came flocking in, and not only Hmong, but also Khmu [another hill tribe], and even some [ethnic] Lao," Vang Pao said. "They all wanted weapons." The village of huts around Vang Pao's headquarters in the mountain valley of Long Cheng seemed to be growing daily. Long Cheng was situated smack in the center of the wide northern part of Laos, near Vientiane and the Vietnam border. The flat valley would prove perfect for a runway, though foggy in rainy season, and the surrounding mountains made it challenging for an enemy army to attack it. New fighters and their families were hastily putting up wooden homes with thatched roofs and holes in the middle for Hmong clay stoves. Across the runway from the village of thatched houses, the CIA and Vang Pao's lieutenants erected more modern concrete buildings with iron roofs that had communications technology, rooms for food and ammunition, strategy rooms with safes for CIA documents, and beds for pilots who needed to rest before their next flight.[34] The army was expanding so rapidly that many of the new arrivals did not even have the time to hold proper traditional Hmong house-construction cere-monies, where chickens would be sacrificed near the doorstep, an ap-peal to spirits who could menace the home.[35]

Vang Pao demanded loyalty from his soldiers, but not spit-and-polish discipline.[36] The Hmong leader didn't seem to care if his soldiers sat in his hut all night arguing about plans for the next at-tack or what marriageable girls would be around after the dry sea-son. Hosting his men was an obligation, and being able to sit down with Vang Pao—rather than merely taking orders from some distant figure—seemed to motivate men to fight.[37] The Hmong leader had a vast wooden table installed inside his home, so big that eighty to one hundred men could sit or squat around it, eat, and talk.[38] Sometimes groups of Hmong picked their officers, a process that Vang Pao usu-ally allowed, at least at the beginning of Momentum. According to Vint Lawrence, who served as a case officer in Laos as a young CIA operative, Vang Pao's "men would come in every day . . . they would just expect Vang Pao to listen, and they would just argue and argue and argue. It was almost like a Hmong kind of town meeting . . . dif-ferent from the politicians I met in Thailand or Vientiane, who were usually accompanied by a whole retainer of people and demanded they be treated like kings."[39]

Still, what had seemed like a ragtag force had proven itself capa-ble even in battles larger than an ambush. In December 1961, accord-ing to a classified CIA history of the operation, Hmong forces fought off a determined attack by North Vietnamese troops just outside the town of Xiang Khouang, despite relentless North Vietnamese shelling of the Hmong's positions.[40] The next year, in August 1962, North Vietnamese troops attacked hills around a Hmong base called Phou Koup, in northeastern Laos. According to a classified CIA history of the battle, the Hmong at Phou Koup were not even among Vang Pao's most experienced men. Many were in excellent shape, and had been hiking over the high, stone peaks and narrow river gorges of the area for months, but few of them had received any formal training, and they lacked enough ammunition for their small arms, mortars, and rockets. Communist forces dug what they called spider holes in the ground, which allowed them to fire on the Hmong without being hit by return fire.[41] The Hmong defenders used up much of what they had firing on the North Vietnamese, as the morning fog burned off and visibility remained poor, without realizing that the spider holes made the enemy virtually untouchable.[42]

As the Hmong ran even lower on ammunition, the North Vietnamese launched a frontal attack, trying to overwhelm the Phou Koup defenders. Yet "despite the paucity of training, the Hmong held off the enemy with small-arms fire long enough" to save the civilians at Phou Koup and keep communist forces from advancing farther, a classified history of the battle reported.[43]

In early 1963, Vang Pao notched by far his biggest triumph to date. The Hmong leader's spies had told him that communist forces in the town of Sam Neua had become vulnerable to an attack. Sam Neua was one of the largest Laotian towns near the northeastern border with North Vietnam, and the Pathet Lao considered it and the surrounding area its safest stronghold in Laos.

North Vietnamese officers had taken troops away from Sam Neua to launch attacks in other parts of the country. Hitting Sam Neua might force the joint North Vietnamese–Pathet Lao force to retreat from other parts of Laos to defend the town, and scare them away from attacking farther into the heart of Laos. A successful attack on Sam Neua, Vang Pao thought, also might demonstrate that his army was capable of taking sizable towns.

Tony Poe also had heard from several Hmong who had captured communist soldiers that Sam Neua was vulnerable. Vang Pao launched a plan to divide and overwhelm the communists. The Hmong leader would send three battalions to surprise a small communist stronghold just north of Sam Neua, gambling that the main force in the city would leave Sam Neua to reinforce the garrison, allowing the Hmong to take the city and then trap the communists outside Sam Neua.

The tactic worked just as it was drawn up. Vang Pao's three battalions took the small garrison outside the city, and the communist forces inside Sam Neua began to panic. As communist troops ran to reinforce the garrison, Vang Pao's fourth group of men snuck into Sam Neua town from the west, while other Hmong quietly surrounded the communists on the roads north of town. The Hmong took Sam Neua with almost no resistance and then snuck up on the enemy troops that had hurried north, capturing or killing much of the communist force.

The CIA's own classified analyses of the Hmong exulted over the rapid learning curve demonstrated by Vang Pao and his men. "The Hmong who constituted the bulk of the manpower had, in the space of two and a half years, undergone a transformation," noted one CIA classified report. "Tribal irregulars previously uncomprehending of any technique or tactic beyond ambush at the approaches to one's own village could now be deployed, in relatively large units, far from home . . . With some expert help, they could mount a sophisticated, coordinated offensive operation."[44]

After the Sam Neua battle, Vang Pao's renown spread throughout Laos. The government promoted him to the rank of general in the national army, and lowland military leaders, who normally disdained the Hmong, flew up to Vang Pao's base to honor him and hear the story of the Sam Neua ambush. Vang Pao received the lowland generals at his home, exulting quietly as they clasped their hands together and bowed slightly before him. Stories spread to Vientiane of ethnic Lao volunteering to serve for Vang Pao.

Laos's monarch, King Savang Vatthana, the epitome of cultured and royal society, traveled to Vang Pao's headquarters at Long Cheng to observe Operation Momentum in person. Long Cheng was, in the relative center of Laos, close enough to Vientiane, the western border, and the eastern border to be strategic. The king was not the actual ruler of the country, but he still commanded respect among many Laotians. The king disliked rough journeys outside of the city where he resided, Luang Prabang, a small gem of temples, Buddhist statuary, green hills, and lemon-yellow French villas, on a peninsula jutting out into two rivers. The king preferred to spend his time receiving visitors in a long chamber room behind an iron gate with guards standing stock-still in the heat, which could top 110 degrees Fahrenheit. So the fact that he had flown up to Long Cheng to honor Vang Pao and the Hmong was especially notable.[45] The monarch reviewed a Hmong military parade and was welcomed by flocks of Hmong waving Laos's royal flag, which had on it drawings of white elephants, the symbol of Laos's monarchy.[46] Although the stocky, ruddy Hmong general bowed his head down to the Laotian king, many people in Long Cheng noted that Vang Pao later stood right next to the monarch and addressed him directly, an uncommon frankness toward a king still regarded by many Laotians as semidivine.

For Bill Lair, and for many other CIA clandestine officers working in Laos, Operation Momentum in the early 1960s was an almost ideal arrangement. The agency was fighting a war with potent and hungry allies, struggling for a cause that was easy to believe in. The Hmong suffered losses, but they won more than Lair had expected, and their victories made the decision to initiate Operation Momentum look right.

Lair was happy as 1963 came to an end, and the normally reserved Texan admitted as much to several of his colleagues. He was happy at home, and he was happy with the Laos operation, in the same way he had been happy when he first officially joined the Thai police paratroops and was working alongside them.

Later, many CIA operatives would talk about the beginning of the Hmong operation as if it were almost holy. CIA officers felt a "great effervescence, a sense that we had finally found people who would fight the communists and occasionally defeat them in guerilla warfare," former CIA case officer James Lilley remembered. "It was a sacred war. A good war."[47]

Bill Lair was not a boaster, but even he told several of his aides that he'd been given a long leash by the American Embassy in Laos, a sign of respect for him. The American ambassadors before 1964 were, generally, cautious diplomats, and they appreciated Lair's experience in Southeast Asia. Leonard Unger, the ambassador from 1962 to 1964, had great respect for Lair. He invited the shy Texan to the ambassador's residence in Vientiane for dinner several times. Lair, who seemed uncomfortable in any formal clothes, would show up in the same dark suit and tie clip each time.

Lair found it difficult to make small talk, but Unger could put him at ease. At the end of the evening, in typical Lair style, after other conversation had been exhausted, Lair would come around to his main message and remind the ambassador of what he saw as the central lesson of the operation: "Don't ever let the locals think mighty America will fight their battles or solve all their problems for them; focus on getting them ready to fix their own problems."[48] It was the same reminder he delivered to younger CIA men coming to Laos.

Director of Central Intelligence John McCone seemed supportive of the operation too, as much as the agency's Far East division could tell, since McCone had been preoccupied with Cuba. Momentum seemed to be working, but Laos was still too obscure for anyone to make his career at the CIA by boasting of having managed the Laos operation.

And yet very soon, Laos would become much better known in the agency. Indeed, in 1963 Laos already received more American aid, per capita, than South Vietnam or any other countries in Southeast Asia.[49] Money was power: it meant that CIA officers could at least claim they would be supported all the way up the chain of command. "The money for Laos was going up; that meant the operation had patrons at higher levels in CIA," explained John Gunther Dean, a longtime diplomat in Southeast Asia.

Lair and several of his most trusted Thai paratroop officers were now flying up to the Hmong base at Long Cheng to meet with Vang Pao regularly. They would fly up on the special Helio Courier plane. The Helio did not seem like much, with its rickety-looking propeller and tiny fuselage, but it was perfect for ferrying supplies and CIA men into a hilly country with few maintained airports.[50] Though its engines were not powerful, it had flaps on its wings that helped it go from full throttle to gliding in just seconds, which allowed the pilot to shoot down quickly into a remote valley and take off again just as easily.[51] The pilots would rumble just a few feet on the ground and catapult into the air again like magic.

For his part, Vang Pao seemed happy with the deal he had made, though it was sometimes hard to tell. Many times, when Lair would arrive in Long Cheng, he would find the Hmong leader walking in circles, manically moving his legs, issuing orders, and waving his arms at the same time; he would stop for a few seconds to welcome Lair and then go back quickly to talking and walking again. Some of the other Hmong would seem overwhelmed by the general's pacing and rapid-fire speech, punctuated by gestures that looked like he was shadowboxing. Others walked with him, circling back and forth and talking all the while as fast as their legs churned. Lair stood and watched, saying nothing.

Still, Vang Pao was confident that American aid would indeed help the Hmong hold off communist forces. And he liked working with Lair. "The Americans, Bill Lair, they were trying to help us, not to use us," Vang Pao said. In 1963 the Hmong leader said he believed that the Hmong and the United States were true partners.[52]

Vang Pao often welcomed the Helios personally when they flew in, but he wanted more supply drops—and other kinds of air support too. With American bombers clearing the way for them, the Hmong could be much more than a guerilla army, he suggested to Lair. The Texan said little in response. The agency was coordinating Vang Pao's training and his supplies, but Lair and his bosses were not, yet, in the business of finding bombers to help Vang Pao.

Chapter 8

The Not-So-Secret Secret: Keeping a Growing Operation Hidden

OPERATION MOMENTUM WAS, BY 1964, UNKNOWN TO most of the world but not completely hidden. The Laos war remained a kind of not-so-secret secret war, in which a small circle of people in Washington and Southeast Asia understood the growing operation but did nothing to publicize it to Americans. CIA directors, members of presidential staffs, and members of Congress were aware of Momentum; its budget came from the CIA's appropriations, as well as from the budgets of other agencies. Unlike the Iran-Contra operation in the 1980s, where money for Nicaraguan rebels was raised through arms sales and then funneled through European banks, the financing for Momentum was as aboveboard as any CIA operation could be.

The fact that the actual fighting on the ground was being done by the Hmong, a foreign proxy army, allowed the agency and American presidents to sidestep constitutional requirements that Congress had to approve any wars involving American forces. Still, sidestepping did not mean that members of Congress were totally ignorant about Operation Momentum, as many would claim later. Although

CIA leaders denied in open congressional hearings anything about the agency's operations in Laos—the CIA's guidelines instructed CIA officials to deny classified operations in public hearings—in classified hearings with members of Congress who oversaw intelligence, agency directors did, in fact, reveal some details about Momentum.

Some foreign reporters who came through Laos also sensed that Vang Pao's large, increasingly better-equipped army must be getting much more American support than anyone let on. But information about the operation trickled in piecemeal—to aid workers and to some reporters. The agency could prevent them from ever seeing the the full picture. No one but Lair, the US ambassador in Vientiane, senior advisors to the president, and a few other CIA clandestine officers in Laos and CIA officials back in Washington had the whole picture of Operation Momentum anyway. Reporters who came to Laos never saw the Helio flights to Vang Pao's base. The flights came in to Long Cheng from Thailand, and Thai air bases remained off-limits to American outsiders. It was hard to get anywhere in Laos, too; unlike Vietnam, where the roads were passable, there was a growing US military presence and military transport, and you could usually travel almost anywhere in the South.

A few reporters were allowed, in secret, to visit some of the Hmong areas, but always after signing an agreement with US Embassy officials confirming that they would keep the sites secret, and would focus, more generally, on the Hmong's struggle against communism. These trips never included briefings with CIA operatives or any discussion of the CIA's role in the war. A former *Los Angeles Times* correspondent in Southeast Asia noted that when the US Embassy was worried that a reporter might expose the extent of American involvement in a country that was, theoretically, still neutral and hosting no foreign force, someone there would ask the correspondent to use "discretion" in his reporting. Until the late 1960s, American journalists, not wishing to alienate the ambassador and unable to find any solid sources on the CIA's involvement in Laos, followed the embassy's advice.[1]

In addition to Tony Poe and a tiny group of other CIA case officers in up-country Laos, the agency in 1964 was also working with a select group of contractors. For now, the contractors were pilots, mostly: men who could fly the Helios to Vang Pao's men and land on tiny plots of dirt that passed for airstrips in Laos.

Bill Lair mostly trusted the contractors. Even though there was only a handful of Laos contractors, and they were not official CIA employees, the contractors usually had been working with agency operations for over a decade. Lair felt they could be trusted not to boast about their flights to American friends back at the bars on Petchburi Road and Soi Cowboy in Bangkok, where the pilots congregated to relax. The screening process for finding these contractors was relatively rigorous, Lair believed, and he treated the pilots and other contractors no differently than he would actual agency employees.

Lair had particularly come to trust the contractors from the agency's Asia airline, Air America, which had a thin cover as a charter airline but relied mostly on agency money and agency flights to survive. The pilots and mechanics usually were Southeast Asia lifers, just like Lair; they usually had Thai or Laotian wives, like Lair; their wives usually knew that the men didn't really work for a regular charter, but they didn't ask too many questions. Lair also liked that the contractors treated the Thais and the Hmong with respect, like equals.[2]

Lair's trust in the CIA contractors would soon ebb.

To maintain secrecy, the CIA tried hard to ingratiate itself with certain members of Congress who had been supportive initially of aid for the Hmong. By 1964, Lair, CIA case officers based at Long

Cheng, and General Vang Pao himself had become used to occasional congressional delegations flying up to Hmong country in the mosquito-like Helios. The congressmen and senators would fly in from Vientiane or an air base in northern Thailand for a quick consultation with Vang Pao, who was usually smiling and dressed in fatigues and a jaunty kind of camouflage cap, which looked like a green cowboy hat adapted to the jungle.[3]

The visiting US politicians would have had to dig a bit during their trips to understand how rapidly Operation Momentum was growing, since the agency tried to play down the size of American aid, and members of Congress would be whisked out of up-country Laos after a day or two at most. CIA case officers created an entire fake "headquarters" for Vang Pao to host dignitaries. It was located away from Vang Pao's actual base at Long Cheng, so that he could portray his war as a tiny Hmong-run guerilla fight that received only food assistance and other humanitarian aid from generous US funds.[4] The general usually gave all congressmen and senators the same briefing: telling them that the Hmong could beat the Pathet Lao and the North Vietnamese as long as they got American aid, and laying out maps of northern Laos filled with complicated diagrams of the places Vang Pao planned to take from the communists. The congressmen and senators almost always came away impressed with the Hmong leader's planning and seriousness. Sometimes, when members of Congress visited, CIA officers and Vang Pao would arrange for a few Hmong villagers to approach the Americans, seemingly on their own initiative, to drape wreaths of flowers around the beaming congressmen's necks and to praise US leaders for helping the Hmong. Vang Pao somehow always picked the prettiest young Hmong women to drape the flowers on the congressmen.[5]

Senator Stuart Symington, a powerful Missouri politician who served on the Senate Armed Services Committee and the Senate Foreign Relations Committee, was one of the members of Congress given access to details of Operation Momentum, both in Washington briefings and on trips to Laos. He attended numerous classified CIA congressional briefings on Laos. A Democrat who was running for a third term in 1964, Symington prided himself on his knowledge of intelligence and spying; in Laos, he even stayed at the house of the CIA's Vientiane station chief, with no illusions about the chief's thin diplomatic cover. Symington praised the agency in closed-door meetings with senior agency officials, including the CIA head, for achieving results while spending relatively little American money.[6] An internal CIA history of the 1960s concluded that, for most of the decade, Symington was probably Congress's strongest champion of the Laos operation.[7]

By the end of the 1960s, the task of keeping a war from the American public would become too hard even for the CIA. Too many people would learn too much about Operation Momentum, and the genteel consensus in Washington—among reporters, members of Congress, and the CIA—to keep intelligence work quiet would be shattered by the Vietnam War. The CIA would have to take far more extreme measures to hide its aid to the Hmong, and to punish anyone who tried to reveal just how deeply involved the United States was in Laos's war.

Symington himself would become transformed: a senator worried about how the voting public would react if it knew that he had, for so long, just accepted the agency's version of events in Laos. He would hold hearings to investigate US involvement in the kingdom. He would call agency leaders to testify, and would pretend he had known nothing about Momentum when it began. The CIA would respond to Symington's hearings with fury—"a deeply felt sense of having been betrayed by a trusted friend," the agency's own classified internal history of its relations with Congress reported.[8]

But in 1964, the Central Intelligence Agency had no reason to believe that the trusted few who knew about Momentum would leak information to the public. Bill Lair thought that even if the American people found out somehow about the Laos operation, they would support it anyway. But Lair did not want to involve the public: by

1964, he had worked for the CIA for nearly fifteen years, and he did not question the need for secrecy. Still, Lair believed, Momentum was basically a way to help a small tribe on the run fight communism and hold on to their lives. He felt certain that if America's role in Laos was found out, it would reflect positively on the United States.[9]

Chapter 9

Enter the Bombers

THE WORKDAY IN VIENTIANE STARTED EARLY, SINCE THE early morning contained the few daylight hours where humans could tolerate working outdoors. As in other tropical countries, daybreak and sunset varied little from season to season, and the sun would go from down to up, and up to down, in what seemed like a few seconds. When the sun rose over dusty Vientiane, with chickens scratching in the dirt around even the most elaborate French-style villas, there was little of the bustle of Saigon or Bangkok, where motorcycles and three-wheeled *tuk-tuks* clogged road overpasses and crowds poured through the dirty main streets. On a Vientiane morning, busyness meant something else entirely. Monks wandered down the alleys with begging bowls for people to give them scoops of rice to eat. A few money changers laid out piles of Laotian currency in front of the morning market, diagonally opposite the revered That Luang *stupa*, a triangular Buddhist shrine. The That Luang resembles one golden spike atop hundreds of smaller shining golden spikes. An occasional pedicab puttered in and out of the morning market, and some of the market vendors hauled baskets of small chilies and bags of rice over their shoulders. Only two miles from the city center, farmers raised pigs and cultivated small plots of rice.

At the US ambassador's residence, a few blocks from the Mekong River, Bill Sullivan defied the slow Laos routine that many diplomats fell into after coming to Vientiane. Sullivan woke early for a light breakfast at home. He rarely went to the street-side cafes serving fresh baguettes and drip coffee sweetened with condensed milk, where many junior American diplomats liked to take the morning and enjoy Vientiane's tranquility before the heat and the dust of the day covered everything in a thin layer of grit and dried sweat. When he arrived at the embassy, Sullivan read through the cables that had come in overnight from other embassies in the region, and then leafed through a pile of summaries of foreign news reports aides had prepared for him. In the late morning, Sullivan received the US military attaché, the embassy deputy chief of mission, and sometimes top Laotian politicians. The late-morning individual meetings were usually short and intense; despite his patrician manner, Sullivan would have a list of questions prepared for his guests, and he would spit them out quickly. Later, Sullivan would hold a bigger meeting, which he chaired, of all the chiefs of American government outfits in Vientiane, including the CIA, USAID, and many others.

This was a practice that no previous ambassador in Laos—or ambassadors in most other countries—had ever established, since few agency heads were willing to attend a meeting every day to listen to the ambassador tell them how exactly to do *their* jobs. But Sullivan quickly cowed most of the American mission in Laos. Within months of his arrival, he got most of the agency heads at his meeting each day, where Sullivan would give orders about every aspect of their work.

In the afternoon, Sullivan often took his car out to the airfield on the edge of Vientiane, which featured large billboards with the face of the king and red letters on its sole terminal, a crumbling concrete building with bags of luggage strewn outside. Planes traveled out to up-country Laos with bags of American rice, tools, seeds, and sometimes aluminum sheets for the Hmong to use to build simple homes. Sullivan squeezed into one of the row of seats in the back of the bulky transport planes shuttling in and out of Vientiane, alongside the USAID officers who regularly traveled up-country. Even in the heat and smoke of the airport, where baggage handlers and even traffic controllers often fell asleep at midday leaning on the side of the terminal, Sullivan rarely took off his suit jacket. He kept the handkerchief in his pocket neatly folded, with the top triangle peering out, and his cuffs always seemed freshly pressed, no matter how much Sullivan had walked around that day or how humid the air had become.

The ambassadors in Laos before Sullivan had not demanded that CIA operatives run every single Laos plan by them—and they probably could not have gotten the agency to agree to it anyway. From the time he came to the kingdom, Sullivan demonstrated that past practices would no longer apply. He would approve, and even choose, battle targets for the Laos war. He would decide, along with the agency and Vang Pao, where the Hmong should attack, how they should attack, and how the US would help them—or not. He warned his own aides, and the CIA officers he met in Laos, that if he found out agency staffers were going around him, as they had before, he would ensure they were punished by being transferred out of the Laos operation and buried in some desk job or some horrific posting elsewhere in the world. Sullivan's connections at senior levels of the White House gave those threats power.

Within months of Sullivan's arrival, the message had clearly sunk in: the CIA station in Vientiane sent word to clandestine officers in Laos that no one should go around the new ambassador.[1] The agency also recognized that Sullivan didn't just have to be briefed—he was going to make as many decisions about the operation as the CIA would. As one of the agency's own historians admitted, in a retrospective of the Laos war, "William Sullivan was the most important and influential man in the twenty-year history of America's military assistance program in Laos. For more than four years, Sullivan ran . . . the [Laos] war."[2]

Sullivan worked closely with the CIA but not with the American military; he and the CIA station in Vientiane went to extraordinary lengths to keep the US Army out of Momentum. Ambassador Sullivan did not allow the army colonel whose job was to provide counsel for running the war in Laos to do much more than make plans to "sup-ply rice and bullets," in the words of the Pentagon officer who worked with Sullivan.[3] Using his influence in the Johnson administration, Sullivan made sure that this colonel, who had four times the wartime experience as Sullivan and the CIA station chief together, could not even reside in Laos. The advisor, Sullivan insisted, had to live in Bang-kok, where he had to rely on secondhand intelligence about what was happening in Laos, passed to him from foreign diplomats and a few sympathetic American diplomats.[4] "Sullivan's authority over US mili-tary activity in Laos went largely unquestioned," wrote CIA historian Timothy Castle.[5]

So, as Castle wrote, in the most diplomatic way, a "unique" situa-tion resulted. The war in Laos grew larger, with almost no input from actual warriors. The military men who were supposed to advise on the war lived in a kind of exile in Bangkok and were treated, at best, by the CIA and Sullivan as "clerks," as Castle put it. Soon the United States would start bombing extensively in the kingdom. Still, Sullivan retained the "galling presumption that a diplomat knew more about the employment of airpower than trained airmen."[6]

By the first months of 1965, as Bill Sullivan was settling into his post, Bill Lair continued following his own regular morning routine. At Udorn Air Base in northeastern Thailand, Lair woke up at sunrise, when roosters crowed and packs of scrawny wild dogs howled and rummaged through garbage. For all but a few days in late December and early January, when the mercury dropped into the 60s in Fahren-heit and Thais donned parkas as if they were climbing the Alps, the temperature fluctuated between moderately hot and blazing hot. Lair didn't much care—he might not have wanted a job in oil drilling, but he'd always loved the heat of the Texas Panhandle, and Thailand's tem-peratures did not bother him.

Lair shaved and had a small breakfast of an egg and rice, or a bit of soup and rice. He cleaned his thick glasses, which always somehow looked cracked—a counterpoint to his stiff, military-style appearance. He put on a pair of tightly creased tan slacks—he had ten or twelve pairs that all looked pretty much the same and a rack of dress shirts that were indistinguishable from one another. Indeed, Lair's appearance seemed virtually identical from day to day, and that was fine with him.

Lair arrived in his office at the base by eight o'clock, usually to find his deputy, Pat Landry, already there. The two men had a boxlike office in the small wooden bungalow that housed the CIA operation at Udorn, and they sat so close together that their shoulders often touched. The wood hut, shaped like a traditional Thai building, with a steeply sloping roof, had no decorations save for a sign above the door that read AB-1 when the CIA took it over; Lair and Landry and everyone else in Operation Momentum would forever refer to the Udorn station as AB-1.[7] Lair and Landry used their proximity to speak on the two phones to different officials in Laos or Thailand or Washington, using hand signals to coordinate their messages and responses at the same time as they spoke.

Every morning, Lair called the Vientiane and Bangkok stations and read through cables that had come in from Washington overnight. He took a cigar out of a box he kept on his desk and chewed on it as he read; he was an occasional smoker but also liked to simply gnaw the cigar ends. Lair opened the office safe and took out one of his spiral writing notebooks, in which he jotted down supply requisitions and how much supplies would cost. He stuck it in his pants pocket. Lair took a kind of pride in keeping all the operation costs in these small spiral notebooks. Any operation where the accounting was done in cheap notebooks, he thought, was an operation that hadn't been taken over by Washington bureaucrats.[8]

Although Lair would never admit to being introspective, he liked to take a few minutes after reading the cables to walk around the base and think about the operation's future. Midday, he often had to fly up to Long Cheng to meet with Vang Pao; although the CIA had clandestine officers stationed there, the general liked to see Lair almost every day as a matter of course. It seemed to reassure Vang Pao that America's commitment to the Hmong remained strong. And when Lair landed at Long Cheng, dropping into the valley's airstrip, he often felt a surge of pride seeing Hmong troops drilling, or Hmong boys and girls learning to read in small makeshift classrooms along the slopes of the Long Cheng hills.

By the first months of 1965, Lair's pride still swelled when he flew into Long Cheng, but the Texan was beginning to have grave doubts about the direction of the operation he still considered his personal project. Lair kept his doubts to himself—not even sharing them with Landry, with whom he spent more time than he did with his wife—but he couldn't shake them from his mind.

The CIA station chiefs in Laos and Thailand in the early 1960s had known Lair before the operation started and had trusted him. They had allowed Lair to keep the number of CIA case officers involved to a handful. And in the early 1960s, Laos, though an obsession of Eisenhower's and Kennedy's, was still considered a backwater for career-oriented agency men. It was thus not surprising that mediocre, less career-minded station chiefs had not questioned Bill Lair, a man with more than a decade under his belt in Indochina, fluency in Thai and Lao, and more contacts in the region than any station chief.

But Vang Pao's victories, and reports of how much power the CIA wielded in the kingdom, had made Laos a much more desirable place for clandestine officers. At agency training, recruits in 1965 already knew that the CIA was in full charge of the war in Laos. A new agency man could personally make a real difference, not be some tiny cog in a huge operation in a place such as Saigon or Berlin. So Laos started to attract a different type of recruit: company men. "The success with Vang Pao was so good that everybody wanted to get into it. Reputations and big promotions were to be made for those Americans working with the Hmong," said Lair.[9] "Laos was the promised land" for clandestine paramilitary operatives, recalled James Parker, a former CIA officer who served with the Hmong. "The CIA ran the war there . . . We heard throughout training that we were getting the most out of our resources and were actually accomplishing our mission there."[10]

Lair thought that the CIA officers now coming to Southeast Asia did not care to learn much about the region or about the Hmong. They didn't understand the lean, Hmong-owned plan Lair had put into place. They didn't trust or really respect the Hmong; they mocked their traditions, such as not bathing regularly for fear of washing powerful spirits off of one's body.[11] "We didn't own [the Hmong] . . . they needed us, but if we lost their respect, we didn't have any other decent army in Laos," Lair said. "Then what?"[12]

Lair also noticed that, increasingly, the agency was turning to contractors as the war expanded. The contractors were, in many cases, similar to Tony Poe, but for the agency's management, they came without the hassles of having Poe as your actual employee. The contractors were often men with army and air force training and experience in previous wars. Yet if contractors grew stressed in wartime jobs that were often dangerous and isolating, and began displaying insane behaviors like Poe's, they could simply be fired. Using contractors was generally cheaper than actually hiring men like Tony Poe. It also made it easier to conceal the war.

In this hiring deluge, many contractors were recruited knowing nothing about Laos—or, Lair realized, about the risks involved in Operation Momentum. That made them dangers, not assets.

CIA operatives and the air force pilots loaned to the Laos operation mostly understood the dangers of the secret war. Many of the pilots had received extensive combat training during their time in the air force or other branches of the military, before they came to Laos. But the expanding operation also required other types of contractors—engineers, forward air controllers, surveillance technicians—who were hired through private companies or sometimes loaned from other branches of the armed forces. These men had only minimal combat training in the private sector or the uniformed military before coming to the kingdom.

The technicians, engineers, and others would travel to Bangkok to have the records of their air force or army backgrounds deleted. Then they would be given false identities as workers for a number of different American companies, a practice the agency in Laos called "sheep dipping." (Sheep dipping was a common term in intelligence circles for giving someone a new identity. On farms, dipping sheep in insecticide helped remove bugs and parasites from their bodies, leaving them clean; thus, "sheep dipping" operatives was supposed to "clean" them of any details of their former identities.) The sheep-dipped workers were given uniforms of technicians for Sears, or Lockheed Martin, or other major American companies, They were flown into Laos to service or set up surveillance and radar sites, or to work on planes, mortars, and other equipment. These men were then expunged from official records. Even when the king of Laos attempted to give awards to them, the embassy declared that no Americans in the kingdom could accept such decorations, even in private.[13]

Though sites in Laos where engineers, air controllers, and technicians were needed increasingly drew enemy attacks, most of the sheep-dipped men had only sidearms—if that—to defend themselves and did not know how to use bigger weapons. As several classified CIA analyses concluded, the agency simply did not naturally see the technicians as fighters and was not used to taking the kinds of precautions that the armed forces did for anyone who served in a combat zone. (For example, army medics in World War II or Vietnam received significant combat training before going into the field.) "The sheep-dipped technicians, unarmed and posing as civilians, were not really combatants, yet they were in a position where close combat was almost inevitable," concluded one CIA retrospective of the war in Laos.[14]

Lair warned his bosses at the Far East division that sheep dipping men who were not fighters and sending them into Laos was asking for Americans to be killed, and dead Americans could expose the entire operation.[15] The Far East division ignored Lair's warnings.

———

The spate of new men was one worry for Lair. There was a bigger worry, too, consuming his thoughts as he ate breakfast by himself or walked the base or lay in bed at night. Laos wasn't just full of new CIA operatives that Lair did not understand and did not really trust. The operation there was becoming a new type of war.

Vang Pao had Laotian generals and even the king almost worshipping him, but he wanted more. He repeated his one big demand to Lair and to other CIA officers at Long Cheng, like a mantra: he wanted American bombers and fighters, which he knew were housed at air bases all over northeastern Thailand, on call for him to win larger battles. Vang Pao's shocking victory at Sam Neua had strengthened his conviction that his army could take towns and drive whole North Vietnamese divisions out of the country. "We could stop the North Vietnamese if we had air cover," Vang Pao insisted.[16]

Although the United States was the most powerful nation in the world, Vang Pao and his men were almost always outgunned, in terms of rifles and artillery, by North Vietnamese soldiers. The Hmong sometimes skirmished with the Pathet Lao, who were not so well equipped, but much of the fighting in Laos was done by the North Vietnamese army, not the Pathet Lao. The CIA had provided Vang Pao with World War II–era American rifles and machine guns, but the North Vietnamese had newer Chinese- and Soviet-made weaponry. This was not necessarily because the Chinese and Soviets had more money to fund their allies. During the French Indochina War, US weaponry provided to the French forces was far superior to the weaponry supplied to Ho Chi Minh's forces. But now the latest American guns were hard for Lair to obtain: the US military saved them for its own soldiers and close military allies, not for a tribal army over which American generals had no real control. Airpower might alter this imbalance, but for now, the Hmong were *always* outmanned; whenever they fought a battle that was more than a hit-and-run, the communists usually had four or five times as many men.

Foreigners often saw Vang Pao as a man driven only by instincts, but the Hmong leader enjoyed reading and thinking about war. He could read some French, and he had read books and newspaper accounts of the power of new aerial weapons, including napalm and the heavier, bunker-busting bombs that the larger American bombers could drop. Vang Pao had heard firsthand, too, from some of the French officers in the 1950s, how the new American bombs could turn any battle and save almost any desperate situation.

One story of deliverance stuck in Vang Pao's mind. During the earlier French Indochina War, French and pro-French Vietnamese forces dug in around the town of Vinh Yen in early 1951 were nearly overrun by waves of Viet Minh soldiers. France's troop commander ordered vast air strikes, relying on a new air weapon that had been utilized in World War II. The air assault, the biggest of the war, stopped the Viet Minh advance at the last minute by dropping napalm, an incendiary that stuck to the skin of men as it fell from the sky like a curtain of fire. Thousands of Viet Minh infantrymen were roasted to death in a wall of chemical heat that split the battlefield in two.[17] The entrenched French fighters shot down the fleeing Viet Minh en masse.[18] French soldiers who had been at Vinh Yen said it felt less like war and more like hunting animals or executing men as part of a firing squad. The defeat was probably the Viet Minh's worst of the war.

Now Vang Pao hoped that American airpower could even his own people's odds against the North Vietnamese.

———

When he was at Long Cheng, Vang Pao was addressed either by his military rank or as "Uncle," a Hmong term of respect, according to one account of the Laos war. Several CIA officers had taken to calling the Hmong leader "the Wizard" for his mastery of fighting and his almost supernatural ability to survive close combat.[19]

He had gained a following that seemed, to visitors who came to Long Cheng, to give him not just the traditional respect that Hmong gave to a clan leader but also almost the worship due to a god. Historically, clan leaders could be powerful, but they usually had only tens or hundreds of people in their clan, and they did not feed their clans, or clothe them, or really do much to protect them; they helped make decisions and represented the group to other clans, and sometimes they helped shamans who divined the clan's future. Vang Pao was much more powerful than any Hmong leader had ever been. His former mentor, Touby Lyfoung, remained involved in Laotian politics, but without the massive US support, Touby Lyfoung could no longer match Vang Pao's influence. Although most Hmong fought on the side of the national army and the United States, a handful of Hmong leaders had allied themselves with the Laotian-Vietnamese communist forces. However, Hanoi and the Pathet Lao could not give them the amounts of food and bags of cash that the CIA could provide Vang Pao.

One reason for this was that the CIA directed much of its food and arms drops through Vang Pao rather than spreading the assistance around. In fact, the general frequently flew in a low-cruising helicopter throughout northern and central Laos, looking for Hmong refugees in the jungle and forest. When Vang Pao saw refugees, he would yell out the chopper window for the Hmong to stay in place; then he would return with drops of food and essential supplies to keep them alive.[20] The agency's strategy of dealing only with Vang Pao made it easier to distribute guns and food, but it concentrated power in one person. "We wanted to just deal with Vang Pao, simple . . . We didn't care what that meant for the Hmong," Poe said.[21]

The result, as one observer recalled to a *New York Times* reporter after visiting Long Cheng, was that a people who "hardly knew wheeled transport" before the war believed that Vang Pao was in control of stunning, almost incomprehensible power. He could summon death or food in ways that, in Hmong lore, only deities could do. "It awed them," the visitor recalled. "They thought the man who commanded all this power . . . was General Vang Pao . . . He was real, while, to most of them, the Americans [who controlled the airlifts] were shadows."[22] Hmong flocked to Vang Pao with a devotion reminiscent of a personality cult.[23] In Long Cheng, "Vang Pao held court every morning, playing Solomon with supplicants, some of whom wanted redress for offenses committed by neighbors or militiamen, while others, the unfortunate, were simply looking for help," noted one CIA history of the Laos war.[24]

Without any big battles against the North Vietnamese, Vang Pao's power within Laos's politics would always be limited. But if the Hmong could win those larger battles too, who knew how much power he and his fellow tribesmen could amass?

The Hmong's political power, Vang Pao's own power, the capacity to fight Hanoi directly—all of these goals rested, the general was convinced, on those American fighters and bombers. He had been entranced by the power of air warfare and large artillery warfare since early in his fighting days, certain that he could command large armies, aircraft groups, and heavy weaponry, which together would make him more than just a guerilla leader. He also saw air strikes as more precise than they were, at least at that time in US warfare. "Vang Pao looks upon air [strikes] as a magic wand. All he has to say is 'Kill all the enemy,' and it's done," Larry Devlin, one of the agency's station chiefs in Vientiane, told CIA historians in a classified interview.[25]

Top American officials were willing, by 1964, to give Vang Pao some of the air support the Hmong leader wanted, but they remained cautious about unleashing the full power of American fighters and bombers. Hanoi's growing incursions into Laos in 1964, and the increasing involvement of US forces in Vietnam, convinced some of the more skeptical aides to President Lyndon Johnson that American air support was worth trying in Laos. The Ho Chi Minh supply trail through Laos had been widened repeatedly by Vietnamese engineers, and North Vietnamese units could now move men, heavy weapons, and supplies into South Vietnam much more easily. After Kennedy's assassination in November 1963, Johnson had taken over the presidency, but had mostly left Kennedy's circle of national security advisors in place.

US military involvement in South Vietnam, which had been focused on advising the South Vietnamese forces, had expanded dramatically, in 1964 and early 1965, to include US Army and Marines ground operations. Johnson had, at times, been skeptical of increasing the US presence in Vietnam, but he felt trapped, by his advisors and his desire not to back down. The political situation in South Vietnam seemed increasingly insecure—former president Diem had been assassinated just before Kennedy, and a junta had taken power in the South. As David Halberstam's iconic portrait of the origins of the Vietnam War showed, Johnson's circle of advisors had absorbed lessons from the "loss" of China to communism during the Truman administration—most importantly, that the Democratic Party's leaders had to make a strong, even military stand against the spread of communism in Asia.[26] Johnson had seen US government studies suggesting that the United States would need to send as many as one million American troops to turn back communist advances in Vietnam, a number impossible to sell to the American public. The new president suspected that a smaller commitment, though politically feasible, might not stop Hanoi. Still, Johnson approved the insertion of US ground forces into Vietnam, made easier by claiming that North

Vietnamese naval boats had attacked a US destroyer in the Gulf of Tonkin. Johnson approved, then, the escalation of the US commitment. With US ground forces committed in Vietnam, it became even more essential to US policy, many of Johnson's aides believed, to close the Ho Chi Minh supply trail as much as possible.

In mid-May 1964, Leonard Unger, the US ambassador in Vientiane before Bill Sullivan, made what a classified CIA history of the war called "an unprecedented suggestion . . . that T-28 fighter-bombers flown by American pilots be deployed against the advancing enemy," the Laotian and Vietnamese communist forces moving south and east in Laos, and against the supply trail through Laos.[27]

The senior management of the CIA's Far East division supported Unger's proposal enthusiastically. Bill Lair, however, thought it was a dangerous idea. An air war, he believed, would lead inevitably to greater demands by Vang Pao for more bombers and fighters, and a bigger war overall—a losing war.

A bigger war did not suit the Laotian forces or Vang Pao, Lair warned the embassy and the Far East division heads after the bombing began in earnest in July 1964. The Hmong had never really fought in terrain they barely knew, in other parts of Laos. They had not conducted multiple large battles in one year, as the North Vietnamese had. Many of Vang Pao's men, though tough and willing to learn, came and went from the army several times per year, sometimes leaving to farm or to participate in clan meetings or to see their families. Even if paramilitary instructors trained many more Hmong, it would still be hard to predict how many soldiers would even show up for a big battle with the North Vietnamese. And Washington certainly wouldn't be giving the Hmong any American ground forces to help.

In 1964 the CIA station chief in Vientiane, Douglas Blaufarb, agreed with most of Lair's arguments. His view, as he wrote in a secret cable to headquarters, was that proponents of a bigger war with American air support "were being 'carried away by visions derived from [World War II] experience,'" in which larger, much-better-armed groups of insurgents, such as the French Resistance, had played major roles in places such as France.[28] In Laos, he asserted, "such an approach would inevitably end in disaster."[29]

But by 1966, Blaufarb had left Laos. The new CIA station chief would be willing to approve far more bombing raids per day, and would oversee the bigger ground war that Lair and Blaufarb had warned against.

———

Lair's objections were overruled by Johnson's top aides. "A week later [after Unger's recommendation], Air America pilots were bombing and strafing enemy positions both east and west of the Plain of Jars," the CIA history noted.[30]

Still, Unger, and many Johnson aides, did not see the bombing campaign over the Plain of Jars as necessarily the beginnings of an extended air war. In May and June 1964, debate raged around the president on how much air support, if any, the United States should commit to Laos for the long term, according to classified CIA accounts of the war. Some American officials worried that too many bombing runs would compromise Washington's ability to preserve the fiction that the United States was not fighting in Laos; they wondered if airmen shot down over Laos could be held as hostages by Hanoi and the Laotian communists. Some also believed that Laos would be an extremely tough environment for bombers to hit targets. Secretary of Defense Robert McNamara supported sending fighter-bombers into Laos authorized to attack and return fire. However, Director of Central Intelligence John McCone was more reluctant, even though his deputies in the Far East division supported the air campaign. McCone was concerned that the Pathet Lao and North Vietnamese would be difficult to attack from the air. President Johnson himself, the CIA recorded, "acknowledged his own doubts" about sending fighter-bombers into Laos.[31]

These concerns about the limits, and the effects, of bombing in Laos would be proven prescient. North Vietnamese and Pathet Lao troops moved at night, or in excellent camouflage, or spread out over a significant distance. These tactics made it hard for bombers to attack a large number of communist troops at once. "Even though the US had air supremacy [over Laos], the targets were highly elusive," a military retrospective of the Laos war concluded ruefully, after the United States already had been bombing Laos for nearly a decade.[32] Also, much of the country was mountainous and poorly mapped. And weather conditions such as long stretches of fog and intense rain made it hard for even the most experienced pilots to hit targets. Ambassador Bill Sullivan, despite approving bombing operations later, admitted in a classified 1965 cable that Laos's "impenetrable tree canopy which high-speed, high-flying jets literally cannot see through" was a significant obstacle to an air war. "Significant quantities of logistics [in other words, Communist arms, nonlethal supplies, and men] can still be moving over routes which . . . our strike aircraft are unable to discern."[33]

For a year after the strikes in July 1964, the US government would limit the use of American airpower in Laos. But those limits would be shredded by 1966.

Chapter 10

The Wider War

TED SHACKLEY ARRIVED IN VIENTIANE IN JULY 1966 AS
the new CIA station chief. Shackley's arrival crystallized all of Lair's
worries—about how the operation might shift into a total war, about
how Hmong fighting only for the United States would not fight well,
about the new type of CIA men in Asia who knew ideology but not
people. Suddenly Lair saw all these diffuse concerns personified,
fairly or unfairly, in the figure of one man.

Shackley was the opposite of the old hands-off station chiefs who
had deferred to the great Bill Lair. By the time he came to Vientiane,
Shackley was already a favorite at CIA headquarters, destined for even
more prestigious postings. After the 1961 Bay of Pigs debacle, Shackley had taken charge of the Cuba program and reformed it. Under
Shackley, the Cuban operation uncovered the Soviet ballistic missiles
that had been secretly deployed on the island, an enormous intelligence coup. Shackley would eventually rise to become the deputy director of covert operations at the agency. He personified the type of
clandestine operative the agency now preferred: someone who could
move from country to country, never becoming too personally in-
vested in any one place. Shackley would never "go native," as some in
the Far East division quietly said had happened to Bill Lair.

Shackley, like many of the up-and-coming men in the clandestine
service, also worked maniacally. He spent many nights in his office,
reading secret cables from CIA stations, cables sent by US diplomats
from all over the world, and memos prepared for him by field officers

summarizing the latest fighting in Laos.[1] "Shackley is a 'driven' person . . . ambitious, tough-minded, and ruthless," said former CIA operative James Lilley, who worked in Laos. "He wanted to win wars. His inclination was to drive ahead."[2] Sometimes, Shackley would sleep on the floor of his bare office rather than go home, even though driving through Vientiane's vacant streets at night took only five or ten minutes.

He also had little tolerance for the cultural norms of Southeast Asia: the elastic sense of time, the kind of quiet deference that Lair had mastered, the fake jocularity that some clandestine officers assumed in the field when they encountered other CIA men. Many of the clandestine officers in Laos and Thailand recalled that their first impression of Shackley was one of iciness, calmness, a cold stare, and ghostly white skin.[3] (Some of his CIA colleagues nicknamed him the "blond ghost.") In a country where government officials and diplomats routinely arrived for meetings more than an hour late, Shackley demanded that subordinates arrive on the minute—even if that meant precisely at 1:37 p.m. or 4:23 p.m.[4] On his first visit to Lair's operation in Udorn, Thailand, Shackley flew in, landed, didn't eat or drink a thing, and then spoke for two hours about his plans for Operation Momentum before taking any questions from Lair or anyone else.

The beginning of the air war in Laos had signaled that Operation Momentum was shifting, but in 1966 Shackley announced that the war would change on the ground: the Hmong would now "take the war to the North Vietnamese army."[5] This larger war strategy required, in Shackley's words, "wrest[ing] areas of Laos from enemy control"—using the anti-communist forces to take territory and hold it.[6] To train the Hmong to stand and fight, the agency would wrap barbed wire around positions that Hmong troops held.[7] Holding this territory would force Hanoi to commit more of its forces to Laos and make the fight in Vietnam easier. In other words, this plan called for the type of conventional fight that Shackley's predecessor, Blaufarb, had equated with the Free French in World War II—and which he said would be a disastrous strategy in Laos.

Larger battles would also allow CIA clandestine officers to command the battlefield much more directly, which many of the CIA men had desired. In 1965, when Tony Poe intervened in the firefight that wounded him severely, Lair had applauded Poe's bravery but admonished him for taking command of the military operation. Soon no one would criticize clandestine officers working with the Hmong for taking a more direct battlefield role.

The idea of building a wider war was gaining support at the top of the agency. Desmond Fitzgerald, who had been instrumental in getting Lair's original proposal for a Hmong operation approved, now advocated for a larger Hmong force. Fitzgerald believed not only that a bigger war could bleed Hanoi but also that Vang Pao's men provided a unique opportunity for the CIA to widen its military capabilities vastly. Meanwhile, the new CIA head, Richard Helms, who took over the agency the same year that Shackley became station chief, did not have the kinds of doubts about a bigger war in Laos that his predecessor, McCone, had laid out in mid-1964.[8]

Helms's "support for the Laos program was highly visible to the Far East division and a source of assurance" as the war escalated and the CIA's role increased, said the agency's classified history of Helms's time as director.[9] Helms "took particular pride in that [Laos] program. You could tell it was sort of his baby," William Nelson of the CIA's Far East division told interviewers.[10]

In this new type of war, the Hmong and other anti-communists in Laos would build up their forces, and their physical defenses, in towns rather than in the countryside. They would build these towns into bases that would, in theory, draw attacks from the North Vietnamese; then they would trap and crush Hanoi's troops. Bill Sullivan approved of the plan to establish bases, but in public he tried to hedge his support for a larger war. In his memoir, Sullivan wrote, "The kind of war I undertook to direct was strictly defensive and essentially of a guerilla nature."[11] In other words, the kind of war Lair had originally imagined in Laos. But Sullivan's State Department aides—former CIA operatives who dealt with the ambassador—and the now-declassified embassy and CIA documents about the Laos war suggest that the ambassador went along with the plan for an enlarged, conventional war.

In fact, Sullivan backed the agency repeatedly in 1966 as it pushed the White House to let it use Vang Pao's men in bigger battles that included massive airpower.

———

In August 1966 about forty Hmong clan elders visited Vang Pao in Long Cheng. They were worried about the direction of the war and about how many young Hmong men were being sucked into battle. Although the general had become a figure of reverence for many of the refugees in Long Cheng, Vang Pao was two decades younger than most of the clan leaders; Hmong tradition, with its respect for age, required that even Vang Pao at least pretend to listen to them.[12] He welcomed them with piles of bananas, rice, and pieces of chicken and pig; he calmed his legs long enough to squat down in his home, with the elders around him, and just listen for more than two hours.

The danger to the Hmong wasn't just from the constant need for more young male bodies for the war, warned the clan leaders. The foundations of Hmong culture, which had survived so many centuries of wars and foreign occupations of Laos's land, were threatened like they had never been before.

Since the territory controlled by Vang Pao's army and the communist forces was always shifting, it had become hard for many Hmong families to plant crops; the farmers never knew if their land would be held by friendly forces by the time harvesting season came. The draw of expanding US airdrops of rice and other staples had lured Hmong families to Long Cheng.[13] Most of the vegetation of the Long Cheng Valley had been ripped up to make room for the runway, for huts, and for the bald areas manned by large guns.[14]

To visitors, including some of the clan leaders who had never before come to the general's base, Long Cheng looked like an increasingly decrepit and depressing place. The town's high mountain valley, protected on three sides by peaks, had made it an excellent choice for a base, but Long Cheng was not a particularly pleasant place to live. In monsoon season, the dirt tracks that led through the hastily built village turned quickly into quicksand-like mud, and it became hard to drive or even walk. The rains made Long Cheng beautiful: Ireland-green moss grew on the jagged limestone walls of the surrounding mountains, and yellow flowers, tall as a person, popped out of the ground. Flowers even bloomed out of some of the crevices in the irregularly shaped peaks, which looked like giant white-gray pieces of coral, with tiny holes in them. But the monsoon rains also made it harder for planes to land on the runway, endangering food supplies.

Medics and Hmong grunts carried wounded and dead bodies through the town to field hospitals and graves. Children played with empty rifles and pieces of ammunition strewn in the streets. Antiaircraft guns sat everywhere: on top of buildings, near the runway, up the sides of the valley. Down by the runway, men ran back and forth to planes and helicopters constantly, loading and unloading supplies and fighters, or fuelling and repairing planes. The din of landing and taking off went on all day.

Long Cheng's cold weather and cramped, flat ground made it a poor site for farming or raising animals. To survive, many turned to waiting on the foreigners—Americans and Thais, mostly—who worked in the valley or passed through it. Long Cheng was becoming "a desultory megalopolis, an unpaved, sewerless city . . . where Hmong ran noodle stands, cobbled shoes, tailored clothes, repaired radios, ran military-jeep taxi services, and interpreted for American pilots and relief workers," wrote Anne Fadiman, an American reporter who chronicled the Hmong's existence in Laos and subsequent migration to the United States.[15] During the day, soldiers of different ethnicities and nationalities bargained for goods in the muddy central market where Hmong women sat on the ground selling long eggplants and baskets of rice, or sipped beers in thatched huts turned into makeshift bars, recalled former CIA officer James Parker.[16] "Thai mercenaries, taller than the other nationalities, were heavily tattooed and wore distinctive unit scarves; the [ethnic] Lao forces looked like the French Foreign Legion, with their berets and camouflage tunics; and the Hmong, the smallest and the youngest, looked like dirty mountaineers."[17]

Some Hmong families used their huts not only to sell beer and rice liquor but also to offer young Hmong women as prostitutes to the foreign soldiers. Prostitution had not been common in Hmong culture before, in contrast to the cultures of lowland Lao and Thais. Hmong families could historically expect sizable dowries from Hmong men—usually, in silver—for marrying off daughters who were virgins.[18] But now, in this culturally mixed up and economically desperate situation, prostitution flourished.

Yet Hmong families kept coming to Long Cheng. An entire generation of young Hmong was growing up in the valley, disconnected from traditional culture and eating food that had been dropped from the skies, the clan elders complained to Vang Pao. Several Americans who worked with the Hmong thought the Hmong who'd grown up on the general's base had come to believe that they ate when rations fell from the air. They had a dangerous lack of survival skills in a country that remained largely wild and impoverished, and where few Hmong had attained the education to do urban jobs.[19]

———

By nightfall, Vang Pao was growing restless and was struggling to hide his exasperation at what had become a long lecture. He stopped squatting and circled around the inside of the house. His wide smile, which he had kept pasted on his face as an expression of good will, was gone. The elders finally fell silent. Vang Pao stood in the middle of the room. Why wouldn't he want the CIA to care more about Laos?

Vang Pao asked the elders. The Hmong wanted more US support; if more support required more fighting, that was a trade-off the Hmong had to make.[20]

The general warned the elders that if the Hmong didn't accept the CIA's new plan to fight big battles, no one else was going to save the tribe. The national army certainly wouldn't. Vang Pao and several of his officers had often journeyed to Vientiane to meet with the lowland Lao generals, and they always returned to the Hmong highlands extremely unimpressed. The Royal Lao Army generals enjoyed a lush existence in the capital, often trading away army supplies to Thai arms dealers who were happy to offer the generals stacks of Thai, American, and Laotian cash. RLA generals, who supposedly drew salaries from the national treasury that would have barely paid for small huts, had built themselves lavish villas in Vientiane. Many had continually stocked their homes with imported new televisions and radios from Thailand and wine and beef from France. Revelations of the vast misuse of US aid in the *Wall Street Journal* in 1958 had not embarrassed the Laotian army leaders into giving up expensive habits, though they tried to be more cautious about discussing their purchases with reporters.[21] They often had their favored monks on call to bless them at any time, in exchange for a few dollars or piles of the Laotian currency.[22]

And if Hmong civilians were caught by communist forces, they would be treated brutally, Vang Pao said. Many top communist leaders in Laos and Vietnam reviled the Hmong for (mostly) cooperating with the French in the past and with the United States now, and twenty years of fighting had hardened the North Vietnamese forces in Laos to the point that abuses had become increasingly tolerated.

Since 1964, both the Pathet Lao and the North Vietnamese troops in Laos had appeared to adopt a take-no-prisoners approach toward Hmong civilians. Ban Ban Valley was one example. In April 1964, when communist forces had driven one group of Hmong fighters out of the valley on the northeastern side of the strategically vital Plain of

Jars, the surviving Hmong soldiers had fled south with around fourteen thousand Hmong civilians. One group of Hmong refugee families halted in a valley and made camp for the night.

Combined communist battalions caught up with the troops and
the thousands of fleeing civilians around midnight and started firing
rockets into their camp; the refugees awoke to shells exploding. Families herded their children, on the run, from one side of the valley to
the other, looking for a spot not guarded by enemy troops. There was
none. Then the communist soldiers ran at the civilians, tossing grenades and slashing with bayonets. Several picked up small Hmong
children and swung them around in the air. The soldiers swung and
swung and then, once they had created enough force to kill with the
swings, smashed the little children's heads into rocks.[23]

Massacres like the one at Ban Ban Valley made the elders fear for
the Hmong people's safety; they knew that when Vang Pao said captured civilians would be treated brutally, he was probably right. The
general also assured the elders that Hmong spirits visited him in his
dreams frequently and had personally confirmed to him that a bigger
war could be won. Vang Pao believed that the spirits sent him signals for which battles to pursue, which deals to make with the United
States, and which fights to join. His repeated escapes from near-death
encounters in close fighting had convinced the Hmong leader that
the spirits had rendered him invulnerable so that he could lead the
Hmong. Later, living in America, Vang Pao reflected on his communication with spirits, telling Stephen Young, a longtime advisor when
Vang Pao lived in the US, "I must have been saved by the spirits, by
some reason to do good for my people."[24]

Once, when Bill Sullivan visited Long Cheng, Vang Pao took the
ambassador to the site of an ongoing battle with North Vietnamese
forces so that he could lead the fight himself. He left the ambassador, called together a group of Hmong soldiers who were planning
a new assault, ran up the hill at their head, lay in the dirt just a few
feet below an enemy sniper's nest, and handed his men grenade after

grenade from a box, which they chucked into the Vietnamese hide-out.[25] When the grenades ran out, Vang Pao sprinted with his men into the hideout, firing when they got only about five feet from the surviving snipers.[26] All the North Vietnamese were killed. After-ward, Vang Pao sat in the snipers' former hideout and told Sullivan that he knew he would survive because spirits had been watching over him.[27]

Vang Pao assured Sullivan and Shackley that with much greater American airpower, and more men in his army, the Hmong could do what US officials wanted. The hill tribe could take over whole chunks of Laos. They didn't have to just fight in rainy season, when the com-munists found it hard to move and couldn't drag their artillery—the Hmong could fight all year round. In fact, Vang Pao had already tried to make the Hmong forces more disciplined, more like a conventional infantry. He had reorganized his army with officers and battalions, like a national army, though he still let the men mostly choose their own officers.[28] In addition to sending groups of Hmong to Thailand for training, Vang Pao made his men go through formal training in Laos too, including learning how to fight on open ground, drilling in marching and saluting and using other types of military regalia, and firing heavy artillery. "Was any of this really relevant to fighting in the highlands of Laos, in the jungle?" asked Tony Poe, who observed the stepped-up training. "Some . . . Were they going to whip out their regiments and blow bugles? I don't think so. But it was Vang Pao's way of saying that he was ready to lead the whole war."[29]

There was, at least initially, some reason to believe that this plan for waging conventional war could work. Vang Pao had already, at times, fought brief open-field battles, had held small towns, and had even made his great capture of Sam Neua. Since 1964, the North Viet-namese had been forced to send more battalions of crack troops into Laos to deal with Vang Pao and his men. This was exactly the type of diversion of forces from Vietnam that could benefit the United States and South Vietnam in their war against Hanoi. If Vang Pao could take more territory and actually hold it, he might draw even more of Hanoi's finest fighters away from the war in Vietnam.

––––––––––

Ambassador Sullivan, Shackley, and the CIA's Far East division concluded that one of the first places to take the fight to the North Vietnamese was at Nam Bac, a town in the north, about forty miles from the Vietnamese border and ringed by high mountains. Anticommunist forces had dug in at Nam Bac, and the plan was to increase the size of the army holding the town and to build up the defenses with howitzers and other heavy guns. This buildup might draw the communists to the fortified Nam Bac, and the Laotian army could then slaughter them as they attacked entrenched defenses and faced American bombers. After a victory, Nam Bac could be a model for other sites in northern and northeastern Laos.

Lair already regarded plans for a wider war as suicidal, but even if a bigger war was inevitable, he still objected to making a stand at Nam Bac. In July 1966, shortly after he became station chief, Shackley flew to Udorn and asked Lair what he thought of the Nam Bac plan. Lair did not hesitate with his answer. He told his new boss that Nam Bac would be a trap where the anti-communists, who had trouble defending positions, would be surrounded by the North Vietnamese and subject to a devastating siege. The Laotian generals who had already committed more than three thousand men to Nam Bac were incompetent and should never have put their fighters there. Nam Bac was surrounded by mountains, which would allow the North Vietnamese—masters of moving artillery across even the roughest terrain—to drag mortars up to the mountaintops and then rain hell onto the town below. Nam Bac was also close enough to the Vietnamese border that, even if Hanoi suffered some losses in the fighting, it could replenish its forces with tested, veteran troops from inside Vietnam. Meanwhile, the town could not be reached by road from the rest of Laos, forcing its defenders to be relieved only by air—a dangerous proposition.

In fact, Lair said, the idea of setting up troops in a place like remote Nam Bac, inviting the enemy to come to high points around the town, and planning to relieve the defenders through airdrops seemed eerily reminiscent of the biggest disaster, to date, anyone had suffered against Hanoi. Nam Bac seemed much like Dien Bien Phu, where in 1954 the Viet Minh had slaughtered the French with an artillery bombardment and siege against a similar type of fortress, located on low ground that allowed attackers to position themselves above it, and that could only be resupplied by air.[30] At Dien Bien Phu, the air resupply had eventually been closed by a combination of Vietnamese attacks on the fortress's airstrip and poor weather, leaving the defenders isolated and vulnerable. The exhausted Dien Bien Phu troops, forced into a smaller and smaller perimeter, had eventually been overrun and taken captive.

Sullivan and Shackley ignored Lair's counsel. Shackley "listened to me, and he didn't really comment on it. They went ahead with the operation," Lair recalled.[31]

Chapter 11

Massacre

THE LAOTIAN MEN DUG IN AT NAM BAC TOWN HAD BEEN living on the brink of mental breakdown for months now. It was the beginning of January 1968, and the town's defenders were waiting for the North Vietnamese troops and the small numbers of Pathet Lao with them to finally attack Nam Bac directly. The defenders had little hope of stopping the enemy, but at least an attack would mean the end of more than a year of daily misery. Shells from the North Vietnamese artillery's heavy guns rained down on Nam Bac constantly, and they seemed to come from nearly every direction; even the officers in Nam Bac were convinced that communist troops had totally encircled the town. Lowland Lao and hilltribe men among the defenders had constructed makeshift shrines in the town where they prayed for survival, leaving bites of food or Buddhist amulets in front of the shrines. A few soldiers who could write had jotted notes and stuck them in their clothes, identifying themselves in case their bodies were blown apart.

The shelling drove some of Nam Bac's defenders mad. Discipline had never been solid among the Nam Bac forces. Ammunition stocks were low, since officers had sold off bullets and guns and pocketed the cash. By January, at least one-sixth of the men who had been in the town a year earlier had deserted, slipping away at night, when they had the best chance of evading the tightening North Vietnamese vise around Nam Bac. Men defecated anywhere they wanted and slept in holes or even out in the open—they were so tired that they risked being killed by shells in their sleep.[1] If the besieged Dien Bien Phu in 1954 had been, in the words of French journalist Bernard Fall, "hell in a very small place," Nam Bac was awfully close to the same state.[2]

As 1968 began, most of the soldiers at Nam Bac had little idea of why, or how, this town in the remote northeast had been chosen as a stronghold. They knew only that some officers were promising double pay for men who stayed. Nam Bac had become an American priority. The CIA and Bill Sullivan had built up the anti-communist troops there to about seven thousand men by the end of 1967. In the town, soldiers had dug trenches, built up fortifications, and positioned guns in the valley toward the hills around it.

The anti-communist soldiers did not know that Hanoi had sent one of the toughest divisions in its whole veteran army, the 316th, to Nam Bac. The 316th, led by some of Hanoi's most experienced officers, had played a major role in many of Hanoi's victories over the French. The 316th also had the newest Soviet 122-millimeter mortars, lumbering giant guns that had never been unleashed in Laos before.[3]

In the last two months of 1967, North Vietnamese gunners trained mortars on the valley, seeking out the weakest points of the defenders' fortifications. At sites northeast of Nam Bac, the North Vietnamese also bloodied the Laotian forces in small skirmishes. The Laotians had run, dropping their weapons.

Laotian commanders begged the Americans and their own government repeatedly for more men and for bombers to batter the North Vietnamese and the Pathet Lao. But it was hard to get supplies to Nam Bac on many days, when cloud cover shrouded the valley. In September 1967 two battalions of Laotian paratroopers jumped into Nam Bac, giving the defenders some rest. But the defenders got no further large deployments of fresh troops. American F-4, F-105, and A-1 fighter-bombers attempted to strike the North Vietnamese and Pathet Lao again and again in December, and on January 3, 1968, American planes flew forty-five times to Nam Bac to strafe and bomb the communists.[4] However, the communist forces proved adept at digging into the ground, as they had before in Laos, as well as using trees to hide from bombing.

By the end of the first week of January 1968, the North Vietnamese had surrounded the runway at Nam Bac, threatening any planes that tried to land by battering the airfield with mortar fire. No more did; now American pilots could only drop parachuted food and ammunition into the area. As in Dien Bien Phu, Nam Bac was basically cut off from the outside world.

A month earlier, in December 1967, the US Embassy in Vientiane had begun to distance itself from a potential bloodbath in Nam Bac. An embassy memo sent to Laos's leaders suggested that although the Americans had been so enthusiastic about Nam Bac before, now the embassy believed the site should "not be defended at all costs."[5] Bill Sullivan also drafted documents suggesting that the idea for a big battle at Nam Bac had been the Laotians' plan all along, not the Americans'.[6] Still, the embassy and the CIA did not push the Nam Bac defenders to attempt to retreat. The siege continued.

On January 13, North Vietnamese and Laotian communist infantry finally attacked directly, surging toward Nam Bac from the north and west and killing at least 200 of the defenders in a day of close fighting. After that one day, the men at Nam Bac lost whatever discipline they had left. Few of the officers tried to organize a coordinated retreat, and several had run from the town as soon as the attack began. The Laotian general in charge of the garrison, convinced on the first day of close fighting that communist forces had already taken the town—they had not yet—fled south into the jungle. Over 3,000 of the anti-communist troops soon ran off in a panic as well.[7] The fleeing men dropped over $1 million worth of American-provided weapons on the ground, leaving a bounteous haul for enemy troops. They also left fifty mortars and thousands of rifles scattered throughout the town, as well as modern communications equipment far more advanced than what Hanoi had.

Overall, about 2,400 of the Nam Bac defenders were captured by the communists in the jungles outside the town. Many of those who managed to escape the enemy never reported for army duty again.

As Laotian generals and politicians sifted through the reports of the battle with the Americans in Laos, they learned more about exactly how badly the army had disintegrated.[8] The Laotian army and the US Embassy realized that the anti-communist forces had actually deployed nearly twice as many men at Nam Bac as the combined Pathet Lao–North Vietnamese contingent. And the Laotian infantry, along with its general, had fled the town without even informing the paratroopers who had dropped in to help hold Nam Bac. The paratroopers had been fighting hard in another part of the valley and had no idea that the rest of the army was on the run. With no backup, they were slaughtered. Of the more than 400 paratroopers who came to reinforce Nam Bac, only 12 or 13 survived.[9]

———

Even before the catastrophe at Nam Bac, Lair had felt increasingly isolated in his job. The growing war on the ground and in the air had meant expanding American operations at Udorn and other bases in Thailand, and Lair found himself resenting even the minor details that this growth entailed.

The air bases in northeastern Thailand, just across the border from Laos, were expanding rapidly to handle bombing runs into Laos and Vietnam, as well as to supply flights to Vang Pao's men and the refugees in Laos. Several bases, including the one in Udorn, had morphed into mini-Americas, as pilots and other men working for the operation re-created small segments of US life in the midst of the poorest and, previously, least urbanized part of Thailand.[10] Squat new concrete buildings, costing millions of dollars to build, were springing up at Udorn to house US pilots and other Americans working on the operation. Pilots and other contractors rambled around the northeastern plains on their days off, cruising in pickup trucks past the crumbling *stupas* and other ruins of ancient Khmer and Laotian civilizations. So many American pilots were arriving in the northeast, and adopting mainstream business practices, that some wanted to form a pilots' union.[11]

The runway next to Lair's office, which had been relatively quiet when the operation started, now rumbled with jets and prop planes taking off regularly. Crews worked night and day fueling and cleaning planes, as well as taking steps to keep the planes' identity secret, such as painting over the US Air Force tail numbers.[12] (Although leaders of many nations, including all of the communist powers, obviously knew about the vast US war effort in the country, obscuring the tail numbers allowed Washington to maintain the fiction of Laos's neutrality.) Hamburger joints with bars selling Singha Thai beer and whiskey, ladies' clubs for wives, swimming clubs with long oval pools, rec rooms with pool halls and movie rooms and cooks trained in serving classic American fare—they all sprang up on the bases. A Thai company also had built a squat, blocky hotel in Udorn, right next to the firehouse and the town center, specifically to house US pilots and other contractors coming for short stays in the northeast.[13]

On weekend evenings, CIA contractors and the agency operatives in Udorn held regular parties at clubs on the American compound. Pilots and air controllers smoked cigars and used knives to carve their names into the long wooden bar.[14] Weekday nights, pilots and other contractors would eat dinner at the base, watch films, or cool off with a swim. On one of his first evenings at Udorn, Charles Davis, a contract helicopter pilot for the agency's airline, had dinner at a club restaurant with one of his friends. "I order some sort of veal dish with all the extras," Davis recalled. "They appear to have a good chef."[15]

The CIA's airline would not actually drop bombs—that would be done by jets, often at the direction of the agency and Bill Sullivan, and in areas of Laos coordinated by CIA-run forward air control-lers—but it would, by the end of the decade, be dropping millions of pounds of military supplies and food into Laos: rice, wheat, salt, cornmeal, and canned meat.[16] "The war is going great guns now," one CIA helicopter pilot wrote to his parents.[17] The CIA's airline also would run wounded Hmong soldiers, and some Americans, to hospitals in Thailand. It searched for downed American pilots, it conducted surveillance photography missions over Laos, and, in-creasingly, it moved Hmong troops en masse to battle sites in other parts of Laos.

Lair had never paid much attention before to how Udorn had looked. But Lair could feel himself getting angry at the changes all around him, an irritability he could not remember ever having be-fore. The agency asked that Lair and his deputy, Pat Landry, move out of their squat, tiny office and into a newer, larger building at the base that would be designed by an architect brought in from Wash-ington.[18] Usually willing to take any orders loyally, Lair grumbled and grumbled about the move, and offered to design a new, mod-est office for himself that would cost around $100,000, if the agency wanted to spend more money on his office so badly. "This didn't sat-isfy them," he recalled. "Instead, they designed a big air-conditioned building that must have cost a million dollars."[19] His bosses at the Far East division in Washington ordered him to work in the new building; Lair and his deputy took to calling it the "Taj Mahal."[20] Lair said, "You know what they did with all those empty rooms" in the large new office? "They filled them with Americans, who sat at desks and created paper on the increasing number of Americans working in Laos."[21]

Lair's annoyance at the base's appearance and the new office and the arrival of so many Americans reflected a broader unhappiness. He knew he was losing the debate about why the operation he had initiated existed at all. Lair had always believed, as Eisenhower had, that Laos mattered on its own as a bulwark against communist ad-

vances and potentially as an example of US-backed democracy. Since
Laos mattered, he did not want to simply sacrifice Hmong troops in
big battles, because the Hmong would be critical to saving Laos. Now
he had to answer to men who believed that Laos meant little on its
own, and that making it America's war was just fine—the country was
just a place to bleed Hanoi as long as possible, even if that bleeding
decimated Laos's own army.

Lair struggled to maintain even the pretense of cordial relations
with the two men who had to approve his operation on a daily basis:
Sullivan and Shackley. Bill Sullivan had come to Laos hearing about
the great Bill Lair: the man who knew the local people as well as
they knew themselves, the man who could speak Thai and Lao like a
native, the operative who was winning while losses piled up in Vietnam. Sullivan seemed to resent Lair's reputation. At one of their first
meetings, Lair remembered, Sullivan took care to invite Lair for a
briefing at the embassy in Vientiane and then have him wait for two
hours in an outer room, with no clear reason why the ambassador
was delayed.[22]

And as Sullivan stayed in Laos longer, he seemed even less interested in Lair's opinion about the direction of the operation. "It became quite tense" between him and Sullivan even before Nam Bac
fell, Lair said in an interview years later. Instead of coming to Vientiane and waiting to see the ambassador, Lair found himself not invited at all to Sullivan's regular meetings to plan the operation.

Even the smallest things about Lair seemed to irk Sullivan, and
Shackley as well. They both told aides that Lair was too deferential to
the Hmong, who depended on US support to survive, not the other
way around. They complained that Lair spent too much time every
day shuttling to and from Long Cheng to placate Vang Pao and not
enough time at Udorn managing the war. They also complained
about Lair dressing in flip-flops and loose, Southeast Asian–style
clothes—which were much more comfortable in the tropics—rather
than a suit.[23]

Lair began to dread briefing his bosses. Shackley had installed several men loyal to him at key posts in the Laos operation. He assigned Thomas Clines, who had worked with him at the Cuba station in Miami, to Udorn Air Base to work alongside Lair.[24] Clines acted publicly deferential to Lair, but his loyalties were clear. "[Shackley] looked at the big picture . . . our national interest," said Clines. "Bill [Lair] . . . [his] concept of national interest was too Lao oriented."[25] Meanwhile, Sullivan demanded that Lair travel to Long Cheng less often, and Shackley became the new primary liaison for the Hmong leader.

––––––––

The pace of American bombing in Laos had sped up since the air war began in earnest in July 1964, and the pressure to cut the Ho Chi Minh Trail would eventually become paramount. Lair recognized that bombing might play some role in stopping the movement of supplies along the Ho Chi Minh Trail, but he doubted it could be very successful, and he thought the air war was undermining any hope of victory in Laos itself. By January 1968, American planes were flying fifteen to twenty sorties per day into Laos. At times, such as during the height of the battle for Nam Bac, that number could increase to forty or fifty missions per day. The bombers supported the Hmong's battles, but US planes also flew attacks on targets that had little to do with the Hmong's survival—against North Vietnamese supply lines to South Vietnam, for example, which ran through eastern Laos. Thousands of North Vietnamese engineers maintained the Ho Chi Minh Trail through Laos and Cambodia to South Vietnam, so that North Vietnamese trucks could drive the basic road through rugged terrain. The North used caves along the trail to hide supplies moved by truck or handcart, and pumped oil and gas along the trail route through hidden pipelines and concealed metal drums.[26]

The agency did not even inform many top Laotian leaders about when and where they would be bombing the trail. "US officials considered it desirable, but by no means essential, to keep [Laotian Prime Minister] Souvanna [Phouma] informed on US actions," noted the US Defense Department's Pentagon Papers history of the war.[27] American officials also did not inform Vang Pao about many of these missions, but the general didn't have much leverage to complain, anyway. "US ability to control (including veto) a Lao operation is to all practical purposes complete because US materiel and air support are [now] vital [to Vang Pao's strategies,]" one National Security Council memo to the president's senior staff declared.[28] Vang Pao never saw this memo, but he surely would have understood what it meant.

The bombing runs were, in a way, also creating their own rationale for existing—and for expanding. "Once the air war started in Laos, the agency could go to the president's staff and say, 'This is our number of sorties per day now; we can't go less than that, because we'll lose in Laos' . . . and that figure steadily increased, since it was assumed we couldn't go back to less," said Campbell James, a longtime CIA clandestine officer in Southeast Asia. "No one took into account whether the war could be won, or stalemated, in Laos without increasing the bombings, but every time there was a setback, it started to be assumed the solution was more bombing."[29] And while the agency offered senators and congressmen occasional briefings on Operation Momentum, the briefers avoided going into detail about the skyrocketing number of bombing runs in Laos or the total tonnage of bombs being dropped on the kingdom.

When the defenders of Nam Bac turned and fled, Lair said nothing about the debacle to Sullivan or Shackley or anyone else.[30] Instead, he took weeks to write a report on the siege, detailing the buildup at Nam Bac and the defenders' total breakdown in the face of a numerically weaker enemy. His postmortem spared no one. He noted that using Vang Pao's forces as a conventional army was a mistake in general, and that Nam Bac was a particularly poor place to make a stand—the same critiques he had offered before the decisions were made.[31] Lair faulted the anti-communist fighters' officers and generals too; he faulted them for weak organization in the face of artillery, for allowing the reek of desperation to poison the minds of their men, for fleeing themselves and letting their men run with no plan for retreat. But while much of Lair's report outlined the deficiencies of the Laotian generals, anyone in the US government who read his words would know that the agency and Bill Sullivan had pushed the guerillas into a bigger, more conventional battle and had chosen Nam Bac as the first place to try the strategy.[32] "To me [Nam Bac] was a prime example of [Sullivan and the CIA] . . . not taking the advice [of caution], because the advice was there," Lair said many years later.[33]

By contrast, the reports issued by Sullivan and Shackley about Nam Bac placed the blame for the defeat squarely on the local forces and mostly avoided discussion of who had decided to make a stand there. "[Sullivan and the CIA] immediately made steps to say that they had nothing to do with [the Nam Bac debacle]," Lair added.[34]

Lair locked his Nam Bac report in his office safe at Udorn, along with the dossiers on American airmen and technicians who'd vanished in Laos and a few rubber-banded bricks of dollars and Thai baht that he kept there in case money was needed quickly for some reason in Long Cheng.

But there was one thing about Operation Momentum that he no longer kept in that safe: the accounting of its cost. Early on, Lair had jotted down the details of Operation Momentum's finances in his spiral notebooks. An operation that now had become the agency's biggest, and that now cost around $300 million per year (in 1968 dollars), couldn't have its bookkeeping kept on three-ring notebooks pulled out of Bill Lair's pockets.[35] There was little doubt, he believed, that the cost would keep rising. And, indeed, by 1970, Momentum would cost around $500 million per year (in 1970 dollars), and the CIA would devote a bigger percentage of its budget to paramilitary operations than at any time in its history.[36] Operation Momentum needed accountants and office managers and, Lair said, all the clerks he'd never wanted in his life.[37]

Bill Lair looked around his office at Udorn Air Base. It was the summer of 1968. Though the agency had moved him into the bigger office, the new space was about as bare as the old one. It contained a safe to store secret documents, phones, and a few scattered wooden chairs and maps. Lair had put up no family mementos or other artwork. New concrete was being poured for another expansion of the blocky buildings that were colonizing Udorn. So many men were coming into Udorn, with the contractors hiring so rapidly, that Lair knew virtually none of the new faces. The demand for men had grown so vastly that some of the contract organizations had taken to advertising positions openly in the English-language newspapers in Bangkok—their ads barely concealing who the hires would ultimately be serving.

Lair had been going on a lot of aimless drives, thinking about Operation Momentum and about his life. Driving relaxed him. Years later, still haunted by Laos and needing income, he would work as a long-haul trucker back home, driving the numbingly straight roads of Texas while replaying scenes from Laos in his mind.

For seven years, since 1961, Lair had stuck with the war. Even if he disagreed with the decisions being made above him, even if his loyalty to his country and to the CIA was questioned, Lair had stuck. He had continued to hope that he could exert enough influence to stop the worst, deadliest plans from ever happening, and to keep Momentum as some kind of partnership. Lair also had believed that, of all the CIA officers, Vang Pao felt a special fondness for him and listened to him. As long as Lair stayed, he could keep the Hmong general on an even keel.

Lair had never considered himself an idealist; he had always seen himself as a concrete guy, a doer. But he'd had ideas for Momentum. And, he recognized, they had failed.

Lair had failed to do anything to stop Nam Bac. And even after Nam Bac, the agency and Vang Pao were not planning to dial down the conventional war; they were simply trying to think of other ways to fight big battles.

Sullivan, and even Lair's bosses in Washington, seemed to think Lair was expendable. They believed Vang Pao needed US assistance so badly that the Hmong leader would listen to any American. There was some truth to this, but once Lair was gone, Vang Pao, who had never been the most stable character, would become harder to control—rasher and less sensible. Eventually, in a classified history of the Laos war, the agency would admit, "Lair seemed to have enjoyed unique standing with Vang Pao."[38]

To get out of Operation Momentum, Lair found a gig where the agency would pay for him to attend the United States Army War College back in the States. After that, he thought, maybe he and his wife could settle in Bangkok again. He had little interest in using his CIA connections to become a well-paid contractor for the agency, as many former clandestine officers were doing in booming Thailand. Lair had the connections there to build a profitable contracting network—training Thai troops, or doing intelligence work all over Southeast Asia, or moving supplies for the agency. But he did not trust many of the new contract organizations affiliated with the CIA, and he did not want to add to their ranks or spend his life marked as someone who had cashed in on his agency tour.[39] For now, he chose to leave the area entirely.

Even though he was walking out of Momentum, Lair remained loyal to the agency and its chain of command. In the next three years, multiple men who worked on secret operations in Laos and Cambodia, despairing about the expansion of the war and the management of battle strategy, would leak information about the wars to Congress or the media. But not Bill Lair. He could not see himself as a whistle-blower; as someone standing up and attracting attention. Perhaps, since he had started the Laos operation, Lair just could not bring himself to destroy it.[40] He eventually retrieved the copies of the scathing Nam Bac report and burned them.[41]

Before he left Operation Momentum for good, Bill Lair flew up to Long Cheng one final time. In place of slacks, he had donned long, black silk trousers and a black silk vest, like many Hmong wore for special occasions. The high mountain valley looked little like it had when he'd first helped select it as Vang Pao's base nearly a decade earlier. Then, Long Cheng had been deserted; just a flat mesa and a thick forest. Now the CIA had built its operation station on the side of the slopes of Long Cheng, the building's jutting radio antennas a telltale sign that it was not a typical Hmong home. Hundreds of new wood-plank houses dotted the slopes by the runway. Still, many of the same men who had been with Lair when they first began to look at Long Cheng were there now at the air strip: Vang Pao, his top lieutenants, and Edgar "Pop" Buell. A USAID worker also close to the general, Buell, like Lair, had planted roots in Hmong country and had become something of a local legend for his intense devotion to the people's schooling and basic survival.

Vang Pao, also dressed in black silk, knelt before Lair and tied the *baci* strings around the American's wrists, one after the other up his forearms. The Hmong had held a *baci* when the operation began, as they did for all important occasions, but back then the strings were supposed to bind the Hmong to America. Now the *baci* strings would provide Lair with luck and ensure that spirits were watching him as he departed. Lair found it difficult not to cry.

Chapter 12

Going for Broke

IT DID NOT TAKE LONG AFTER BILL LAIR LEFT LAOS FOR the impact of his departure to be felt. Vang Pao, the man whom the French had praised as fierce but cautious in his fighting, was becoming reckless, with no Hmong who would contradict him and no Americans left who knew him well. By 1968, the Hmong leader not only had been made a general in the Royal Lao Army but also had been given command of the entire royalist army in northeastern Laos.

Vang Pao was even invited to Washington as an honored guest of the US government, the ultimate reward. In late September 1968, the Hmong leader and a small entourage traveled to the US capital. On October 1 they met several top White House aides, including National Security Advisor Walt Rostow.[1] Vang Pao also met with CIA head Richard Helms. The general was introduced, repeatedly, as a great military leader. After his tour through Washington, he was escorted on to Disneyland in Anaheim, California, where one of his CIA handlers led him and his entourage through the park.[2] (Vang Pao also made another, work-related, secret visit to the United States to see training programs at Fort Bragg, North Carolina.)

The foreign press, though it had not reported on the CIA's extensive support of the anti-communists in Laos, ran hundreds of stories about the Hmong general and his army. The articles lionized Vang Pao as a brilliant strategist and served to stroke his ego. Several newspaper and magazine pieces featured photographs of him wearing his wide-brimmed cap and pointing into the distance like he was about to lead a vast assault. The articles usually mentioned that Vang Pao led from the front and had taken bullets in several firefights.

The articles didn't mention that after the loss of Nam Bac, communist forces had moved steadily across northern Laos, destroying multiple Hmong strongholds and killing at least a thousand Hmong fighters. Several of Vang Pao's key commanders had been killed as well.[3]

One of the communists' most brutal attacks came on a vital radar site installed by the United States on the top of a mountain called Phou Pha Thi. While the agency helped set up the site at Phou Pha Thi, it could not send US troops to defend it. The only Americans at the site were the "sheep-dipped" radar technicians, who were not combat forces. "This was a problem we had many times [in the war]," Vang Pao remembered. "CIA wanted to be like the military, running a war, but when I needed help, they couldn't help me like a military could."[4] A US Air Force analysis of the battle at Phou Pha Thi concluded that even before fighting erupted, it was well known among Americans running the Laos war that the men defending Phou Pha Thi would be "greatly outnumbered by the potential forces which the enemy could draw upon" and probably were not going to be given any backup if attacked.[5] Meanwhile, Hanoi might not have known that the radar at Phou Pha Thi was guiding a majority of American air strikes from Thailand into Vietnam, but the North Vietnamese surely understood that the site was important to guiding US planes and could be playing a role in the Laos bombing.

In early 1968, American reconnaissance planes reported that North Vietnamese engineers were diligently building a basic road toward Phou Pha Thi, probably so that Hanoi could move artillery to batter the site. When anti-communist forces conducting a patrol southeast of Phou Pha Thi killed several North Vietnamese soldiers, they discovered a notebook on the body of one that contained details of Hanoi's plans for a coming attack on the Phou Pha Thi.[6] In fact, the North Vietnamese road to Phou Pha Thi took long enough to build that American planes easily tracked its construction as it moved closer and closer to the radar site and its small band of defenders. And US reconnaissance planes noticed communist troops encircling Phou Pha Thi and slowly tightening the circle until they formed a tight ring.

Anti-communist leaders, including Vang Pao, pleaded with their CIA handlers to send more guns or other troops to Phou Pha Thi to avert a massacre of the Hmong and Thai and American technicians at the site. Ambassador Sullivan refused to let US Special Forces be air-lifted in to defend the area, because sending in troops would directly involve the US Army, compromising secrecy and allowing the military to possibly take over Sullivan's and the CIA's war.

The CIA office at Udorn Air Base became so concerned about the men at Phou Pha Thi that, without the ambassador's knowledge, it secretly sent assault rifles and grenades to men stationed at the mountaintop communications site. The heavier arms would be of little use, though, since there were still too few men there to stop Hanoi's troops, and several of the technicians did not even know how to use the heavier guns.

As night fell on March 10, 1968, with communist forces clearly drawing near the mountaintop (known in agency parlance as "Lima Site 85") and bombarding Phou Pha Thi with artillery, the men on Phou Pha Thi warily went to sleep after cabling Udorn Air Base, "See you later . . . I hope."[7] They prayed for an evacuation, or reinforcements to save them. But in the middle of the night, North Vietnamese Special Forces and regular infantry attacked. Within hours of first light, they had driven the Hmong, Americans, Thais, and lowland Laotians off the top of the mountain. When the American technicians ran out the front door of their hut, three were killed by gunfire.

As the site's defenders retreated to the edge of a mountainside cliff, they found themselves cornered. According to several accounts of the battle by survivors, the North Vietnamese fired at them and tossed grenades toward the trapped men. One man's body was blown in half, and "two pieces of his body lay on my legs," remembered Stanley Sliz, one of the few US survivors of Phou Pha Thi.[8] Before Sliz could pull his former colleague's body parts off of himself, another grenade exploded and blew what was left of the man into the air and down the mountain.[9] As the Vietnamese drew nearer, they fired into the body of anyone still groaning. Some reports from survivors of Phou Pha Thi said that the Vietnamese took out knives and slit the throats of many of the mountaintop's defenders, bleeding them to death.[10]

US planes arrived near daylight to strafe the site, trying to destroy the radar to keep it from being captured, and obliterating much of the top of the mountain. But they came too late to change the course of the fight. By the end of that morning, at least forty Hmong and Thais had been killed on the mountain, along with eleven American technicians. Some sixteen thousand Hmong refugees, fearing a further communist advance, fled the Phou Pha Thi vicinity after the site was captured.

The casualty reports were sent to Bill Lair, a few months before his decision to leave Operation Momentum. As he had feared from the beginning, the sheep-dipped technicians had been slaughtered like sheep, and it was he who would have to essentially hide the bloody details of their deaths. His office's safe became like a morgue roster— one that, if it were found by anyone outside Momentum, would not only expose the operation but also make the US government look like it had basically sacrificed these contractors.[11]

Even after Nam Bac and Phou Pha Thi, Vang Pao hoped to stop the North Vietnamese advance with a massive surprise attack. He wanted to launch it somewhere that would allow him to combat the North Vietnamese in large numbers and possibly capture whole divisions of the enemy. The Hmong leader, who had lost more than eighteen thousand men in the last seven years, was convinced that he had to land a big blow before his forces dwindled further. The general believed he could get the knockout—and after 1968, there was no Bill Lair left to caution him to think smaller. Between 1965 and 1968, US bombers already flew fifteen to twenty sorties a day—a substantial number in a country only about ninety thousand square miles in area—but Vang Pao told the agency that he needed more frequent bombings, and more control of when and where the planes flew.[12]

The general wanted to go for broke.

Vang Pao would do so at a time when his decision would be aligned perfectly with changes in US politics. In January 1969, Richard Nixon was inaugurated as the thirty-seventh president of the United States.

The Nixon White House had come into office promising to keep South Vietnam from being overrun by communist forces, while also slowly extricating the United States from Southeast Asia. And so, Nixon cared less about Laos than his predecessors did.[13] He and National Security Advisor Henry Kissinger believed that, ultimately, their biggest goal was to reset the balance of great powers in the world. Moscow and Beijing already had begun to turn on each other, fighting along their borders, and Nixon hoped to take advantage of the divisions between them, boosting US ties with China and utilizing the split between the Soviets and Chinese to weaken North Vietnam and make ending the war easier. And ending the war with Vietnam would make it easier for Washington and Beijing to forge a long-term relationship, which Nixon could then use as leverage against the Soviet Union in a continuation of the strategic game. At the same time, Nixon and Kissinger believed that they could warm ties with Moscow, and then use improved US-Soviet relations as a hedge against Chinese power, leaving the United States at the apex of the international order.

Yet Nixon's disinterest in Laos actually would allow the war in the kingdom to grow, at least for a time. Nixon and Kissinger argued within the administration that increased bombing, even though it required more US resources for a time, would be an effective way to bludgeon North Vietnam and its allies in Laos into agreeing to a peace deal for all of Indochina. Nixon would show Hanoi, the Pathet Lao, and the Soviet Union and China, that he would bomb without the qualms and restraints of the Johnson administration. He would hurt Hanoi and its allies in Laos, Cambodia, and South Vietnam mercilessly until Hanoi agreed to a peace settlement on US terms. The CIA and the embassy in Vientiane had already launched a larger ground war by the time Nixon was inaugurated, but the White House would approve an even bigger conventional fight in Laos.

Nixon also had an almost pathological distrust of the press, of Congress, and of most US government agencies that served under him, which he saw as dominated by the elite Northeastern men who had, generally, held the working-class, socially awkward, and politically opportunistic Nixon in low regard. Nixon loathed the State Department; he named a secretary of state, William Rogers, whom he then consulted rarely.[14]

Nixon had a similar visceral distaste for Richard Helms, the CIA head. The tweedy Helms was, to the president, emblematic of the East Coast establishment that Nixon despised. Helms had prepped at a school in Switzerland, gone on to Williams College, and then on to the OSS and the agency. Helms "was well liked by the liberal Georgetown social set," according to the agency's classified internal history of Helms's time as Director of Central Intelligence.[15] Nixon also believed that the CIA had played a role in his narrow defeat in the 1960 presidential election. Before the election, someone in the agency had given Democratic nominee John F. Kennedy overly inflated estimates of the USSR's missile capabilities, perhaps because these agency analysts and officers disliked Nixon as much as he disliked them. Kennedy used the inaccurate numbers to attack Eisenhower and Nixon, who had been Eisenhower's vice president, for supposedly allowing a "missile gap" to emerge between the United States and the Soviet Union.[16] Helms had played no role in providing these false missile estimates, but that did not matter to Nixon, who believed that the whole CIA had screwed him. Helms said that "it was bound to be a rocky period [for the agency] with Richard Nixon as president . . . He had a barb out for the agency all the time."[17]

Helms knew that Nixon disdained the CIA, but he also knew that Nixon preferred to conduct foreign policy secretly, presiding over missions around the globe like the ultimate spymaster. The president was obsessed with secrecy and often exploded at aides whenever any important stories—about foreign or domestic policy—made their way into the press from leaks in the administration. Nixon would eventually become so obsessed with secrecy and preserving a record of conversations for himself that he would have the now-infamous taping system installed in the Oval Office and the Cabinet Room. The new president also had even less interest than his predecessors in linking ideals such as promoting freedom and human rights to US policy. The foreign leaders with whom Nixon got along best, like President Agha Muhammad Yahya Khan of Pakistan, were almost always authoritarian strongmen.[18] In private, captured on the secret tapes that Nixon kept of his interactions in the White House, the president told his aides that most poor countries were not ready to become real democracies, anyway; he disdained India, the largest of the poor democracies, as a country of "slippery, treacherous people" who would use their vote to put incompetent leaders into office.[19]

So, while Nixon personally disliked Helms and deeply resented the CIA, leaving the agency in charge of Laos and expanding the air war suited the new administration. If ramping up activities in Laos multiplied civilian casualties and also solidified the dictatorial tendencies of Vang Pao, that was of little concern. "How many did we kill in Laos?" Nixon asked Kissinger in one taped recording of a conversation three years into their bombing campaign. "In the Laotian thing, we killed about ten, fifteen [thousand]," Kissinger replied.[20] The national security advisor did not seem to have a very clear figure and seemed blasé about exactly how many people—civilians, mostly—the bombing had killed to that point.

Before January 1969, the United States had been maintaining its rate of about fifteen to twenty bombing runs per day in Laos, although sometimes this figure would increase during the middle of a major battle such as Nam Bac.[21] By the end of 1969, less than a year into Nixon's first term, US planes were conducting roughly three hundred sorties per day over Laos. At the same time, the Nixon administration began a secret bombing campaign targeting bases in Cambodia for Hanoi's army and for the Vietcong, Hanoi's allies operating in South Vietnam.

The bombing runs increased over Laos even though US pilots as well as some in the agency's Far East division admitted that there was not a greater number of targets in Laos in the end of 1969 than there had been in January, or five years earlier. If anything, there were fewer potential targets for bombers to hit, since much of the tiny country's infrastructure had already been ripped apart by the previous five years of bombing, and the North Vietnamese were getting much better at hiding men and supplies along the Ho Chi Minh Trail. Even under the pressure of daily bombing, North Vietnamese engineers operating in Laos were still able to build makeshift roads in the country at the rate of one mile per day, working at night and undercover.[22]

The bombing became increasingly disconnected from political events on the ground in Laos. Laotian leaders were also less and less involved in the bombing campaign. The Johnson and Kennedy administrations had, at times, acted in Laos without consulting Laotian politicians, or offered only the pretense of consultation, but Nixon made it the norm. His administration bombed areas of the Ho Chi Minh Trail or other parts of Laos regularly without telling any Laotian leaders in advance what the United States was doing.

Massive bombing seemed to hold an appeal to Nixon beyond its direct merits as a policy tool, and even when the president and his national security advisor wondered whether the bombing was effective in changing the direction of battles in Laos, Vietnam, or Cambodia. (On one memo to Kissinger, Nixon wrote in his own hand that he wondered if bombing had achieved "zilch" in Indochina, yet he continued the bombing campaign nonetheless.)[23] In memos and on tape-recorded conversations, the president seemed, at times, to believe that by severely punishing enemies of the United States in Laos, Cambodia, and Vietnam, he would not only get a better settlement at the peace table but also might distinguish himself as a man, and a kind of antiliberal. In a memo he would write later about his decision to approve intensive bombing of major military targets in North Vietnam in 1972, Nixon noted, "I cannot emphasize too strongly that I have determined that we should go for broke . . . We have the power to destroy [the enemy's] war making capacity. The only question is whether we have the will to use that power. What distinguishes me from Lyndon Johnson is that I have the will in spades."[24]

After bombing Vietnamese bases in Cambodia in early 1969, Nixon exulted privately not only in his policy success but also in the power of such a harsh tool of war. We should crack the hell out of them, Nixon told Kissinger, according to a tape of their conversation.[25] "Nixon saw bombing as part of being strong, and being strong was the most important characteristic to him," said John Gunther Dean, a former US diplomat who served in Laos and other countries in Indochina. "Bombing in Laos, Cambodia, North Vietnam, was strong, and he always preferred a strong move . . . He always wanted to play the card that he wasn't like Johnson or Kennedy, and bombing would convince the communists of this."

As the air war grew, US officials still insisted, when questioned by members of Congress or senior staffers around the president, that the Laotians were running their own war and that the Hmong leader was his own man. The United States was just helping out. "We don't run

Vang Pao. We advise him," claimed Larry Devlin, who served as CIA station chief in Vientiane after Shackley, in a classified interview with agency historians.[26] But that was a fiction: although Vang Pao had finally gotten the stepped-up air campaign he wanted, increasingly, the Hmong leader was not in control in Laos at all anymore.

Chapter 13

The Victory and the Loss

TONY POE WAS NOT A STRATEGIC THINKER, AND HE HAD no interest in the politics of CIA headquarters. He occasionally read cheap thrillers and biographies of military heroes. He rarely read the newspapers, even when he was taking a trip to Bangkok. But he was pleased with what even he could see as the direction of the Laos war. "Making the war bigger but with CIA still controlling it was going to mean they needed me more, guys like me . . . CIA people with military skills," Poe said. "They couldn't get rid of me."

Poe had become much harder to control. He had been a teetotaler early in his career, but by 1969, he was infamous within the agency's Far East division for his drinking. He had married a Hmong woman, but this marriage, he said, simply made it easier for him to drink to excess, since he could spend nights getting wrecked and trust that members of his extended local family would carry him home safely.[1] In typical Poe fashion, after the marriage met with strong disapproval from the Far East division and the station in Vientiane—which worried about Poe becoming compromised by his local ties—he reportedly cabled back to bosses at Far East, "I'm married . . . She's mean as hell . . . doesn't smell too good . . . but she's mine now."[2] He also noted that he had arrived for his wedding ceremony wearing "my .357 Magnum, like always," but he took the hand grenades off the vest he wore normally, in honor of his wedding day.[3]

A longtime US aid worker in Laos, Howard Lewin, remembered that, by the time Poe had been in Laos for nearly a decade, he had made it a requirement that foreigners staying overnight with him in up-country Laos had to get drunk by the end of the evening. "I got drunker than I had ever been in my life, before or since," Lewin said about the one evening he spent with Poe. "I vaguely remember an argument and a gunshot," Lewin said of that night, adding that he never found out who fired the shot and whether the bullet hit anyone.[4]

Poe also admitted cheerfully to his bosses that he had been carrying out extreme measures to scare veteran North Vietnamese troops. The CIA operative had started sticking heads of dead communist fighters on spikes and leaving them out by the roadside like a Southeast Asian Vlad the Impaler. One time, he convinced an American pilot to fly over communist-controlled territory in Laos. As the pilot zoomed low, Poe tossed the severed heads of dead North Vietnamese soldiers down onto enemy forces.[5]

Yet Tony Poe, for all his faults, had remained an important cog in the Laos war—which was why his drinking and head dropping had not gotten him fired. The decision to expand the war meant that Vang Pao, other Laotian leaders, and their US allies had to find more troops somewhere. They needed recruiters who could track down anyone left in Laos willing to fight, and to turn those men into actual fighters.

A man with Poe's skills at recruiting and training could be perfect for the job of finding these tribesmen and launching these new units. So the Far East division sent him into northwestern Laos, a region even wilder than most of the country. Poe was based out of Nam Yu, an outpost in which his station was a thatched-roof hut atop a steep climb of over two hundred steps. Unlike nearly every other CIA station in Asia—even ones in relatively remote places such as Long Cheng—Nam Yu had virtually nothing of the modern world, not even hot showers.[6] Stilts let rain wash under Poe's home; palms and giant ferns nearly covered the slanted roof. Several of Poe's most loyal men in Nam Yu guarded the house at all times, carrying clips of ammunition and rifles and sleeping in front of the house on mats or on the ground.

Well before Poe arrived, the northwest had become infamous for drug smuggling and gunrunning. The area had few towns of any size, and was sprinkled with peaks over six thousand feet. It was home to tigers and several types of leopards, as well as gaurs, a kind of wild Asian bison. It had few passable roads, even during the dry season. Many of the tribes in the northwest regularly planted opium, and it was rumored that some of the northwestern tribal leaders had gone into business, in the early 1960s, with the international crime syndicates—French Corsican syndicates, Chinese gangs, and many others—transporting opium and heroin through Laos, Thailand, Burma, and Vietnam. This expansion of the drug trade added another element of uncertainty to the region. Nationalist Chinese soldiers who had fled China after losing their civil war in 1949 had set up fiefdoms in the Burmese and Thai portions of the Golden Triangle; several of the Nationalist leaders had reportedly become major drug barons as well. Abutting the largely unmarked border with China, the northwest was also strategically valuable. Its unpatrolled borders could provide an avenue for the agency and its trainees to sneak into China, or for Chinese troops to sneak into Southeast Asia.

Poe's mission was to corral the fractious hill tribes in the northwest into fighting militias that could defend the area and be moved to other parts of Laos to join larger ground battles. By 1969, Poe had put together a force of around six thousand men, cobbled together from the Yao, Lahu, Shan, and other tribes. He would build up the group to ten thousand by the next year. He'd outfitted many of the men in surplus US military garb—jackets with jungle camouflage and old green army pants. He'd manage to train some of the six thousand, who had been used to shooting flintlock muskets or homemade guns, on M-1 rifles and a few Korean War–era pistols and some rusty pieces of artillery.

But Poe had also found the task of uniting the tribes and building a real working army nearly impossible. In the northwest, he soon discovered, no charismatic and unifying leader, like Vang Pao, seemed to exist.[7] The vast array of northwestern hill tribes, many of whom harbored toward one another ancient grudges as fierce as their feelings about the communists, made it hard for Operation Unity, as Poe's mission was named optimistically by his CIA bosses, to actually achieve much unity. The northwestern tribal leaders would accept the handouts of dollars that Poe would deliver to them about once a month, after planes dropped into Nam Yu from Thailand carrying bags of agency cash. But Poe couldn't pay them enough to truly work together.

In fact, Poe was spending much of his time in the northwest trying to get tribal leaders not to shoot or stab one another with the weapons they'd been given, or sell off their guns and ammunition.[8] His army of six thousand, and later ten thousand, looked substantial when written up in a cable or listed on a payroll, but in reality, Poe said, "They couldn't fight a real battle . . . they weren't really useful for anything against anyone."

Poe, who had plenty of experience coming between tough characters, was not always even successful in keeping tribal leaders from attacking one another. On at least four occasions, Poe said, Shan and Lahu leaders in the force stabbed one another with long knives. Poe even got the agency to pay to build separate seating areas in the dining house in Nam Yu for men from the different ethnic groups, since he feared that more knife fights would break out if men from the different tribes spent considerable time eating together.[9] The reasons for the fights were never clear, but Poe presumed that several of them were over control of the growing heroin and opium trade. He believed that there was little he could do to stop the drug trade in Laos or to halt Vang Pao's participation, and he always denied reports that he himself had fostered the expansion of the narcotics business.[10] He told the television news show *Frontline*, "I'm sure we [CIA operatives] all knew [of the opium and heroin trafficking in Laos], but we tried to monitor it, because we controlled most of the pilots" for the CIA's airlines.[11]

Vang Pao had hoped that armies from other parts of the kingdom, like Poe's men from the northwest, would help relieve the pressure on the Hmong. Although the general couldn't stand working with Poe, he had been convinced that the American could at least recruit a few thousand more men and get them into fighting shape. Vang Pao's army was hemorrhaging fighters at a much higher rate than the rest of the anti-communist Laotian forces. As the war grew in Laos, with the bigger ground battles and the nonstop bombing, Hanoi no longer sent its less capable officers and weaker divisions into the kingdom. North Vietnam's decision to assign more men and better officers to Laos was exactly what Washington had wanted, since it diverted those troops from Vietnam. But drawing more, and better, Vietnamese battalions into Laos also meant harder fights for Vang Pao and his men. Indeed, by the beginning of 1969, Vang Pao's men were suffering about 70 percent of all the casualties taken by the anti-communist forces in Laos, even though the Hmong still comprised but a fraction of the total anti-communist army.[12]

In the summer of 1969, Vang Pao told several of the CIA case officers stationed in Long Cheng that the Hmong could not last more than two or three years if they continued losing men at this pace, even with more support from US bombers and fighter planes. By then, he was losing about ten men for every three new recruits he could muster, and many of the new men were actually boys of thirteen or fourteen, who were incapable of handling the physical and mental pressures of war. In a recruiting drive launched in the first months of 1969, Vang Pao found only three hundred military-age Hmong men for the army.[13]

Vang Pao was also worrying more about defections. He had not previously faced the level of defections that the lowland Laotian army did; he had never seen his men flee in droves as many Laotian soldiers had done at Nam Bac. But in the first four months of 1969, small groups of Hmong officers, angry that they had not been promoted higher in what Vang Pao had once promised was an egalitarian army, had defected to the communist forces. Other Hmong had gone to fight for the lowland army or had simply quit fighting altogether. Some men who had fought with Vang Pao left the army angry not only about the staggering toll in blood but also about how the army's basic mission had changed. "The Hmong would fight for themselves, for their land," said one of Vang Pao's lieutenants. "I think that's why they fought well for a long time, but it's not the same push to fight for the United States, and people are not going to fight as hard fighting for someone else's war."

The agency and the Thai government paid for a growing stream of Thai troops to fill the gaps in Vang Pao's divisions. Bangkok, worried about the possibility of communist forces getting closer to the Thai border, dispatched battalions of troops to fight alongside Vang Pao's men, with most of the Thai troops' salaries paid by the United States. The Thais were well trained, but they had minimal personal attachment to Laos. Vang Pao and other Laotian leaders knew that the Thais were only a stopgap measure. The Thais were not fighting for their own land, and eventually they might be needed back in their own country.[14]

Hanoi seemed to sense the desperation of Vang Pao and the other Laotian leaders. Emboldened by victories at Nam Bac and other sites, the North Vietnamese and the Laotian communists had been grabbing large swaths of Laos since the dry season began at the end of 1968. In January, February, and March 1969, communist forces overran several Hmong bases in northeastern Laos. At one garrison, Nha Khang, four thousand Hmong troops barely slipped out and avoided being massacred before the communists took over.[15]

The communists also moved onto the Plain of Jars, stationing troops across the vital area.

Before 1969, North Vietnam, which dominated decision making on the communist side, had been content to attack but not hold the Plain of Jars, keeping control of the area just long enough to move men and supplies through the kingdom, and often withdrawing during monsoon season. But Hanoi had seemed uneasy about trying to hold a high, relatively scarcely vegetated plateau where troops would be exposed fully to US bombers; their Pathet Lao allies had only small numbers of men and could contribute relatively little to holding the plateau. The communists' seizure of the Plain in 1969, then, was taken in Washington as an ominous sign of the enemy's extreme confidence—a confidence, even in the face of US bombers, that could mean Hanoi's next move would be to march into Laos's biggest towns or destroy Vang Pao's base.

As the dry season stretched into April and May, communist forces moved antiaircraft guns, engineers, and other support divisions onto the Plain, suggesting that they were planning to hold the area for good. American bombers that had been trying to stop the communists from holding the Plain had faced trouble hitting their targets because of long stretches of cloudy, rainy weather, unusual for the dry season. And Vang Pao received intelligence from several spies suggesting that the North Vietnamese were going to attack his base imminently. Humiliated, in late June 1969 Vang Pao allowed the United States to assemble a force of helicopters at Long Cheng in order to evacuate Vang Pao, his top aides, and as many refugees as possible from the Hmong base.[16] The prime minister of Laos, Souvanna Phouma, warned the embassy in Vientiane that a joint Laotian-Vietnamese communist force was planning a huge assault to finally topple his government.[17] "Laos is grim. It really looks like we are going to lose a big portion of it," wrote Air America pilot Harry Casterlin, as the CIA's airline and Vang Pao prepared for the possible evacuation.[18] Women, children, and the elderly left their huts on the base and went into the jungle surrounding the base to sleep, fearing that communist forces could storm Long Cheng during nighttime.[19]

But as the rains came in the summer of 1969, drenching Laos every afternoon, the communists' offensive slowed, buying enough time for Vang Pao to go for broke. In June and July, dirt tracks throughout Laos turned to impassable mud that even the resourceful North Vietnamese could not drag trucks or artillery pieces over.[20] The North Vietnamese had amassed ammunition, guns, and supplies for a possible attack on Long Cheng, and had nearly made it to the Hmong base. But now all that weaponry and food was sitting, stuck, with communist troops in and around the Plain of Jars.

Vang Pao saw his chance. This was the moment for the big knockout punch he had hoped to deliver—the surprise attack that would stun Hanoi and halt any plans to take Vang Pao's base. "There are not enough Hmong to fight for all of Laos," Vang Pao told the embassy in Vientiane.[21] The Hmong needed to win a big battle that would demoralize Hanoi, and for that, they needed airpower like the United States had never used before in Laos—what Vang Pao called "massed air sorties."[22] The general proposed moving the largest possible force of his men onto the Plain of Jars, where North Vietnamese officers, who believed they could never lose a conventional battle in Laos, would not expect an attack.

It would be an enormous gamble: Long Cheng, and all the Hmong civilians beyond it, would be only lightly guarded. Before the assault, US planes would have to obliterate routes off of the Plain, making it harder for the communists to flee. Apprised earlier in the year of Vang Pao's ideas for a massive assault, US Embassy analysts concluded that the general's idea was impractical—"an act of desperation" that would be sure to fail.[23]

But at senior levels of the CIA and the White House, and in the office of the ambassador himself, the view was different. Senior administration officials worried that details of US involvement in Laos could leak out to the American public at any time, making it even more important to land a decisive blow before the operation was exposed—and possibly curtailed by Congress. In February 1969 Prime Minister Souvanna Phouma had slipped up badly in an interview with United Press International, the wire service. Though he had not intended to, Souvanna admitted that American planes had been bombing communist forces in northern and central Laos, the first time any Laotian or US official had said so publicly. Warned by Nixon's aides to quash the UPI report, the US Embassy in Vientiane denied the claim of American bombing throughout Laos (as US officials had done for years), and Souvanna quickly backtracked. But the admission added to the feeling of urgency in the CIA and the White House.[24]

Vang Pao's plan also was a chance—maybe the best chance—for the new Nixon administration to prove that its idea to intensify the war in Indochina, for the short term, would help produce the longer-term goal of peace and withdrawal with a sense of pride. In addition, a real victory might stiffen the resolve of Laos's government, which Nixon and Kissinger feared might at any point give in to a negotiated political settlement that would essentially allow the Pathet Lao to take over Vientiane. The White House, the embassy, and the CIA gave Vang Pao the approval to launch his audacious attack—with the carpet bombing he needed for it to work.

During the first week of August, Vang Pao began the attack, which he and the Americans had named About Face. As the general had hoped, his men totally surprised the North Vietnamese on the Plain of Jars. A small band of Hmong commandos snuck behind the communists' lines and attacked them from the eastern part of the Plain, destroying much of the North Vietnamese supply lines. Then several Hmong battalions totaling as many as six thousand men rushed into the Plain from the south.

The US air assault, meanwhile, was unrelenting, just as Vang Pao had wanted. Virtually every man-made structure on the Plain of Jars was destroyed, as American planes launched up to three hundred bombing sorties per day over the Plain.[25] After the bombers emptied their payloads, US planes flew over the Plain and dumped chemicals to kill any vegetation and make it impossible for communist troops—as well as civilians—to grow rice or anything else there.[26]

The combination of airpower, surprise, and a Hmong force willing to stand and fight in the open proved decisive. But the Hmong got lucky, too: the normally resourceful North Vietnamese and Pathet Lao spies failed to anticipate About Face. The rainy season, one of the heaviest in Laotian history, came at just the right time to favor a counterattack and make retreat harder for the Vietnamese. And communist commanders had stretched their supply lines too much, opening themselves to attack.

It was Vang Pao's biggest win. The Hmong and the American bombers shocked and overwhelmed the North Vietnamese and a smaller group of Pathet Lao. The communist troops were disoriented by the carpet bombing, which rattled the earth night and day. Unsure of where the ground attacks were coming from, they put up little resistance as Vang Pao's men clambered onto the Plain. The general and his men set up machine guns and howitzers along escape routes, of which there were few, and mowed down North Vietnamese troops as they tried to get off the high plateau. The Hmong leader personally directed his troops to place four 155-millimeter guns in the path of escaping North Vietnamese and fire shells above their heads, so that shrapnel would splinter in the air and rain down everywhere, creating a wide shower of hot death.[27] US bombers also attacked Vietnamese ammunition dumps, causing secondary explosions that killed many more fleeing North Vietnamese and could last for hours at a time.[28] "The Plain had become a mass graveyard . . . The twisted and charred hulks of more than three hundred [North Vietnamese] armored vehicles, tanks, amphibious personnel carriers, and transport trucks lay scattered" across a wasteland of denuded fields and bomb craters, wrote Keith Quincy, a historian of the Hmong.[29] Hanoi's 312th Division, which was made up of relatively inexperienced troops, was

almost totally destroyed; in one battalion of the 312th, only three survivors made it back to a communist stronghold.

As the North Vietnamese burned and died, Vang Pao sent several
groups of his most trusted soldiers to march onto the middle of the
Plain of Jars. "A fantastic sight—3,000 men [part of Vang Pao's army]
walking upright across the Plain of Jars," one CIA contractor responsible for directing bombing runs, Karl Polifka, wrote after watching
Vang Pao's men take the Plain.[30]

With communist forces on the run, in early September Vang Pao
asked US bombers to move east and hit communist strongholds
near the border with North Vietnam. Emboldened by Vang Pao's advance, the Nixon administration agreed to assault these border forts,
even though launching this bombing close to North Vietnam while
Hanoi and Washington were in a cease-fire risked scuttling a settlement. American planes attacked the makeshift buildings erected by
the Pathet Lao and North Vietnamese in the northeastern mountains.
One complex in the joint Laotian-Vietnamese communists' stronghold comprised fifty-two small buildings linked together by multiple paths and tunnels. Airmen flying out of northeastern Thailand
hit it with several five-hundred-pound bombs. "In the blink of an
eye, an area the size of three football fields erupted in a massive chain
reaction . . . The explosions continued sporadically for twenty-four
hours," wrote Quincy in his history of the secret war, *Harvesting Pa
Chay's Wheat: The Hmong and America's Secret War in Laos*.[31] The entire complex of fifty-two buildings was leveled.

By October 1969, Vang Pao and his men controlled the entire five-
hundred-square-mile Plain of Jars, probably the most important military site in Laos. Unable to retreat effectively, as US bombers blocked
routes out of the Plain, Hanoi's fighters fled into the surrounding hills,
where they often faced brutal revenge attacks. The North Vietnamese soldiers were hungry and wounded, their supplies running out
while US planes zoomed low over the hills, looking for isolated bands
of North Vietnamese troops to kill. Hilltribe men and women who

hadn't fought on the Plain but were hardly fans of the North Vietnamese captured some of the fleeing infantrymen and murdered them, shooting them or cutting their throats with long knives.[32] Vang Pao regretted only that the Hmong did not have enough men available to systematically chase the North Vietnamese on foot and kill them all.[33]

In taking the Plain of Jars, Vang Pao and his men also captured twelve Soviet-made tanks, mortars, antiaircraft guns, and other heavy weapons, and some two thousand tons (three million rounds) of ammunition.[34] The CIA estimated that the captured equipment, ammunition, and other supplies amounted to a loss of around $12 million worth of goods for Hanoi.[35]

"It is hard to believe but the [Plain of Jars] has been recaptured . . . I am flying in areas that I have never been before," Casterlin, the Air America pilot, wrote in a letter.[36] The Plain was critical to controlling the country; holding it could cut off multiple routes through Laos used by communist forces. Besides capturing territory critical to North Vietnamese supply lines, sending Hanoi's troops fleeing, and seizing ammunition and weapons, Vang Pao had ensured that as long as the Hmong held the Plain, residents of the area could not be used as porters along the Ho Chi Minh Trail. (The CIA had estimated that about ten thousand Laotians in and around the Plain had been used as porters, hauling supplies for the enemy and doing other manual tasks.)

Vang Pao celebrated with several Hmong officers atop the Plain, firing guns into the air and preparing a celebratory meal of rice balls, soup, chicken, pig, and other meats. The general appeared radiant; he walked up and down lines of Hmong soldiers, sticking impromptu decorations on their chests and occasionally handing one a captured North Vietnamese rifle. He dictated an account of the battle to several CIA officers walking with him through the ranks of his troops. "Vang Pao has successfully occupied the Plain of Jars . . . He personally fired the first twenty or thirty rounds into the enemy and then directed the troops in the final assault," exulted CIA head Helms in a secret memorandum to National Security Advisor Kissinger and President Nixon.[37]

Taking the Plain of Jars seemed to erase the memory of Nam Bac and, for now, hold off any possibility that the Laotian government would agree to some political deal with the Pathet Lao that might allow communist ministers to take over control in Vientiane. For some US officials, the victory also seemed to prove finally the theory that the Hmong could bring the fight to the North Vietnamese. For the Hmong leader, taking the Plain seemed like the heavy blow he had hoped to land against the communists; one that would force Hanoi to reconsider sending more troops into Laos.

Yet only days after Vang Pao's triumphant march across the Plain, he worried privately that he could not afford many such "victories." By November, the Hmong general was actually asking his CIA contacts for an even heavier American bombing campaign. Without it, he insisted, the communists would quickly regroup and launch a successful counterattack. And in the battle for the Plain of Jars, even with the element of surprise, the desperate and heroic fighting of the Hmong troops, and the support of bombing runs as intense as any in the history of warfare, Vang Pao had lost several battalions' worth of men. His forces were stretched too thin to hold the Plain for long, and the victory did not immediately lead to a huge recruiting drive that could swell the Hmong army. Despite Director of Central Intelligence Helms's celebratory note to President Nixon, CIA analysts predicted, in a confidential internal memo, that Vang Pao's offensive would only disrupt the communists' movement and supply routes on the Plain of Jars for a few months.[38] Agency analysts believed that despite the humiliation and retreat of the North Vietnamese's once-prestigious 316th Division, Hanoi would soon send fresh new divisions into Laos to demonstrate that one defeat would not set it back. The counterattack would potentially decimate a Hmong force that Vang Pao had already spread over too wide an area. Taking the Plain of Jars "certainly was not worth the high price [the Hmong] paid," concluded one classified analysis of the campaign by Doug-las Blaufarb, who had been the CIA station chief in Laos in the early 1960s and was now an Indochina analyst.[39]

The bombing of the Plain had temporarily demoralized the North Vietnamese, cut their supply lines, and helped force them to retreat. But more than any other air attacks during the war, it also had come at a great price. The civilian toll on the Plain of Jars was the highest of the war, with all but 9,000 of the 150,000 people who had lived there either killed, wounded, or forced to flee the area.

The Nixon administration had supported massive bombing of the Plain out of worry that the war's cover would soon be blown, but Op-eration About Face would actually speed up leaks about the war to the American public. The size of the offensive on the Plain was so large in terms of combatants, deaths, and territory fought over that the Hmong, the agency, and the embassy in Vientiane just could not keep some details about the fighting from getting out to the press and to Congress. And the intense bombing of the Plain of Jars, which left the region virtually uninhabitable, turned the Laotian civilians who managed to stay alive into refugees. Many headed for the capital. With so many people pouring into Vientiane, it was almost inevitable that American reporters, who spent most of their time in Laos in the city, would finally come face-to- face with Laotians caught in the war.

The CIA's gloomy analysts, who had worried that the Hmong could not hold the Plain, were soon proven right. By January 1970, only three months after Vang Pao's jubilant celebration, two North Viet-namese army divisions, supported by tanks, artillery, and minelayers, had overrun the Plain of Jars again. As they marched forward, the North Vietnamese routed overstretched and tired Hmong units in their way, with every force of Vang Pao's soldiers taking heavy casualties. Overcast weather prevented US planes from bombing the North Vietnamese and helping stop their advance.[40] "Both the north and the south are under heavy attack by Communist troops . . . We continue to take a beating," said Ken Hessel, a clandestine operative in Laos.[41]

As suddenly as they had taken the Plain, the Hmong retreated from it. They had to stop the Vietnamese, now on the move again, from overrunning Long Cheng. The US Embassy, seeing that the Hmong could not hold onto the Plain of Jars, also advised Vang Pao and his men to retreat.[42] By February 1970, the North Vietnamese, along with small groups of Pathet Lao, had not only taken the Plain again but also built a headquarters on it. Their move onto the Plain suggested they weren't worried about being pushed off again. Bangkok frantically flew in fresh Thai troops to reinforce Vang Pao's base at Long Cheng. In the first weeks of February, US planes, which only months earlier had been on the attack on the Plain, now scattered throughout Laos to ferry Hmong fighters and more than five hundred other anti-communist Laotian troops to Long Cheng.[43] Some days in February, the airstrip at Long Cheng was so busy that planes took off and landed every two minutes.[44] Meanwhile, Vang Pao reluctantly allowed civilians at Long Cheng to flee, at least temporarily, in case the communists attacked.[45] The general had worried that allowing civilians to flee might signal desperation and prompt his soldiers to desert, but he gave the order anyway. Although the CIA had never kept files listing the names of its operatives at Long Cheng, or the details of what its men were doing in Laos, the agency still had maps, some copies of cables, logistics reports, and other documents at Long Cheng that could prove incriminating.[46] Now clandestine officers rushed to empty the CIA's offices in Long Cheng of any documents, stuff them in large metal trash cans outside, douse them with gasoline, and light them on fire.[47] Some of the clandestine CIA officers were so convinced that the base was about to fall to Hanoi that they hung signs that read "Shove It Up Your Ass, Ho Chi Minh" on some of the buildings in Long Cheng.[48]

Worried that a Laotian-Vietnamese communist force could move on from the Plain to attack not just Long Cheng but also Vientiane, seriously imperiling Thailand and South Vietnam, the White House ordered an even larger escalation of the air war in February 1970. "We did go farther than ever before," admitted Secretary of Defense Melvin Laird in a National Security Council meeting.[49] The White House sent B-52 bombers, the biggest in America's aviation arsenal, to attack the North Vietnamese troops stationed on the edge of the Plain—the ones who could possibly march on Vientiane. The B-52s, America's immense long-range Stratofortresses, were the ultimate air weapon, their payloads vast and terrible. Neil Sheehan, the war correspondent, wrote that, when the B-52s bombed North Vietnam, a formation of just six of the giants could, in one run, destroy every object in an area approximately five-eighths of a mile wide by two miles long.[50] The planes also flew at a high enough altitude that they could not be seen from the ground by the North Vietnamese and Laotian communists, even in clear weather. Indeed, the North Vietnamese troops never saw the planes as they dropped over a thousand tons of bombs throughout the night of February 17. "To those on the receiving end, the explosions seemed spontaneous, as if the earth had erupted on its own in a thousand places," wrote historian Keith Quincy in his account of the bombing.[51]

The Pathet Lao and the North Vietnamese did not move on to the capital. (Although Vietnamese forces were doing the majority of the fighting, Hanoi was careful to ensure that the Laotian communists seemed to be leading marches through central Laos, especially as the communist forces drew closer to Laos's bigger cities.) And Long Cheng would not fall. Not yet.

Chapter 14

The Secret War
Becomes Public

BILL SULLIVAN LEFT LAOS IN MARCH 1969. HIS LAST DAYS in Vientiane did not end with a teary, hours-long *baci* like Bill Lair's good-bye, or an all-night moonshine-quaffing fest like Tony Poe had with some of the Hmong he loved the most before he headed up to the northwest. The ambassador had loyal aides but few close friends in Vientiane. He had won respect from Laotian leaders for his influence over policy, but he had never taken a great interest in Laotian culture or society, the way that Lair had. Sullivan was often openly dismissive of Laotians and seemed to have little respect for how they ran their country. Speaking to a group of US senators in January 1968, Sullivan said that Laotians were "very charming, pleasant, lovable, gentle people, but I can't say they have much zip and zoom."[1]

In February and March, Sullivan made the usual round of diplomatic farewells, calling on Prime Minister Souvanna Phouma, Western European ambassadors, and some of the ambassadors from communist countries who had remained friendly with US diplomats in the tiny Laotian capital. He gave a reception for his staff at the embassy. Then he flew to Long Cheng for a short meeting to prepare Vang Pao for the change in ambassador. The general thanked Sullivan but held no ceremonies for him and made no speeches as Sullivan left the Hmong base.[2]

To acquaintances who met him after his return to Washington,

Bill Sullivan seemed even more confident in his skills as a diplomat and a politician, and in his thinking about Indochina, than he had been before he left for Vientiane. His longstanding conviction that he would become an ambassador, a position that most Foreign Service hands never attained, had been proven right, and he still had many years left in his diplomatic career. However, working in a climate of unrelenting heat and eating unclean food had worn Sullivan down physically.[3] He had lost weight, and his thick shock of wavy hair had gone gray and white. "The endless business of running [a war] against the North Vietnamese" left him with what he called a "bedraggled look," as well as a series of gastrointestinal infections that ultimately put him in a US military hospital for two weeks.[4]

However, he did not seem to have lost anything mentally. Sullivan soon began working long days, and even overnight, at the State Department back in Washington.[5] If anything, his mind had grown sharper in Laos, as he had taken on not only the burdens of an ambassador but also the duties of a military commander, an aid expert, and to some extent, a top spy.

William Sullivan, a lifelong Democrat, had no personal relationship with Richard Nixon; he was well known as a protégé of Harriman, a Democratic Party fixture. Sullivan had served in Italy when Nixon was Eisenhower's vice president, and Nixon had not run for office between 1962 and 1968, the period when Sullivan had held his most influential positions.

Shortly after Nixon was elected in November 1968, Henry Kissinger quietly called several of Lyndon Johnson's aides who had dealt with Sullivan. From what he understood about Laos, Kissinger considered the operation, so far, a success story. Momentum had tied down North Vietnamese forces, and with more US bombing, the operation could kill even more of Hanoi's best troops. For his part in expanding Momentum, former Laos station chief Ted Shackley had been rewarded recently with a promotion to running the CIA's operation in Saigon.

Kissinger and his aides had heard from Sullivan's acquaintances that the ambassador had taken an unusually large interest in how Laos policy was made at the highest levels, that he had considered it his job to decide what to do about Laos, even on the military side. If Sullivan was allowed to handle the Laos war from Washington, would he create a problem for the White House if the president demanded a strategy of intensifying the war in order to eventually leave it? Don't worry, Kissinger and his aides were told, Sullivan is no ideologue; he wants to manage Laos policy, but he will go along with the changes.

Kissinger, who already knew Bill Sullivan informally, took in what he heard about the brilliant micromanaging ambassador and how much Sullivan already knew about bombing and fighting in Laos. Kissinger was impressed. Sullivan was made the deputy assistant secretary of state for East Asian and Pacific affairs. The Nixon administration installed a new ambassador in Laos, G. McMurtrie Godley, who had also made it clear that he would support the increased bombing campaign.[6] Sullivan's job, as the "DAS," as people in Washington called it, would be to manage Indochina policy. Although he was supposed to focus on Vietnam, the job necessarily included Laos policy. With Bill Lair gone from Laos, a new US ambassador in Vientiane, and few other Laos experts in the administration in Washington, Sullivan would retain influence over the kingdom.

In theory, the ambassador was to manage the policy at the State Department, but the administration wanted to make sure that Sullivan really worked for Kissinger and the president, and not for the State Department. Sullivan admitted that Kissinger and Nixon, "with a fetish for secrecy, wished to bypass [Secretary of State Bill] Rogers and the [State] Department," which was a highly unusual way to make foreign policy. But he was used to operating differently from the way the Foreign Service normally did. He would manage Laos policy for Kissinger personally rather than for the State Department, if that was the way to retain his influence.[7] I "spent more and more of my time in the [White House] Situation Room and acting more and more as an executive arm . . . for Kissinger," Sullivan recalled.[8]

Even after being taken into Kissinger's circle, Sullivan did not expect to become the public face of America's Laos war. Yet not long after he returned to Washington, he would be the man called before Congress to explain what really was happening in the kingdom of Laos.

In 1967, the *New York Times* had run a story that mentioned that the Hmong were getting American help in fighting the Pathet Lao and North Vietnamese. But the *Times* only hinted at CIA involvement and did not uncover the scope of the US war effort in Laos.[9] At that point, the paper could find no one who could confirm US bombing in Laos or CIA involvement in the kingdom at all.[10]

However, by the time of Vang Pao's victory on the Plain of Jars in September–October 1969, internal agency memos noted that reporters were getting close to uncovering the extent of US operations there. They were stumbling across CIA contractors in Thailand and Laos, as well as gaining access to the agency's secret sites. There were so many men and women involved with the operation in Laos that it was becoming harder for the agency to monitor everyone who came in and out of Long Cheng, the way that the CIA had done in the mid-1960s. It was also becoming tougher for the CIA to keep Vang Pao, who increasingly enjoyed his press coverage, from boasting about Operation About Face and how he got US bombers to help him win the battle.

And after the Plain of Jars battle, the stream of refugees flooding Vientiane was hard to miss. Some reporters had long suspected that the scale of American assistance in the kingdom was much greater than Washington had let on but were unable to confirm their hunches. Now, with so many refugees living in makeshift encampments on the outskirts of Laos's capital, reporters finally had faces and stories to confirm their suspicions.

The refugees had gruesome stories to tell.[11] In 1969 alone, according to several accounts, the United States dropped more bombs on Laos than it did on Japan during all of World War II. By 1973, when the bombing campaign ended, America had launched over 580,000 bombing runs in Laos.[12] A high percentage of these bombs were antipersonnel or fragmentation bombs—which exploded into hundreds of small, deadly metal pellets on impact—antipersonnel mines, and bombs that caused widespread fires.[13] The antipersonnel mines thumped into the ground and were almost impossible to see from the surface, so that even when bombers moved on to other targets, villagers—including many children—were constantly stepping on mines and being killed or maimed.[14]

"Laos is deeply forested, and the only 'targets' visible from the air were villages," recalled Fred Branfman, a former aid worker in Laos who became an antiwar activist and helped journalists meet refugees from the bombing campaign. "The main victims of the bombing, every refugee explained, were civilians—particularly older people, mothers, and children who had to remain near their villages to survive. The soldiers moved through the deeply carpeted forests of northern Laos and were relatively unscathed by the bombing."[15] Before fleeing, most of these mothers and children had been living each day simply trying to gather any food and avoid bombing. "Our lives became like those of animals desperately trying to escape their hunters," one refugee from the Plain of Jars told Branfman.[16] "The society living in and around [the Plain] no longer existed."[17]

Branfman could have filled multiple books with stories of atrocities in the air war. In the most heavily bombed part of the country, the Plain of Jars, the bombing runs almost never paused. The Plain, a series of massive stone megaliths resembling jars without lids on a high plateau in central Laos, was believed to be ancient burial grounds created as long ago as 500 BC. Hundreds of the stone jars clustered together in sites across the Plain, amidst scattered trees and grasses and peaks that rose as high as nine thousand feet. In one photo of the

Plain of Jars, taken by Perry Stieglitz, who served as cultural attaché at the US Embassy in Laos in the early 1960s, a Laotian man, dressed in the loose pajama-type pants that were the local style, stares up at one of the jars, which is more than twice his height.[18]

The air war focused intensely on the Plain, because of its importance as a crossroads. By the end of the 1960s, massive, moonscape craters pocked the plateau, alongside the remains of the giant stone burial jars. Out on the Plain of Jars, one compendium of oral histories noted, refugees experienced "enormous numbers of jets which dropped huge bombs upon them day after day, month after month, year after year . . . eventually [destroying] the whole society that had existed for the previous 700 years on the Plain of Jars."[19] People living on the Plain of Jars often survived only by crawling into deep caves. Since the air attacks kept up with little pause, some families lived underground for months or years, only sprinting out at night like animals to try to gather food. "Everything was leveled, and you could see only the red, red ground," remembered one survivor. "The holes! The holes! During that time, we needed holes to save our lives," remembered another survivor. "We who were young took our sweat and our strength, which should have been spent raising food . . . and squandered it digging holes" to hide in.[20]

Even the caves and the holes did not always provide shelter. Nearly all the residents of one village fled into a cave, but a US Air Force bomb exploded into the cavern in March 1968, killing everyone: more than four hundred men, women, and children.[21]

Nai Phoung, the leader of the Plain of Jars village of Ban Bouak, had told most of Ban Bouak's children that when the planes swooped down, they should run into smaller holes dug in the ground. He advised them not to run for the largest underground bomb shelters, since the pilots would then know the shelters' locations and could drop bombs that killed everyone inside. So when Nai Phoung's twelve-year-old daughter, Sao Ba, and Nai Phoung's nephew were caught outside as planes appeared overhead, they did not run for the biggest shelters. But the children could not find any small holes nearby, either. "Sao Ba was wearing a white blouse. The plane saw them playing in an open space . . . There were no soldiers around," Nai Phoung said. A US Air Force plane dropped bombs right on them, killing both children.[22]

The bombing could be almost willfully random. In the first months of 1970, some US pilots released ordnance over the kingdom without locating any military target, because they did not want to return to bases with bombs still hanging from their planes.[23] Or, it appeared sometimes they dropped bombs on Laos because the United States and North Vietnam had entered cease-fires, so US bombers were idled.[24] "We had all those planes sitting around and couldn't just let them stay there with nothing to do," said Monteagle Stearns, a career diplomat who served in Laos during the secret war.[25] Stearns seemingly rued allowing such widespread bombing, but one US official, who made sure his name was not revealed, joked to a reporter for the prestigious Asian publication *Far Eastern Economic Review* that "we couldn't just let the planes rust" when the United States was maintaining a halt to bombing North Vietnam.[26]

This was not an unofficial, rogue policy. In fact, when the Johnson and Nixon administrations declared pauses in bombing campaigns of North Vietnam, they simultaneously had the State Department send cables to US embassies noting that the bombing of Laos would continue. The cables suggested that planes that were to be taken out of use, for a brief period, in North Vietnam would be diverted to bombing Laos.[27]

It was, in fact, common knowledge among CIA clandestine officers, and surely in the embassy in Vientiane, that bombers sometimes dropped ordnance on Laos because they didn't want to land with the bombs still attached to the planes, or because they needed practice, or because dropping bombs on or near civilian areas might possibly kill some communist soldiers or sympathizers. Ronald

Rickenbach, a former USAID official in Laos during the height of the bombing, called it "an indiscriminate bombing of civilian population centers."[28] A classified 1969 United States government survey of the effects of the bombing, the results of which were circulated among officials working in Laos, found that after interviewing people from villages across the kingdom, 97 percent of the Laotian civilians surveyed had witnessed a bombing attack, and most had witnessed more than one.[29] And 61 percent of the Laotian civilians interviewed for the survey had personally seen someone killed by the bombing.[30]

Laotian leaders knew about the indiscriminate bombing as well. Laotian villagers and some lower-ranking Laotian military officers, both Hmong and lowland Lao, often expressed outrage at what frequently appeared to be wanton bombing and the high percentage of civilians killed in Laos. Former aid worker Howard Lewin remembers that when he was working on an island in the middle of the Mekong River, he saw an air force C-130 plane fly low and suddenly strafe the island's town—basically just shooting innocent people. The local Laotian military commander ran to Lewin, as he was the only American around, and screamed at him, "What kind of people do you think we are? Animals that you can shoot at us for sport?"[31]

Yet Vang Pao and other top Laotian leaders never expressed such anger about the bombing campaign—at least not publicly. Laotian leaders simply tried to avoid being publicly linked to the US air war, a strategy virtually identical to the public position taken by leaders today in countries such as Yemen, where the United States conducts drone strikes in the war on terrorism. Again, the parallels to the modern day are striking: after US planes bombed a hospital in Kunduz, Afghanistan, in 2015, destroying the facility and killing at least twenty-two people, the attack was condemned by rights groups and Doctors Without Borders, which ran the hospital. But many prominent Afghan politicians defended the strike, saying that the causing of civilian casualties (and contravening laws of war) was worth trying to eliminate Taliban fighters alleged to be in and around the hospital.³²

Some top Laotian leaders—including Vang Pao—believed that the civilian casualties in their country were a cost worth paying if it meant that US bombers also struck the North Vietnamese. Apparently other Laotian leaders had become so used to the lifestyle they enjoyed from US aid—many leading politicians would exaggerate the number of employees in their ministries, get US aid to pay all these "salaries," and then keep the money for the ghost employees themselves—that they were willing to keep quiet about the thousands of Laotians dying in the air war.

The increasing information coming out about the Laos war after the big battle on the Plain of Jars was scooped up quickly by the American press. *Time* and *U.S. News & World Report* published articles in October 1969 detailing the US bombing of Laos, and how American assistance for Vang Pao and his army went far beyond the small amounts of aid US officials had admitted to for years. And over the last week of October 1969, the *New York Times* published three investigative articles on America's involvement in Laos: the "twilight war," the series called it. All these articles showed that Washington was much more involved in Laos than any administration involved had acknowledged.³³

In Washington, the stories shocked policy makers who had no clue that the Laos war had become so large, or that US bombers were actually flying more missions in Laos than in Vietnam. Congress noticed all the news pieces about Laos, too. So, in the third week of October 1969, Bill Sullivan found himself sitting before a closed session of a subcommittee of the Senate Committee on Foreign Relations. The hearings, the first serious congressional probing of the war, would run for four days. Sullivan would have to offer some answers about exactly how and why the United States was waging war in Laos, and whether that war was constitutional. After all, Congress was supposed to approve any declaration of war.

Some of the senators on the committee, such as Stuart Symington of Missouri, had been old allies of the CIA; others, like Senator William Fulbright of Arkansas, had already established themselves as critics of the war in Indochina. But even those senators who once had been trusted by the CIA had never learned that the CIA's operations in Laos had become a full-on war; many were surprised by the revelations aired in the press. As Sullivan sat before them, most of the senators still did not know much about the extent of US bombing in Laos, how long the air war had been going on, or how closely the CIA was involved in Vang Pao's battles. And even former congressional backers of the agency were not as chummy as they had once been. In his opening statement, Symington thundered, "It is time the American people were told more of the facts" about the Laos war.[34] "The secrecy surrounding our relations with that country has gone on far too long."[35]

Sullivan knew he would be in for much rougher treatment than he'd ever gotten before from Congress. Some on the committee appeared genuinely concerned about how large the Laos war was becoming, and how many civilians were being killed; they, and their staffs, and some of their constituents, had read the *Times* series and were surprised to find that a whole war being waged under their noses. Others on the committee, who had known about some aspects of Operation Momentum before, acted shocked. If it came out that the CIA had run a war in Laos and that Congress had never said anything about it, members of Congress would look like powerless pawns.[36]

The *New York Times* stories would not turn out to be as big news, at least among most Americans, as the Nixon administration feared. By the spring of 1970, Laos would again be mostly relegated to the inside pages of newspapers and magazines, or to brief mentions on the nightly news. But in October 1969, there was no way for the White House to know that stories about Laos would not resonate with the American public. So Nixon and Kissinger were trusting Sullivan to defuse congressional probing of the war. Secretary of Defense Melvin Laird had already appeared before a secret session of the House Committee on Foreign Affairs to discuss the operation in Laos, and he had failed to pacify them. "They know the past and everything in Helms's operation, but they were really shocked about the increased [bombing] raids . . . It shakes them to the bottom of their feet," Laird told Kissinger in a taped conversation.[37]

The White House had good reason to maintain confidence in Sullivan's ability to mollify the Senate and keep it from asking more questions about Laos. Although Congress had mostly given Sullivan a free pass before 1969, when he was ambassador in Vientiane, Sullivan had been required to appear before Senate and House committees and subcommittees on foreign relations occasionally and give simple briefings about Momentum. When senators asked even relatively unthreatening questions in these secret sessions, Sullivan had stonewalled them effectively, never slipping up and never making any admissions about the true extent of the war. During one closed-door briefing in January 1968, Senator John Sherman Cooper, a Republican from Kentucky, had mentioned that the United States was training Laotian troops and that some of the trainees—the lowland army—were fleeing rather than fighting. Cooper was not trying to break any news, since the session would not be publicized, but Sullivan had interjected quickly anyway.

"I would just like to correct the record: we do not have a military training and advisory organization in Laos," Sullivan said. "We, therefore, do not have advisers with these troops."[38] Cooper, who seemed taken aback by Sullivan's immediate response, assured the ambassador that, yes, he understood that the United States had no military advisors or trainers in Laos.[39]

Now, in October 1969, Sullivan never looked anything but poised, even as senators bored in on him. Bill Sullivan seemed to have an answer for everything, though it would become clear later that his answers did not match the reality in Laos. He started with a long statement about America's role in the kingdom, which omitted any mention of the CIA's activities, and claimed that the United States was observing the rules about Laos's neutrality.[40] When asked by several senators whether the United States was launching bombing attacks throughout Laos, such as on the Plain of Jars or in the north of the country near the Vietnamese border, Sullivan had an immediate and unequivocal response: no. Sullivan insisted that bombers were hitting a narrow group of targets along the Ho Chi Minh Trail in eastern Laos. US planes were, he conceded, striking a few targets in the north, but only when the Laotian government requested air support. He did not mention that bombing in Laos had increased, some days, to three hundred attacks per twenty-four hours, many of which happened without the Laotian government's knowledge.[41] In fact, the US government was spending about twenty-eight times as much on bombing Laos as it was on giving economic and humanitarian aid to the country, although Laos, on a per capita basis, was still getting more US economic aid than nearly any other country in the world.[42]

When senators pressed him about reports of the bombing causing widespread civilian casualties and creating tens of thousands of refugees, Sullivan was just as firm and calm. Reports of civilian casualties were wildly overstated, and the United States was doing everything possible to avoid any loss of civilian life, Sullivan said. He declared, "It was the policy not to attack populated areas."[43] As ambassador, Sullivan assured the committee, he had taken care to ensure that bombers did not target towns, and he had refused to authorize bombing runs that could endanger civilians.[44] In a later hearing, in 1971, where Sullivan was called again before a subcommittee of the Senate Foreign Relations Committee, he admitted that there had been "two or three" times when the Laotian government mentioned to him that US bombers had hit friendly forces or civilians by mistake.[45] In those few instances, "the first thing we did was to send in a team of doctors, and send in a team of USAID people to help and assist the people of the village. We would also send in—" Sullivan was saying when Senator Edward Kennedy, by far the most aggressive questioner on the subcommittee, broke in.

"Well, you couldn't [provide aid and medical assistance] if it [a bombed village] were held in enemy territory."

Kennedy was exactly right: most of the devastated villages had been marked by the CIA, the embassy, and pilots as in "enemy territory," though in reality they were normally in areas, like the Plain of Jars, being contested by both communist and non-communist forces. Still, by claiming that these villages were in enemy territory, the embassy and the agency could justify taking no real action after bombers reduced these regions to wastelands. "No, we couldn't [provide this kind of aid]" in enemy territory, Sullivan admitted to Kennedy before pivoting quickly.

When civilians died in villages marked as enemy territory, Sullivan said, "We [the embassy] requested photographic evidence and also requested an immediate investigation."[46] He never said what kind of investigation was launched, and, in reality, most bombings were never investigated. Kennedy's time was cut short as another senator got his chance to ask questions.

It was true that, in theory, the bombers attacking Laos had to go through an elaborate series of route plans before takeoff, and had to get several approvals—from the embassy and from the bases back in Thailand—before they could launch their missions. Sullivan and his aides at the embassy had indeed created rules of engagement that pilots were supposed to follow. They had drawn what they called "bomb lines" that avoided civilian populations—lines on maps of Laos that were supposed to guide bombers to military targets. They had also ordered US planes, in most cases, not to fire unless fired upon.[47] The bomb lines had forbidden pilots from dropping ordnance more than a few hundred feet from their targets.

Sullivan added that, actually, the US presence in Laos was a very small one, and that Washington had made no military commitments in the kingdom that could not be ended within twenty-four hours. He did not mention that the United States was training and essentially helping command Vang Pao's entire army, or that Sullivan himself had commanded nearly every aspect of the operation in Laos. When Senator Symington pressed Sullivan to admit how much control he had maintained over fighting in Laos, Sullivan said, "I do not have any cognizance over any of the other people in other [US government] departments."[48]

The senators kept on, perhaps hoping to ruffle Sullivan and get him to admit information that would be more revealing. They failed. Pressed by Fulbright to answer whether the United States had military advisors in Laos, the former ambassador admitted there were some advisors but said that they were not engaged in combat.[49] He did not mention the many times US advisors such as Tony Poe or the men on top of Phou Pha Thi had ignored these instructions and found themselves in the middle of battles in Laos.[50] No military men, Sullivan said—the "advisors" did not count as troops—so the United States was not fighting a war in Laos. Laotian leaders did not expect America to maintain any commitment to Laos, Sullivan insisted—a point that would be clearly proven false when the United States left Indochina, blindsiding Laotian leaders.[51] The United States had made no commitment to the Hmong people, either, Sullivan said—and no plan to help any Hmong refugees who tried to leave Laos.[52]

Senator Fulbright tried again. He had apparently heard from some of his staff about CIA officers recruiting and leading hill tribes, including Poe's men in the northwest, in an attempt to form new guerilla armies in Laos. "Are American troops acting as guerillas in the mountains and the jungles of . . . Laos?" Fulbright asked Sullivan.

"No, sir," Sullivan replied.

"They are not leading any Yao [the tribe Poe was primarily re-cruiting] in any expeditions or ventures?" Fulbright asked again.

"No, sir."

"Nor the Hmong?" Fulbright asked—hitting on the tribe that had been, of course, the center of Operation Momentum.

"No, sir," Sullivan replied.[53]

Fulbright pressed on. "We pretend it [Laos] is a sovereign and in-dependent country . . . But we do intervene in a major way . . . We are pretending we are not there . . . You are deceiving the American peo-ple and the Congress."[54]

Sullivan would not concede an inch, however, claiming that he had no knowledge of any significant US intervention in the country.[55] "There is some misunderstanding," he added: he had no control over air strikes and there was no large-scale US role in Laos.[56]

Symington seemed incredulous. "You directed this war for several years, to my certain knowledge," he said. One of his committee staff-ers reminded Sullivan that a group of the planes operating in Laos was colloquially known as "Ambassador Sullivan's Air Force."[57] Al-though no video of the hearing was made, one can imagine the sen-ators grinding their teeth. "We are fighting a big war in Laos, even if we do not have [American] ground troops there," said Symington. "Yet we are still trying to hide it not only from the [American] people but also from the Congress."[58]

Sullivan seemed offended that the committee would even suggest that the administration was concealing anything about Laos. His ap-pearance before Congress showed that the White House was hiding nothing about its Laos policy. "I must say, Mr. Chairman, that I con-sider these hearings as a very sincere token of an open society," Sulli-van said.[59]

News stories about Laos that came out in 1970 and 1971, and some digging by senators' staffers, would make clear that the ambas-sador had been lying to the Senate. (Sullivan would claim later that if the senators had been more specific in asking him about the extent of the secret war, he would have been more forthcoming in his answers.) For now, though, many of the senators seemed to accept Sullivan's answers. He had held off congressional anger for the moment, making it easier for the White House to continue with the Laos war. Kissinger, the national security advisor, clearly appreciated Sullivan's skill. Soon Kissinger would give Sullivan another promotion of sorts, trusting him to handle the critical stages of secret negotiations with Hanoi that would allow the United States to finally pull out of Indochina.[60]

Chapter 15

Defeat and Retreat

AFTER THE DRAMATIC REVERSAL ON THE PLAIN OF JARS, the general was becoming increasingly despondent. Vang Pao had told Thomas Clines, a CIA officer at Udorn who traveled regularly to Long Cheng, that the general had foreseen that he was leading the Hmong people to annihilation.[1] Air strikes had stopped the North Vietnamese from taking Vang Pao's base, but even the B-52 bombers hadn't stopped Hanoi's men from spending the summer of 1970 dragging more artillery into Laos, building roads toward the Hmong homeland, and consolidating their control of the Plain of Jars. They hammered one of Vang Pao's strongholds north of the Plain, a fortress called Bouam Long atop a series of cliffs that the Hmong had studded with mines and razor wire. Many of the Bouam Long defenders dug tunnels into the cliffs to make bunkers, as Hanoi's gunners shelled the fort, but North Vietnamese tunnel specialists dug into the Hmong tunnels, cornered the soldiers, and machine-gunned many of the trapped men.[2] Only when Vang Pao sent about a thousand men from Long Cheng—men he could not spare—did the Hmong hold on to the fort, albeit with more heavy losses.

In the fall of 1970, as the rains began to slow and it became easier to move in Laos again, Vang Pao's intelligence men and US helicopter pilots reported that Hanoi was moving men toward Long Cheng once again. The general ordered his fighters to lay new lines of mines on the sides of the mountains around his base, and prepared to fight for the high mountain valley.[3]

Vang Pao's mercurial nature was well known to the agency, and to anyone who had even had brief encounters with the general. Until the victory-then-defeat on the Plain of Jars, the general's low moods—which might have been called depression had Vang Pao lived in a place where modern medicine was the norm—usually dissipated quickly, replaced by a buoyancy and bravado. Vang Pao would attend Hmong funerals for his slain men, where people would play the *qeej*, a traditional long reed pipe made of polished bamboo, and the families of the fallen soldiers might slaughter a pig in remembrance. An hour or two after the funerals, he would turn optimistic again, or at least summon up enough fake optimism to make battle plans for the future.

The troughs in his mood were getting deeper and longer now. The general knew what many Laotian politicians and even some American visitors to Long Cheng were saying publicly—that the war was all but over, that Vang Pao and his allies could not win. As a group of Senate aides put it in a report to the Senate Foreign Relations Committee after visiting Laos in the dry season of early spring 1971, "Most observers in Laos say that from the military point of view, the situation there is growing steadily worse, and the initiative seems clearly to be in the hands of the enemy."[4] The aides' negative assessment continued: "The enemy has extended his control [of Laos's territory] . . . Over 60 percent of Laos is no longer under government [non-communist] control . . . It has apparently become increasingly difficult in the past year . . . to maintain an adequate level of manpower [in the non-communist army.]"[5]

Vang Pao didn't have to read a Senate report to know his side was losing territory and that the communists were moving tanks, cannons, and more men into the country than they had at any point before. It was not hard to guess that Hanoi and the Pathet Lao hoped to land such a massive blow against Vang Pao and his army that the Hmong leader would give up, and the entire rest of the national army would fall apart, allowing the communists to walk into Vientiane without fighting more battles.[6] North Vietnamese gunners had been firing thirty to forty rockets a week at Long Cheng, from the mountains around the base, for much of the dry season. Vang Pao also knew that just since December 1970, government troops on patrol had seen communist soldiers with surface-to-air missiles for the first time, threatening US pilots and his own small contingent of Hmong fliers. He knew, too, that Hmong scouts had witnessed North Vietnamese Russian-built MiG fighter jets in the skies over Laos, a rare sight in the past. "It's all been running and dying . . . just running and dying [since Vang Pao retreated from the Plain]," Edgar "Pop" Buell, a longtime aid worker in Long Cheng, despaired.[7]

Before the 1971 dry season war began, in the first months of the year, a classified assessment by the US Embassy in Vientiane said basically the same thing as the Senate aides, though the embassy would not make such an admission in public: "If the Hmong suffer severe losses . . . this year . . . it would be difficult if not impossible for Vang Pao to prevent his troops from joining their dependents in a mass exodus."[8]

The general, once able to walk forty or fifty miles a day if needed, was putting far too much weight on his already stocky frame. Constant stress, lack of sleep, and too much walking had bowed his legs and made his leg bones hurt constantly. He often could get only one or two hours of rest a night, since the constant shelling and his intense nightmares woke him over and over. A face already pocked with moles had taken on furrows across his forehead and deep lines in his cheeks. The Hmong leader screamed at his wives constantly and publicly berated his lieutenants, which he had rarely done in the past.

"I think winning a big victory [at the Plain of Jars] and seeing this still wasn't enough, seriously impacted, the general," said Yang Dao, a Hmong historian and biographer of Vang Pao. "He still was losing men at a huge rate . . . [it] drove home to him that the war was [really] unwinnable." The backup plan of moving the Hmong to Thailand en masse appeared gone as well, said Yang Dao. "It was never going to happen that all these Hmong were just going to be moved in some operation . . . but Vang Pao, some part of him really believed it was possible. The idea was like a way for Vang Pao to think the future would turn out okay, no matter what. Without that idea [and with the huge battle losses], he was losing hope."[9]

The air war also was backfiring, which the Hmong leader was realizing only now. Vang Pao had called for the huge bombing campaign, and American planes had helped the general and his men win their biggest victories and defend Hmong strongholds. But as the war was becoming a long series of defeats and retreats, even some of the general's top aides began to question whether the air war was really helping the Hmong at all. Some Hmong civilians were killed by the bombing, and Hmong soldiers, just like Lao civilians, frequently stumbled onto mines and other unexploded ordnance, causing injuries and deaths in Vang Pao's already thin army.

Worse, the high civilian death toll was turning more of the Laotian population against the United States and its allies in Laos. In the early 1960s, the Pathet Lao and the North Vietnamese had probably done more damage to Laotian villages than anyone else, since communist forces had repeatedly gone on the offensive, and the United States was not deeply involved in the war. But by 1971, US pilots were causing more destruction in Laotian villages than the communists were. Losing the support of civilians was devastating to Vang Pao and his men; they needed their people's backing to survive. Though the Hmong now fought larger battles, they still often operated like a guerilla army when they were on the move. Vang Pao's men often depended on local farmers and villagers to help them eat when they were marching, to provide them with information about communist forces, or even to hide them from communist patrols. The more that Laotian civilians turned against the United States and its allies, the harder it would be for Vang Pao's men to live off the land.

The widening use of American power in Laos also made it harder for Vang Pao and other non-communists to keep up their propaganda campaigns, which used radio dispatches and meetings around the country to portray the communist side as stooges of a foreign power. Meanwhile, the Laotian communists—and Hanoi—feasted on the publicity boon provided them by the bombs' destruction. Hanoi's radio station featured almost daily reports of the bombing's impact on civilians in Laos and in other countries in Indochina. The Laotian communists took photographs of civilians killed by the bombs and of villages totally erased from the earth by American planes. They used the photos, as well as firsthand testimony from people who had survived bombing runs and become more sympathetic to the communists, in propaganda and recruitment sessions in rural Laos.

Losing the support of civilians devastated the general in a more personal way, too. The rationale for Vang Pao's army to exist rested on the notion that he fought for what most Laotians wanted. "The general took pride in the idea that he was fighting for the people of Laos, that even if that took hard [brutal] tactics, most people wanted the anti-communists to win," explained Yang Dao. When he or his men were not welcomed in a village—when he thought the communists were actually winning hearts—it paralyzed the Hmong leader, striking at his identity.[10]

The deaths of so many of his commanders, the frequent battle losses, and the clear signals that his men were losing the war seemed to have made Vang Pao more paranoid as well. Whatever Vang Pao's original inclination—democrat or dictator or something in between—he had become, in retreat in 1970, much more of a dictator. The general had always employed his own group of loyalists as a kind of internal intelligence service within the Hmong community. He had also never shied away from exacting brutal justice on Hmong who had spied for the communist side or fought for Vang Pao's enemies or simply showed significant weakness in battle. His top enforcer, a man named Ly Tou Pao, did not do jury trials. Ly Tou Pao reportedly took Hmong who'd been widely accused of stealing in Long Cheng or other towns and brought them out to a runway to have them beaten in public.[11]

When Bill Lair first started working with the Hmong, Vang Pao was killing prisoners of war. "Both sides [communist and non-communist] did it," Lair said. "They automatically killed all the prisoners."[12] According to Lair, he eventually convinced the Hmong leader to stop—a contention disputed by many other associates of the general, who said that Vang Pao and his top lieutenants made a habit of torturing and killing prisoners. (Vang Pao later denied he made torturing and killing prisoners a habit.)

The agency hardly discouraged this torture. One former Hmong soldier remembered, in an oral history of the war, "The CIA selected ten or eleven of us [at a time] and sent us to Thailand. We trained [in interrogation] for three months. Before we interrogated a [communist] prisoner, we knew what unit he was from, where he was located, and we used this to see if he was telling the truth . . . If the prisoner tried to withhold information, we were allowed to beat up the prisoners . . . One method was to wrap wires around their arms and shock [them] into submitting."[13]

Vang Pao had personally meted out punishments, too. Billy Webb, a former Air America pilot, recalled attending a dinner at Vang Pao's house in Long Cheng, where the general hosted large gatherings nearly every night he was at the base. "Suddenly, a Hmong captain, in uniform, was physically dragged into the room for a hearing before Vang Pao," wrote Webb. "Apparently the captain had been accused of not being aggressive in leading his men in the defense of a hilltop position . . . The officer was found guilty by Vang Pao, and sentenced to serve time in an underground tiger pit. [The accused's] legs buckled, and he was physically carried out of the room."[14]

But after the losses mounted throughout 1970, Vang Pao was seeing enemies everywhere. Some of his officers and men had deserted in the past, as happened in any army. Vang Pao's spies now reported that hundreds, even thousands, of his men, sensing the end was near, were not just deserting but defecting to the communist side in preparation for a communist victory. Whether this was true or not was impossible to tell, even in retrospect—there was no way to know how many Hmong defected to the communist side, since when the war ended, the communists took retribution even on Hmong fighters who defected to the Pathet Lao's side, and no one wanted to admit they had served Vang Pao, even if they had switched sides later. Nonetheless, the Hmong leader reportedly had Ly Tou Pao build a larger network of informants within his army, and had men arrested just because the general had heard rumors that they might desert, or that they were unhappy with how the war was going—a sentiment shared by pretty much everyone in the army, including Vang Pao, though most soldiers would not admit it openly.[15] Deserters who were caught, Vang Pao warned his men, would be punished harshly—executed on the spot, possibly.

Vang Pao had been a savvy political operator throughout the 1950s and 1960s. But after the reversal on the Plain of Jars, he replaced many of his close aides and top officers with men from his clan, the Vang.[16] The Vang officers cooperated with Vang Pao's security chief in rounding up any suspects the Hmong leader wanted jailed, sometimes for no clear reason at all. The makeshift detention area at Long Cheng was becoming overcrowded with men and women whom Vang Pao believed had betrayed him in some way. The general did not let many of the detainees leave when civilians were evacuated from Long Cheng.

Vang Pao was becoming paranoid, but Laos was making Tony Poe lose his mind. Up in the northwest, Poe had befriended many hilltribe leaders but had not formed any kind of real fighting force. He received regular reports, from pilots and CIA radio dispatches, of the losses the Hmong and other Laotian forces were taking. He grew increasingly depressed hearing of the deaths, only a few hundred miles away, while he was stuck in his lonely outpost until he could produce some kind of effective hilltribe militia. When Long Cheng was besieged in March 1970, after Vang Pao lost the Plain of Jars, the Hmong general had begged for reinforcements from anywhere. Poe rushed to help defend Long Cheng, bringing a small detachment of his best-trained men from the Yao hill tribe. The Yao men fought valiantly for a day, pushing a group of North Vietnamese from a strategic ridge overlooking Long Cheng, and killing many of the North Vietnamese soldiers with machine guns and highly lethal sniper fire.

But within three days, Poe's fighters had stopped battling the North Vietnamese and had trained their guns on the Hmong whom they were supposed to fight alongside, after a dispute. Poe did not know how or why it had started. When they threatened to shoot Hmong soldiers, Vang Pao stepped in, and Poe had to take his men back to Nam Yu, ashamed at how he'd been unable to discipline most of them, and how he couldn't fight on.[17]

Poe's men were given a second chance to prove themselves two months later. But again, the unit he brought to Vang Pao's region to help battle the North Vietnamese proved useless, spending its time squabbling among itself and picking fights with the Hmong.[18]

Occasionally, refugees from some of the areas around Vang Pao's base would trickle through Tony Poe's outpost at Nam Yu and tell him stories of the latest defeat, as well as the names of Hmong who'd died. Some of the dead were men Poe had trained, only seventeen or eighteen years old. He had no real way to reach their families and no idea how many of the Hmong he'd trained were still alive. Despite his arguments with Vang Pao, Poe had inspired devotion among many Hmong for the same reasons he had won the Hmong leader's respect, if not his love; Poe fought hard and commanded with confidence and lived beside his men and did everything he could to keep them alive. Much later in his life, in the 1990s and early 2000s, when Poe was living back in the United States, former Hmong soldiers, by then also living in America, would drive or even fly to Poe's apartment in San Francisco. They would kneel before him and thank him for having kept them alive, or bring him piles of fruits and flowers and even stacks of American currency as gifts, even though many of the former fighters had little of their own. Poe refused the money, but he invited many of the Hmong to stay in his apartment for weeks, and traveled to the weddings, funerals, and New Year's celebrations of the families of Hmong with whom he had fought.[19]

Throughout Operation Momentum, Poe had always maintained a simpler idea of how he wanted the United States to fight the Laos war than Bill Lair had. Once America got involved, Poe just wanted to do whatever was necessary to destroy the enemy. He had no interest in the kind of coordinated retreat plan that Lair had discussed with Vang Pao, or in figuring out how to balance what was best for Laos and its people and what was best for the United States, the way that Bill Sullivan did naturally. "I just wanted to win . . . if that meant [American] ground troops, more bombing than we were already doing, flatten every town [where] the communists had been, I didn't care," Poe said. "Either have a total win or don't be there."[20] If the war was going to be a meat grinder, slaughtering the Hmong, Poe believed, American leaders should send the American army too. But the United States and its allies were not winning the war in Laos, and though the Nixon administration had authorized the largest bombing runs yet seen in the kingdom, the White House was not going to send a large contingent of US ground troops into Laos.

Bill Lair had dealt with his disgust at the operation by leaving. Bill Sullivan had gotten the war he wanted, and had seen no reason to abandon his involvement in Laos policy. Vang Pao despaired at the direction of the operation, but he had no real choice but to stay—it was his country. So the Hmong leader searched for enemies within his ranks, pretended the best he could that he could conjure another great victory, and planned every morning for the next raid, the next airstrike, the next defense.

Tony Poe dealt with his despair differently. Poe had never been known for his stability, but with the war not going the way he wanted, he began losing his mind completely. Though Poe had wanted to live rough up at Nam Yu, he had become so isolated in the northwest—no television, nothing much to do, few foreign visitors—that he had started having conversations with himself as if he were on a desert island. His brutality, which had always been part of his character and his operation, became much more extreme. "In Nam Yu, I lived like a goddamn pig," Poe said.[21] His job with the northwestern tribes had been to "train these men in basic guerrilla warfare . . . small unit warfare, up to a hundred men," Poe said. But most of the men he'd found in the northwest had been so untrainable that Poe, who once prided himself on his thrice-daily marine-style trainings, now let the men skip training many days.[22]

In the past, Poe had issued a bounty for the severed ears of communists and piled up a bag of ears. In Nam Yu, he amassed whole bodies. He made a makeshift prison that was just a large hole in the ground. When the Nam Yu militia caught some doctors who worked for the North Vietnamese—a rare capture for Poe's northwestern group—Poe stuck them in the hole and gave them nothing but a few bits of rice. When the Vietnamese doctors complained about the horrific conditions in the hole and asked Poe to just let them defect to his side, the American shot them dead. "What was I going to do with a bunch of doctors?" he asked.[23] When the Nam Yu troops captured a handful of Laotian communist soldiers in the summer of 1969, Poe threw them in the hole prison as well. He left the communist troops there for months on just rice and water, and some of the prisoners died of hunger and exposure.[24] "It's war, and war is hell," was Poe's only explanation for his tactics.[25]

Like Vang Pao, the isolated Poe started to see enemies all around him, though in his mind, the enemies were all within the group of Americans in Laos and Washington who were running the war. Poe believed he was stuck in Nam Yu because he was being punished by

US Embassy bureaucrats for having refused so many orders when he worked with the Hmong—orders to treat Vang Pao more delicately, to avoid getting caught in firefights himself. By the beginning of 1970, Poe was telling anyone who came to Nam Yu that Vang Pao was running the war poorly and that the Hmong general should be removed. When stories of Poe's diatribes about the Hmong made their way back to Long Cheng, they infuriated Vang Pao, making Poe's position in Laos even more precarious. Poe had also begun tearing into pilots who flew in, screaming at them for no reason at all, simply because the pilots were often the only Americans Poe saw, and he believed everyone connected to the US government was out to get him. On the few occasions when Poe left Nam Yu for irregular visits to the northern Thai town of Chiang Rai, he usually ended his evenings in bar fights with other Americans working in Thailand.[26]

When he did get a chance to talk, over the radio, to the US ambassador in Vientiane, Poe would unload on him. "Most of the ambassadors were, were zero[s] . . . I was the boss," Poe said. "Anything I received from these idiots, I look at it, uh, crosswise, and uh, up and down, 'Should I do this or not?' And if I said no, I didn't do it."[27] Jim Scofield, another former CIA operative in Laos who worked with Poe, told reporters later that Poe had even flown into Vientiane and come to a meeting at the embassy holding a rifle and a machete, raving at the ambassador.[28]

Only much later—decades later—would Poe realize that the bosses at the agency hadn't really been against him at all, after they gave him their highest prizes and turned much of the CIA into the kind of paramilitary operation he would have loved. But that was far in the future.

About six hundred of the roughly ten thousand men who collected paychecks as part of Poe's program seemed intensely loyal to him. Perhaps this handful was so loyal because he had given them steady jobs, and had been the first commander willing to fight alongside them, and treated them far better than most of the clan leaders did. Perhaps they had become almost trapped by his brutality, mentally beaten into serving him.

This group, which was mostly from the Yao hill tribe but included a handful of men from other tribes, didn't come and go from Nam Yu like many of the others, showing up for paydays and occasional meetings and then disappearing for weeks or months. They devoted themselves to Poe's training routines: shooting practice, running, hiking, learning how to scout the land in a battle. They stuck with the routines even though Poe seemed increasingly uninterested in maintaining the regimen, which he had used effectively in training Hmong fighters earlier in the decade.[29] As Poe became increasingly alienated from the US Embassy in Vientiane and from Vang Pao and other Laotian leaders, and worried about the direction of the Laos war, this small band of men promised Poe that whatever happened in Laos, they would stay and fight with him. A private militia.

And, of course, Poe drank. He drank *lao-lao*, the harsh Laotian rice whiskey, which he kept on a little stool next to his bedroll, to swig in the middle of the night or in the morning as mouthwash. He drank the weaker Thai whiskey that pilots sometimes flew in, before he started hollering at them all the time. He had a case of Thai whiskey under his bed and under a chair in the office in his complex, and he kept a flask clipped to the gray safari suit he walked in, slept in, ate in, and drank in. The flask stayed on his belt, below the thirteen-inch-long Bowie knife he wore in a shoulder holster. "He was sleeping . . . in the middle of the jungle, surrounded by empty White Horse whiskey bottles," recalled Jack Shirley, a longtime CIA clandestine officer in Laos.[30] When Poe had arrived in Nam Yu, he had frequently cut the trees and palms back from atop his house to give the place some semblance of order, like a real marine would. But now they grew wild, almost into the home's windows, and Poe didn't bother to cut the trees and plants at all. The giant jungle foliage looked as if it might swallow the house at any time.[31]

For Bill Lair, who learned about Poe's increasing insanity while

Lair was working in Bangkok, Poe's story showed that the agency should be careful about putting too much power in the hands of paramilitary operatives. Not all paramilitary men, given the power to train thousands or to kill, would build a private militia or retreat into the jungle, as Poe had done. But Lair believed that someone like Poe was needed only occasionally, in times of great crisis. "You need men like Poshepny [Poe's real last name] to fight a war, but what do you do with them?" asked Lair. "They should be locked in boxes" most of the time.[32] Lair would regretfully see, even after the war in Laos was over, that the CIA would not lock up men like Poe; instead, it would find many more Tony Poes.

———

Fred Branfman, the aid worker turned antiwar activist, had hoped that Americans would be shocked to hear stories from the Plain of Jars about villages pulverized and children maimed, and that public revulsion would put pressure on the Nixon administration. At an open hearing in April 1971 before another Senate subcommittee, Branfman had been called on by Edward Kennedy to give a statement. The Massachusetts senator did not believe the stories American officials—primarily, Bill Sullivan—were telling the subcommittee about Laos: that the bombing there was limited and causing few civilian casualties. The Senate staffers who had traveled to Laos, including staff from Kennedy's office, had included in their report that "there are plenty of instances known to American civilian employees who have been in Laos . . . in which civilian targets have been bombed."[33]

Branfman, who was in the audience for the hearing, had spoken to the senator in advance. Kennedy asked him to stand up and give his account of what Branfman had learned from interviewing over three thousand refugees from the Plain of Jars. With television cameras from the broadcast networks rolling and Bill Sullivan sitting right in front of him, Branfman declared that Sullivan and many other American officials were still concealing the massive scope of the bombing campaign in Laos.[34] Branfman launched into a tirade that led the evening news.[35] "What I am trying to suggest . . . is that there is a good deal of evidence . . . that the United States has been carrying out the most [heavy] bombing of civilian targets in history," Branfman declared.[36]

Antiwar activists thought that, after the hearing—after Ted Kennedy, one of the most famous men in the United States, publicly chastised Sullivan in front of hundreds of reporters—a groundswell of outrage would emerge. After all, the press and some of the American public also were becoming increasingly skeptical that Nixon planned to end the wider Vietnam War, as he had promised in his election campaign. Polls taken in 1970 showed Nixon's favorable rating plummeting among Americans, while sharply rising percentages of Americans called the president untrustworthy. (Limited withdrawals of US troops from Vietnam in 1970 blunted Americans' anger somewhat.) The Democrats made gains in the 1970 midterm elections, to Nixon's fury. And protests against US involvement in Vietnam had been building for years, drawing as many as a half million to an antiwar demonstration held in November 1969 in Washington, DC. After President Nixon had appeared on national television in April 1970 and said that the United States had not only been secretly bombing Cambodia—reports of the Cambodia bombing had emerged in the press the previous spring—but also sending in ground forces, massive protests broke out at US college campuses, parks, and other sites. These protests sometimes turned violent, including at Ohio's Kent State University in May 1970, where US National Guardsmen opened fire on student protestors, killing four and sparking further outrage, especially among the antiwar movement.

Even Vang Pao, half a world away in Laos, got news of the hearing. The general asked one of the CIA case officers at his base whether Ted Kennedy was going to become the next president and personally put an end to the United States' Laos war.[37]

Although US ground troops were not moving into Laos, Vang Pao knew that Americans were dying in the kingdom. Perhaps reports of US casualties in the kingdom would spark American public interest in the secret war. In fact, more Americans would die in Laos than during the fighting in Cambodia that so enraged the antiwar movement in the United States.[38] By 1970, besides the men killed at Phou Pha Thi, the radar site where eleven Americans had been killed on the mountaintop, two Americans had died when another navigational site in Laos was attacked and overrun by communist forces.[39] US pilots had been shot down repeatedly while flying over Laos. As the bombing runs increased, the number of dead pilots and forward air controllers—the American men who coordinated air strikes—was growing.

The Nixon administration wondered, too, how the public would respond to news stories of the bombing in Laos and of Americans dying in the kingdom. The *New York Times*, in February 1970, reported the use of B-52s over the Plain of Jars. The White House suspected that someone at the embassy in Vientiane, angry at the damage that could be caused by the massive bombers, had leaked news of this escalation to the press.

At a meeting of his National Security Council in February 1970, shortly after news of the B-52 bombing had leaked, Nixon asked his staff whether he should say something publicly about Laos, to preempt more stories or leaks from Congress about the secret war. Of course, American policy, since John F. Kennedy's time, had been to deny everything about America's war there; saying anything about US involvement would be a major shift. "I want to run through the whole Laos situation," Nixon told the NSC. "We may have to leak some information [to deal with the public revelations of widespread American involvement], but we have a good story to tell . . . We don't have to stop [the war there.]"[40]

Secretary of State William Rogers counseled Nixon to at least say something about the extent of the US role in the Laos war, breaking with the tradition of stonewalling. "Our sorties [in Laos] have been doubled. B–52 strikes have taken place . . . but we have refused to make anything public," he said to the president. "We need some kind of testimony by the administration [about Laos] . . . We are running into a credibility problem."[41] Nixon agreed warily to come out with some public statement on Laos, after several of his other advisors agreed with Rogers. "We must get it [some information on Laos] out," Nixon concluded. "We can't have testimony [in Congress] saying CIA is involved [in Laos.]"[42]

On March 6, 1970, Nixon's office at his home in Key Biscayne, Florida, handed the presidential press corps a three-thousand-word statement outlining the situation in Laos and US involvement there. The statement, in effect the text of a speech without Nixon actually giving a speech, confirmed many of the details that had come out in the hearings and news articles since the battle on the Plain of Jars. Nixon blamed Hanoi for most of the fighting in Laos, but for the first time, a president admitted that the United States had been conducting an air war in the kingdom and that the United States was advising Laos's military. Still, Nixon's statement did not reveal the full scope of Operation Momentum.[43] It did not say that the United States was bombing Laos even more intensely than it was attacking Vietnam and Cambodia, or discuss the civilian costs of American bombing. It did not discuss the CIA at all, and it muddled the story of Americans dying in the kingdom. Nixon claimed that "no American stationed in Laos has ever been killed in ground combat operations."[44] This was true *technically*, though it did not account for the technicians, forward air controllers who helped guide bombings in Laos, and other agency men and contractors who had died on the ground in Laos, even though they were not combat ground troops.[45] In reality, more than two hundred Americans had been killed in Laos by spring 1970.

The White House knew that the statement was not entirely forthcoming; the point of it was to release some information but not all. In private conversations with his staff, and meetings of his top advisors,

Nixon remained worried that at any moment more leaks about the Laos war would lead to a public outcry and would force the president to reveal more about bombing the country or even halt the campaign entirely. Branfman's statement in 1971 seemed to be the embodiment of those fears.

But the revelations about the secret war in Laos did not seem to have much impact on most Americans. The American public, by and large, remained uninterested in the kingdom, at least as compared with Cambodia and Vietnam. Americans held no massive rallies to protest Laos policy. No huge contingent of antiwar celebrities traveled to Laos to highlight the war there, and no famous musicians held concerts to benefit Laotian refugees or Laotian fighters. An occasional columnist published a piece condemning the bombing or calling for a complete accounting of the civilian damage, but that was about it. "Even though it became exposed [the bombing and the US war in Laos], the policy continued. It [exposing it] did not make a huge difference, as far as I can tell," Branfman admitted ruefully.[46]

Americans were dying in Laos, to be sure, and by the end of the war, 728 Americans would have perished in the kingdom.[47] But the US casualty count, though significant, did not climb high enough to affect most Americans. In contrast, over fifty-six thousand Americans would die in Vietnam, while the bombing of Cambodia by the Nixon administration was much more widely covered in the media than Laos was, and generated more public attention.

More important, the Americans who died in Laos were usually not from the regular US army, draftees like those perishing in Vietnam. The list of casualties did not extend beyond a small circle of CIA operatives, contractors, and military men on loan to Laos and cloaked in false identities.[48] And families of the men who died in Laos could usually either be stonewalled about the details of a man's death, since so much information about his mission had been classified, or could be convinced to keep the details of the death secret as part of the bargain that came with the men serving in the CIA or as CIA contractors.

For the families of the eleven Americans who died at Phou Pha Thi, it would take more than two decades after the end of the Indochina War in 1975 to get a full accounting of how the men died on that mountaintop.[49] Some of the Phou Pha Thi families accepted that, because of the men's work, they might never know how their loved ones had died or the nature of their mission in Laos. Other Phou Pha Thi families tried to get a full accounting but hit bureaucratic walls over and over. When several of the wives of some of the Phou Pha Thi technicians confronted the CIA and the air force, demanding to know more, the US government eventually conceded that the men had been killed in action, and awarded them posthumous Purple Hearts. But the US government would confirm nothing about what had actually happened to them or what they were doing in Laos.[50] It would be decades later, long after the war ended—and only following a concerted campaign to reveal the whole story of Phou Pha Thi not only by several of the wives of the men who died but also by CIA historians— that Washington conceded the eleven American men had been killed in combat, on the ground, on that mountaintop in Laos.

It wasn't just the absence of American grunts dying in Laos that made the war so obscure to the public—even as it was still at the center of Washington policy makers' universe. Though Nixon admitted some details about the war, the CIA and other government agencies did enough to obscure stories about Laos and to keep the worst effects of the bombing hidden that the Laos story never captured the American audience, despite all the efforts of antiwar activists such as Branfman. For one thing, since the first big news stories about Laos broke in the fall of 1969, the CIA had been taking extensive measures to prepare for more leaks of information about the secret war. CIA head Richard Helms was clearly worried that, as more was known about Operation Momentum, CIA operatives would face severe consequences. He sought the CIA legal counsel's private advice about the legality of the Laos operation, under the Truman-era legislation that had chartered the agency. The director also wondered whether

Congress or the courts could punish the CIA for actions it had taken in the kingdom. The answer he got was worrisome. The CIA's legal counsel told Helms privately that the "statutory authority"—in other words, the legal basis—for the CIA waging war was "doubtful."[51]

Of course, as an intelligence agency, the CIA had always placed a priority on secrecy. But with Laos, the agency now went many steps further, institutionalizing changes that increased vastly the level of secrecy around its operations. And many of these changes wound up becoming permanent shifts, despite efforts by Congress in the 1970s to foster greater oversight of the agency.

For the remainder of the operation in Laos, when CIA officers sent written messages, the agency started routinely classifying even the most basic of these under legislation that afforded the highest levels of secrecy, ensuring that they would be much harder to obtain by outsiders. Many station chiefs in Indochina, and eventually in other parts of the world, stopped cabling as much as possible and instead relied on oral communications. Station chiefs would then tear up or burn any notes from the conversations.

The policy stuck. When the Senate Intelligence Committee attempted to investigate the CIA's post-9/11 policies of detention and coercive interrogation, committee staffers quickly found that, while some agency operatives still sent cables, whenever the most sensitive interrogation issues were discussed inside the CIA, headquarters would direct operatives in the field to talk about detention and interrogation only in phone calls. CIA operatives involved in detention and interrogation programs also routinely destroyed whatever written and electronic records existed of the operations. In perhaps the most notable example that came to light, in 2005 Jose Rodriguez, who ran the CIA's clandestine operations in the early 2000s, ordered operatives to shred some ninety videotapes of interrogations of two alleged Al Qaeda members, conducted mostly in Thailand. Pressured by US courts and by Congress, Director of Central Intelligence Porter Goss said in a private meeting with Rodriguez in late 2004 that he thought that the tapes should be preserved, but Goss did not insist upon it, probably to allow the evidence to be destroyed. Rodriguez shredded the tapes, a move he defended as consistent with the agency's culture of protecting its clandestine operatives.[52]

In the lack of public outcry about the war, too, the Laos war presaged the counterterrorism battles of the 2000s, in which American casualties and American killings of foreign civilians had little impact on US public opinion. In the 2000s, as with the Laos war, most Americans knew no one who actually fought in Afghanistan, Yemen, Somalia, Pakistan, or other places where the secret antiterrorism battle took place—and where Americans died. Most Americans knew no one who died in the counterterrorism "long war," as many Obama administration advisors called the battle, because, as in Laos, much of the long war was conducted via air strikes (some by planes and some by drones) and via US advisors. This pool of advisors was drawn mostly from professional CIA clandestine officers and Special Forces. This group of advisors made up but a fraction of the total number of American military and intelligence men and women posted overseas, who themselves comprised less than 0.5 percent of the total population of the United States. (By contrast, in the mid-1940s, about 12 percent of Americans served in the military, including in military intelligence units.)[53] The Americans who died in the war on terrorism had their bodies shipped home and often received intelligence and military honors, but the circumstances of their deaths were kept secret, just as the CIA had done when technicians or pilots died in Laos. Most information about the damage done by the air strikes, the local forces advised by Americans, and the drones used in the counterterrorism war was kept secret from the press or got little attention from the American media. Perhaps unsurprisingly, polls taken in 2014 showed that a majority of Americans approved of the use of drones in the counterterrorism war.[54] In contrast, the polls showed that overwhelming majorities of people in countries where the drones were utilized did not approve of using drones.

As the dry season gave way to the monsoon in the summer of 1971, Vang Pao realized that the US public was not going to come out in droves against the Laos war. In December 1970, Congress, worried by what it had been learning about the Laos war, had passed the Cooper-Church Amendment, which theoretically prohibited the White House from putting American troops on the ground in Laos or Cambodia. But Vang Pao's battle was not going to be stopped by average Americans or even by some congressional amendment. The public continued to focus mostly on Cambodia and Vietnam, and the Cooper-Church Amendment actually could not stop the air war or the CIA support for fighters in Laos, since the operation technically did not involve American ground forces. Vang Pao heard from the CIA case officers stationed at his base that there had been no massive protests against the Laos war, even after the Kennedy hearings. The Hmong leader saw further that the United States continued to launch around sixty bombing runs a day over Laos and that in mid-January 1971, the Nixon administration approved a plan to hit the Ho Chi Minh Trail in southern Laos hard. The plan was to attack the trail with a combined force of over seventeen thousand South Vietnamese ground troops, US bombers and helicopters and artillery, and US ground troops operating to help the South Vietnamese while remaining within South Vietnam—and adhering technically to the new congressional amendment.[55]

Although the raid failed to cut the Ho Chi Minh Trail and stop Hanoi's flow of men and arms into the South—the South Vietnamese troops made little headway and eventually had to retreat from Laos—the Hmong leader was convinced that the raid and the air war showed that the United States was still with him, and his war. "The United States was still behind us . . . The stories in the press hadn't made enough feeling [in the US public] to pressure the White House," he said some thirty-five years later.[56]

Yet Vang Pao soon realized that he should have been more worried about the White House and its ultimate intentions than about the American public stopping the war in Laos. The White House—and Bill Sullivan—had worked assiduously in 1969, 1970, and 1971 to defuse public reaction to the Laos operation and its civilian toll. But the White House—and Bill Sullivan—would now end Vang Pao's war.

Chapter 16

Skyline Ridge

SKYLINE RIDGE, A SET OF LIMESTONE PEAKS JUST NORTH of Vang Pao's base at Long Cheng, was the critical point protecting the Hmong in the mountain valley. The ridge, about two miles long at the highest points between mountains, was covered in thick forest along its sides—cover that allowed men to hide themselves and their artillery. The sides of the ridge often gave way to steep cliffs that jutted out at all angles like ominous spikes. Only five miles northwest of Skyline Ridge, along a snaking, winding mountain road, aid workers had established one of the largest refugee camps in Laos at a site called Sam Thong.

Anyone who got past Skyline Ridge and into Long Cheng had few roadblocks between them and Vientiane and the other cities of lowland Laos. If North Vietnamese troops took the ridge, they also could more easily move supplies through southern Laos and into the war in South Vietnam, potentially turning the tide of the Vietnam War. In January, February, and March 1970, as North Vietnamese troops had shelled Long Cheng and threatened to sweep into the Hmong base, Vang Pao and his men had driven them off Skyline Ridge. Hanoi's troops had made it to the top of the ridge.[1] But during the last week of March, the North Vietnamese had retreated from their positions, knowing that the rainy season was coming soon, and fighting would slow down until the monsoons ended in October or November.

Still, Vang Pao knew that Hanoi's troops would be back to try to take the ridge when the next dry season came—and that if the

Hmong could not hold Skyline Ridge, they were done, and the whole war might be over. A major victory, like the 1969 Plain of Jars triumph, was almost surely out of Vang Pao's reach now. Still, the general hoped to fight a prolonged war that could save Laos. He hoped to defend his base, slow any North Vietnamese advance into lowland Laos, and pray that Hanoi would lose enough men that eventually it would find it pointless to commit so much blood to winning in Laos.[2]

In the dry season of early 1971, from February to April, the North Vietnamese attempted once more to take Skyline Ridge and to besiege Long Cheng. Hanoi sent some eight thousand men up to the ridge, along new roads laid by North Vietnamese engineers. Again, the Hmong, backed by battalions of Thai troops, an airlift of fighters from other parts of Laos, and about sixty bombing runs a day from American planes, barely held off the North Vietnamese. In February Hanoi's troops got high enough on the ridge to lob mortar rounds into Long Cheng's valley, but by April, fierce fighting by the Hmong and the Thais had driven the North Vietnamese down again.[3]

The third battle for Skyline Ridge, which stretched from 1971 into 1972, was probably the largest and most critical fight of the entire war in Laos. It involved over four thousand anti-communist troops— Hmong, lowland Lao, Thai, and US advisors—and at least twenty battalions of North Vietnamese forces. The North Vietnamese outnumbered the defenders of Skyline by around six to one.[4] It was, in fact, one of the largest battles of the United States' entire Indochina War, including the fights in Vietnam. Yet Skyline Ridge got little press coverage at the time, as Americans' brief interest in Laos, sparked by the congressional revelations and news stories of bombing in 1969 and 1970, had waned.

Expecting an even bigger offensive from Hanoi by the end of 1971, throughout the autumn of that year, the Hmong and their Thai allies built bases north of Skyline Ridge into fearsome obstacles. The Thais installed giant cannons at the bases, situated so that three or four of the guns could shoot at advancing troops at the same time, murdering them with a cross fire of shells and large-caliber bullets. The Thais and the Hmong laid razor wire, mines, and booby traps in all directions around their bases; and on Skyline Ridge itself, Vang Pao had his men lay multiple layers of mines.[5]

In December 1971, the North Vietnamese attacked the Thai bases outside Skyline, with more than double the number of men holding the bases. The Hmong, the Thais, and their American advisors knew that the defenders would be outnumbered, but they had little idea of how large a force Hanoi was going to throw at the Ridge this time. The Vietnamese leadership also sent one of its most decorated, seasoned generals to manage the new attempt to take Skyline. Vietnamese officers also, this time, had methodically prepared their men in techniques for hiding in caves and holes on the way up Skyline, to avoid US air strikes.

On December 17, Hanoi's long-range guns and tanks simultaneously smashed into positions north of Skyline Ridge held by the Thai mercenaries. The bombs and rifle rounds were fired with great accuracy, the result of extensive scouting. "The background noise on the radio transmissions" from the Thais to Americans at Long Cheng "was deafening . . . One of the northernmost positions went off the air in midsentence"—since the defenders had been blown away, recalled CIA officer James Parker, who was monitoring the radio at Long Cheng.[6] Another American in Long Cheng, Mike Ingham, who had been speaking over the radio with the Thais, said, "I had some really heart-wrenching radio conversations with some [of the fighters] who were in the final throes" of being killed.[7]

The North Vietnamese commander's report of the battle noted that, at four forty-five on the afternoon of December 19, he ordered the ground assault that began the most intense combat of the third battle for Skyline Ridge. "The assault troops of [North Vietnam's] 9th Company, 165th Regiment rushed forward, ignoring the steep slope of the mountainside and the enemy hand grenades thrown down to block their advance . . . The red flag held by Squad Leader Vu Duc

Thanh was unfurled and flapped back and forth like a flame."[8] The North Vietnamese ran toward the bunkers, as machine gun fire cut down one flag holder and then the next. "The flag, now soaked with the blood [of dead men] was passed" to another soldier, the commander reported.[9] The commander had so many troops that the heavy fire could not stop his men from pushing forward. The Thais retreated into underground bunkers that were essentially caves. The North Vietnamese threw grenades and a larger cluster of bombs into the bunkers, while screaming on bullhorns for the Thais to surrender before they died.[10] Finally, after hours of lobbing grenades into the bunkers, and soldiers entering the holes, firing wildly, the North Vietnamese had killed many of the Thais and taken control of most of the Thais' command posts.

"In the middle of the night of 19 December, a number of enemy soldiers crawled out [of the bunkers], handed over their weapons, and surrendered," reported the North Vietnamese commander.[11] We "totally annihilated those who continued to stubbornly resist."[12]

By December 20, the Thais' supposedly unassailable bases, with their mines and razor wire and artillery guns and cave bunkers, were totally in the hands of North Vietnamese troops. Several detachments of North Vietnamese pursued the Thais, who had run south, carrying or sometimes dragging gravely wounded men. "A pitiful sight . . . The majority [of the Thais] are shell-shocked, and most were suffering from wounds, exposure, or shock in one form or another," wrote Edward Dearborn, an American contract pilot who was airlifting aid to the Thai fighters.[13] The North Vietnamese who were not chasing the Thais headed on toward Skyline Ridge, and the Hmong base. US helicopters flying over the ridge to save Thai survivors and pick up bodies landed constantly at Long Cheng, dropping off piles of green body bags.[14]

On New Year's Eve, in the afternoon, North Vietnamese artillery, which now could lob shells that landed sixteen miles away, began to fire on Long Cheng from just outside Skyline Ridge. An American "reconnaissance plane eventually caught one of the [huge North Vietnamese] guns in the open," recalled Parker. "It seemed enormous . . . How could we beat something that evil looking?"[15] Three days later, the North Vietnamese ground assault on the ridge began. The Vietnamese clashed with Hmong patrols on the eastern slopes, and with Hmong defenders at the high points. For days, Parker recalled, fighting went on along the ridge and all around the Long Cheng Valley.

Several groups of North Vietnamese intelligence snuck ahead toward a small peak that looked right down onto Long Cheng, to prepare to seize the Hmong base. Rockets from North Vietnamese commandos hit dangerously close to the most important buildings in Long Cheng. One shattered Vang Pao's home, destroying part of the house but missing the general; another touched the CIA's headquarters in the valley. A third almost blew up the agency's communications station in Long Cheng.[16] Several of the North Vietnamese commandos snuck into Long Cheng, blew up two of Vang Pao's ammunitions warehouses, and got all the way to the Hmong general's house before an alarm was raised. The commandos snuck away.[17]

The Hmong leader pleaded with CIA officers in Long Cheng to help him bring more troops to his base. Under prodding from the CIA, Bangkok agreed to send more men to fight and hold Skyline Ridge, while the CIA's airline rushed a group of raw Thai soldiers up to the ridge to fight.[18] The government in Vientiane answered Vang Pao's pleas for the best lowland soldiers by sending him several battalions from the national government's elite unit.[19] These were some of the only troops from the national army trusted by Vang Pao to actually fight hard. Sensing the urgency, National Security Advisor Henry Kissinger loosened the rules governing B-52 strikes in Laos, allowing the heavy bombers to again target the North Vietnamese on the doorstep of Long Cheng. Still, by January 10, 1972, North Vietnamese troops had gained much of the ridge, and a group had entered Sam Thong, the refugee area up the road, perhaps hoping to scare more Hmong civilians into fleeing and causing general panic among Vang Pao's men.

Informed of each development on Skyline Ridge, President Nixon wondered to Kissinger whether Laos was going to fall to communist forces imminently.[20] Officials at the US Embassy in Vientiane, normally unfailingly optimistic with reporters, admitted—off the record—during the first days of January, that Vang Pao's base would likely fall.[21]

On January 14, Hanoi declared that it had taken the ridge and captured Long Cheng, killing over one thousand non-communist troops and downing ten American aircraft.[22] A front-page headline in a North Vietnamese state newspaper the next day claimed that North Vietnamese troops had inflicted an enormous defeat on the Hmong and on the United States.[23]

The celebration was premature. Most of the civilians coming under Vietnamese fire did not flee; perhaps they thought fleeing was more dangerous, or, as former CIA officer James Parker speculated, perhaps they just hated the Vietnamese so much that they wouldn't leave.[24] No panic broke out among Vang Pao's men. The agency's communications station at Long Cheng had figured out how to intercept and translate North Vietnamese radio dispatches, and had gotten a pretty good idea of where Hanoi's troops were going to move on the ridge next.[25] With the CIA advisors expertly manipulating the B-52s, the bombers proved far more precise than they had in Laos before, taking out several entire North Vietnamese units that were heading for Long Cheng. Vang Pao pressed the Americans to order more and more airstrikes—as many as humanly possible. He personally helped load bombs onto the smaller T-28 planes.[26] "The next day, some Hmong commandos were dispatched down to [see what the bombers had hit] and found [the area] blown completely apart," reported one of the CIA advisors, who went by the code name "Lucky." "All types of mangled enemy weapons and web gear and body parts were lying around."[27] With bombers roaring overhead, a CIA paramilitary officer named Elias Chavez led the group—about twelve hundred in total—as they charged up the ridge. Before the charge, Chavez was dressed in a poncho, with bandoleers across his chest and a cross around his neck like an Old West outlaw, perhaps because he thought the outfit would fire up the fighters' martial spirits.[28] On January 19, as they started up toward the machine gun nests the North Vietnamese had created in bunkers along the ridge, forty of Chavez's men were killed in the first five minutes of running up the hill, and at least seventy others were wounded. The men clustered together, lying on the ground and waiting for a break in North Vietnamese machine-gunning. When there was even a brief pause, Chavez would lead them at a run forward again, tossing grenades and carrying his cross in his mouth for luck and then hitting the ground.[29]

Over three days, Chavez and his men moved toward North Vietnamese positions. Many of the men were shot from two or three feet away. Pieces of stomach, brain, and bone splattered on the rocks near the top of the ridge, visible in plain sight from American planes that flew overhead. The smell of flesh remained in the air for days. But enough of Chavez's men survived to get into the sandbagged bunkers, where they shot, stabbed, and bludgeoned Vietnamese soldiers. Others crawled up to the sandbags and stuffed grenades into the North Vietnamese fortified positions, blowing geysers of dirt and body parts into the air.[30]

The fighting on the top of the ridge went on for more than a week. Over half the men involved, on both sides, were killed or wounded. By the final days of January, the remaining North Vietnamese troops atop Skyline Ridge had been pushed off by the ferocity of the Hmong and Thai attacks, retreating just down the slopes of the ridge. A group of the retreating communist soldiers became trapped in some of the thick banana and bamboo trees that dotted Skyline's eastern slopes. While the North Vietnamese desperately tried to hack through the bamboo with their machetes, American spotter planes saw the communist troops trapped in the thicket. Vang Pao helped drag several artillery pieces up a small peak facing the North Vietnamese and had several of his men haul up machine guns as well.[31] Then he and the other Hmong just let loose, firing like mad into the thicket of trapped men. "The basin was a wreck of bomb craters, shattered bamboo, and shredded banana trees. Among the wreckage lay the bodies of three thousand [more] North Vietnamese soldiers," reported historian Keith Quincy in his account of the massacre.[32]

Still, Hanoi was determined to take the ridge. During the second week of March, after a lull of about four weeks in the fighting as Vietnamese commanders marshaled their troops and planned a new assault, Hanoi tried again. It brought in Soviet-made tanks, along the road from the northwest. The Hmong, who had fought fiercely, did not stand up to the tanks; historian Keith Quincy reported that "tanks terrified the Hmong . . . [They] had little experience [with them] and no training in how to deal with them. Usually when they spotted a tank, they hid or ran away."[33] But American pilots blew up tanks that rolled toward the ridge, and several tanks hit buried mines and exploded.[34] Their rusted hulks lay along tracks to the ridge, actually slowing Hanoi's troop movement.[35] Still, North Vietnamese infantry were able to climb to the top of the ridge. Again, B-52s swooped in. Again, the bombers, well prepared by the CIA officers, landed direct hits on North Vietnamese units on the northern parts of Skyline. US fighter planes, which could fly low and attack with their cannons and machine guns, followed the B-52s, gunning down North Vietnamese wandering along the ridge, senseless, after the concussive effects of the bombs.[36]

Finally, in the second week of April, Hanoi pulled back most of its men from Skyline Ridge, in part because the North Vietnamese military wanted to send them into South Vietnam, where it was launching a massive offensive that would last until October 1972. (The Easter offensive would be Hanoi's largest invasion of the South up to that time, involving as many as three hundred thousand North Vietnamese soldiers.) Of the roughly twenty-seven thousand North Vietnamese troops who assaulted Skyline Ridge, about ten thousand were killed or wounded.[37] Though the North Vietnamese drew back most of its infantry, Hanoi kept men just beyond Skyline Ridge to contain Vang Pao at his base.[38]

President Nixon personally sent the American Embassy in Vientiane a message, to be passed on to those who had led the Skyline defense. Nixon commended them for blunting the North Vietnamese offensive. "You have done a tremendous job under difficult conditions," he wrote.[39] Even the North Vietnamese commanders, in their postbattle reports, admitted that they had been impressed by the toughness of Vang Pao in the face of overwhelming numbers.[40]

Although Vang Pao's men and their allies had driven the North Vietnamese from Skyline Ridge once more, the battle had been so much larger than the previous year, and so costly to the noncommunist side, that in the long run, it hardly mattered that Hanoi's men had briefly retreated. The men sent from Laos's national army to defend Skyline were needed badly to fight the communists in other parts of the country; some units lost three-quarters of their men at Skyline. Overall, about half of the Hmong, Thai, and lowland Lao soldiers who had defended the ridge and Long Cheng were killed or wounded.[41] Six of the men working for the CIA's contract airline were killed during the battle as well. Though Hanoi had not taken Skyline Ridge or Long Cheng decisively, North Vietnamese commanders were convinced that they had inflicted enough damage on the anticommunists that their enemy could not sustain another large battle. Hanoi did not, as Vang Pao had hoped, decide after Skyline Ridge that taking Laos was not worth more Vietnamese blood.

Vang Pao, meanwhile, had finally passed a threshold that he had feared for years. He could not get anyone to join the army during several recruitment drives just after the Skyline battle. The general had been relying on teenage boys, older men, and even occasionally Hmong women, but many Hmong families would not give him their

boys now. "Many [Hmong] families were down to their last surviving male (often a youth of 13 or 14), and survival of the hill tribe was
becoming a major concern," reported a US Air Force study of the situation after the defense of Skyline Ridge.[42] "We were desperate [after
Skyline Ridge]," Vang Pao admitted much later. "There were no more
men to [get to fight] . . . We could only use up what [men] we had."[43]
Some of Vang Pao's recruiters took to simply abducting preteen boys
from homes and Hmong schools at refugee centers, showing up
during school time and dragging away the largest preteens for army
training.[44] Other officials who worked for Vang Pao warned Hmong
villages that unless they sent fresh recruits for the war, they would stop
getting essential rice drops from American planes, a policy apparently
supported by US officials at Vang Pao's base. "I refused to send more
young men from my village to the war," one Hmong village leader
named Ger Su Yang said. "So they [US planes] stopped dropping rice
to [our village]."[45] It was unclear whether Vang Pao knew about his recruiters' actions, but they certainly did not help his army's popularity.

––––––––

Skyline Ridge also made it easier for the White House to accept that,
as part of any deal with Hanoi, Laos was probably going to be lost.
Despite President Nixon's message of congratulations to the Skyline
Ridge defenders, the huge losses of life in defense of the ridge undermined the holdouts in the administration who believed that Laos
could be kept out of communist hands.

By the time of the battle for Skyline Ridge, White House officials,
led by Henry Kissinger, had already conducted eight rounds of secret
talks with North Vietnamese envoys in Paris and its suburbs to discuss potential peace proposals. The Paris talks did not focus on what
would happen to Laos if the United States withdrew from Vietnam.
Kissinger seemed mostly uninterested in Laos's future. Kissinger and
Nixon believed that the key to maintaining the United States' dominant position in the world was to exploit the Sino-Soviet divisions,

further turning Beijing and Moscow against each other. Laos figured only tangentially in this game.

Though he had played a larger role in the Laos war than any American other than Bill Lair, Bill Sullivan seemed to have convinced himself that getting out was the right move. Withdrawal from Indochina, whatever the consequences for the countries in the region, "brought success to the strategy of containment and hence to the end of the Cold War," Sullivan wrote later. The Nixon administration's policy helped unite the world's powers against the Soviets' efforts at "world hegemony."[46]

———

As the monsoon faded in the fall of 1972, the communists, after giving up Skyline Ridge, were back on the offensive in Laos. While Vang Pao and his men scrambled again to keep the Vietnamese out of their homes, Sullivan was in Paris with Kissinger, where the US Embassy and French officials utilized a complex set of maneuvers to hide the negotiations—at times, having the US negotiators fly into a French military airfield and then secretly board the French president's personal jet, which took them to meet Hanoi's envoys while their original American plane continued on to West Germany.[47] Like Kissinger, Sullivan seemed to relish the subterfuge involved. Sullivan, by that point, was "Henry's man," according to Nixon's chief of staff, H. R. Haldeman.[48]

Despite tapping his phone for three years, Nixon and Kissinger had slowly gained trust in Bill Sullivan, particularly after Sullivan's numerous congressional appearances. Since 1968, Kissinger had been leading rounds of secret talks in Paris, mostly with North Vietnamese envoy Le Duc Tho. But as the two sides had moved closer to a deal, a final agreement seemed elusive: Washington and Hanoi squabbled over the details, and South Vietnam's president, Nguyen Van Thieu, refused to go along with the deal after a draft agreement of a peace accord was unveiled in October 1972. As Thieu balked, the North

Vietnamese seemed ready to pull out of the negotiations. To pressure Hanoi, Nixon repeatedly bombed the North in the fall and winter of 1972. Still, by the fall of 1972, just before the presidential election, a deal seemed like it could collapse at any time. While Kissinger negotiated frantically, he needed someone who could work with the North Vietnamese to make an agreement that stuck and who could be trusted by a president who trusted almost no one. He needed someone, also, who could tell Laotian leaders just enough about what was going on in the talks without completely revealing that Laos would be basically abandoned.

He needed Bill Sullivan.

Sullivan proved more than capable. Even Kissinger, not known for his praise of aides, admitted later in his memoirs that Sullivan's "contribution to the final round of negotiations was indispensable."[49]

At the final stage of the talks, in fact, Bill Sullivan was in his element. Since his days as a young diplomat dealing with the Vietnamese, he had maintained a healthy respect for Hanoi's leaders—much more respect than he had for most Laotians. And, since the early fall, when Kissinger picked Sullivan to be the point person for the final rounds of negotiations, the ambassador had, once again, been right at the center of US policy. He accompanied Kissinger to South Vietnam, Bangkok, and back to Paris, among other stops, and Sullivan made sure that the details of the deal remained mostly obscure to Laotian leaders.

The government of Laos, in fact, would not be fully informed about what was going on in Paris until the deal was done. And though he had been ambassador to Laos, Sullivan made no efforts during the peace talks to push Kissinger, Nixon, or the North Vietnamese to protect Hmong and other anti-communists who had fought with the United States.

The Paris Peace Accords, signed by representatives of South Vietnam, North Vietnam, and the United States on January 27, 1973, did not formally require North Vietnam to remove its troops from Laos, despite a promise Kissinger received from Hanoi's main negotiator, Le Duc Tho, that Hanoi would foster a rapid cease-fire in the kingdom.[50] It did commit the United States to withdrawing its forces and also committed both North and South Vietnam to a cease-fire that included holding their militaries in place. And so it fell to Kissinger and Sullivan, again, to pressure the non-communists in Laos to publicly accept that the peace deal had been signed, and to make their own, similar agreement with the Pathet Lao and their North Vietnamese backers—even though they had been given no say at Paris, and though Laotian leaders strongly suspected that the increasingly strong communist forces would never keep any deal they made.

In Vientiane just after the deal was announced, Sullivan met with Souvanna Phouma. The prime minister refused to publicly support the Paris Peace Accords or embrace the idea of a corollary Laos agreement. So Sullivan reminded him, with little subtlety, that the United States was going to pull out of Indochina anyway, leaving its allies in the kingdom extremely exposed. Better to support the Paris deal and come to some accommodation with Hanoi before the United States stopped fighting completely, Sullivan suggested.[51]

Kissinger followed up in the same vein. In February 1973, he flew to Vientiane to pressure Laotian leaders to make a deal with the Pathet Lao, though he did not bother to travel up-country to meet Vang Pao. Kissinger arrived in Laos after a trip to Hanoi to discuss a postwar US relationship with North Vietnam. Kissinger clearly did not want Laos to undermine the delicate peace agreement negotiated with Saigon and Hanoi, and any possible postwar ties with the North, and he made no promises of continued US aid to Vientiane.

Kissinger was relentless in Vientiane. Prime Minister Souvanna Phouma pleaded with the American not to cut Laos off, telling him "the very survival [of Laos] rests on your shoulders . . . Your shoulders are very broad." Through his own channels, Vang Pao sent the same message to Kissinger, telling the national security advisor that without US economic and security aid, Laos would be devastated, and that the United States had to uphold the promises it had made to protect the Hmong.[52] According to his own account, Kissinger told Laotian leaders that he "had not come all this way to betray our friends."[53]

But despite these words of reassurance, it was clear that the pleas from Vang Pao and other leaders made little impact on a man who prided himself on looking at foreign policy coldly and realistically. Kissinger pressed Laotian leaders to sign a cease-fire with communist forces—they had no other choice, Kissinger made clear, since US assistance would be winding down. In his memoirs, even Kissinger would admit that he felt "a pang of shame" at ignoring Souvanna's "wistful plea."[54] Kissinger really was "ramming this thing down Souvanna's throat," recalled former CIA Vientiane station chief Hugh Tovar.[55] There was little Souvanna could do, and he put on his best public face, though privately he condemned Kissinger for the betrayal. On February 21, 1973, the Laotian government and representatives of the Pathet Lao signed a treaty in Vientiane that called for Laos to form a coalition government that included Pathet Lao representatives, and for the two sides to form joint forces to control the major Laotian cities and towns.

Vang Pao said nothing publicly as the leaders in Vientiane reluctantly signed the agreement. The Hmong leader was linked even more closely to the United States than the other Laotian leaders, and he and his people still might need US help to get out of Laos. He did not condemn the deal publicly, though the general raged to several of his aides and refused to see any Americans for days. Vang Pao went on as if the Hmong under him had a future in Laos. He made a brief visit to Thailand shortly after the peace deal was announced. There he toured farms near Chiang Rai, a town in northern Thailand; he

told the Thais that he wanted to copy their modern agricultural techniques back in Hmong country in Laos.[56]

Then the Hmong leader collapsed; he had contracted pneumonia
during the battle for Skyline Ridge, when Vang Pao spent days in cold
and wet bunkers while North Vietnamese gunners were shelling his
base. Vang Pao believed that, in his dreams, he was being destroyed
by the spirits of dead Hmong soldiers.[57] A retinue of the general's
trusted shamans paraded through his house, but no one could determine for sure what the spirits had done to Vang Pao.

Even before the Vientiane Treaty, the general had begun to admit in
public that he and his men were losing the war.[58] It was not a shock
to anyone who studied the military balance in Laos, but to hear it
come from the normally cocky general was like an explosion in the
community. Clan leaders were no longer deferential to Vang Pao
the way they had been in the 1960s; many stood up at gatherings at
the Hmong leader's base to denounce him for getting the Hmong so
deeply involved in the war without more guarantees of success, or to
wonder why the Hmong had become involved in the war at all.[59] One
group of Hmong who had become increasingly worried about the effect of the secret war flocked to a Hmong farmer named Shong Lue
Yang, who some Hmong had come to believe was a kind of prophet,
and who had invented a new way of writing the Hmong language.
Vang Pao welcomed the prophet at first, but as it became clear that
Shong Lue Yang's growing popularity could be a threat, in 1969 the
Hmong general claimed that Shong Lue Yang had ties to the Pathet
Lao and had him arrested. In 1971, some of Vang Pao's soldiers ap-
parently assassinated him.[60]

Vang Pao offered Hmong elders none of the promises and public bravado that he used to show, and none of the impatience he'd
demonstrated with clan leaders who questioned the war in the 1960s.
"I apologized to them," Vang Pao said. He admitted that he almost

never apologized—an open apology was not the norm in Hmong culture. "I apologized to them," the general said again.

Vang Pao admitted that he had trusted US advisors to look at the whole picture of the war. He had believed, up until the Paris Peace Accords were signed, that the United States would continue to give him at least bombing support, even if it was reducing its other commitments in Indochina. Some Americans stationed in Laos seemed to believe that the United States would still do what it could to assist the Hmong, even *after* the deal with North Vietnam. Shortly after Washington signed the Paris Peace Accords with Hanoi, the State Department cabled the embassy in Vientiane "to take no steps which might impair existing US or [non-communist] Lao government military operational capabilities until further notice."[61] In other words, the State Department believed that, even after the agreement, the White House might maintain some assistance to the fighters in Laos. "There was . . . reason to believe that the United States was not totally committed to a significant military withdrawal from Laos," wrote CIA historian Timothy Castle in a retrospective of the operation in Laos.[62]

But the White House was moving on to its priorities: China and the chess game of the great powers. Vang Pao's allies in Bangkok were also pulling Thai soldiers out of Laos. After the Paris Peace Accords were completed, the CIA had been ordered to pull out most of its advisors, and supply flights and bombing support to the Hmong stopped as well. At the end of March 1973, US bombing of Laos stopped. In mid-1974 the last plane from the CIA's contract airline, Air America, flew into Laos and back to Thailand again.[63]

Despite his admission that the war was essentially lost, Vang Pao kept fighting—though he also traveled secretly to the United States one more time to visit sites where he might live if he had to flee. He still kept a photograph of Richard Nixon in his house and praised the president, as if hoping that he would win a reprieve from Washington and aid would start up again.[64] His army, about ten thousand men as the fighting began in the dry season of 1974, took loss after loss. By the end of 1974, communist forces sat atop all the hills around Long Cheng. They made it impossible for many Hmong to even venture out of the small area controlled by Vang Pao's army.[65] If they did, they ran the risk of being slaughtered.

Chapter 17

Final Days

THE WAR WAS NOT ACTUALLY OVER YET, THOUGH IT HAD been all but over after the 1973 accords. Vang Pao's forces, along with other pro-government troops, still guarded the junction called Sala Phou Khoun. Located at the intersection of several major roads and less than one hundred miles north of Vientiane, Sala Phou Khoun was the last bastion protecting Laos's biggest towns from the communist advance. The communists had overwhelmed most of the country.

The country's defense minister begged Vang Pao to send his men to defend the junction. Yet even as it begged Vang Pao to hold Sala Phou Khoun, the government could not offer the general any more air support or reserves of troops called in from anywhere else. There were none. Vang Pao himself had only a handful of planes at his command.

The men at Sala Phou Khoun had no hope. Communist forces outnumbered them by at least three to one, and the communists had been attacking the junction repeatedly since the end of 1974, relying on grinding volleys of fire and infantry charges. In addition to Hanoi's forces, arms, and nonlethal aid, China had been increasing its assistance to the communist side in Laos dramatically since the late 1960s, with three divisions of Chinese troops entering the country to help the Pathet Lao and the North Vietnamese build roads, lay mines, and operate heavy weapons such as antiaircraft guns.[1] Vang Pao's army in early 1975 was a thin shadow of the fighting force it had been a decade ago, when the general could call upon over thirty thou-

sand well-rested, tough, and hopeful fighters to surprise the North
Vietnamese on his territory. Rations were low, and many men had
been fighting with little rest for two years. Some had clear signs of
posttraumatic stress disorder, shell shock from being around artillery
and bombs so often, and a range of physical diseases from drinking
bad water and sometimes eating rancid food. Some of the Hmong
soldiers had shoes worn down to the soles and sores up and down
their legs from untreated cuts and blisters.

Many of the soldiers at the junction feared what might happen to
them after a communist victory, and none expressed even faint optimism that they would hold Sala Phou Khoun.[2] Yet they had fought in
the army so long that they had no other way to make money, or they
had resigned themselves to whatever fate would befall them. Some of
the men had become used to having no food for days even while on
the march.[3]

US bombers no longer flew over to provide Vang Pao and his men
with cover, and US planes no longer dropped him new ammunition,
parts, and weapons. Vang Pao could not rely on many Americans for
advice either: the CIA station in the country had shrunk, and there
were only four Americans left at the Hmong base at Long Cheng.
Many of the Americans Vang Pao had known in Laos, who'd resided
in Long Cheng or in Kilometer Six, the American-favored suburb of
Vientiane, had left the country in fear.[4] The national leadership in
Vientiane was crumbling, with Souvanna ailing—he had suffered a
heart attack in 1974.

Still, the defense minister in Vientiane trusted Vang Pao's men,
even in their haggard shape, more than the royal Lao army under the
ministry's command; in late 1974 and early 1975, the royal army had
reported mass defections. The Defense Ministry did not believe the
royal army would stand and fight for Sala Phou Khoun or for Laos's
cities as the communists drew nearer. Vang Pao had hesitated before
committing his men—he feared the battle would be a massacre, and
he had already witnessed so many gruesome Hmong massacres. He

knew that even holding Sala Phou Khoun for weeks or months more probably would not change the future. Communist forces had several whole divisions in reserve that they could call into the fight.

But he agreed to keep his force fighting at the junction, and he even ordered his handful of planes to bombard the communists again, risking themselves against antiaircraft fire. "I was loyal to the government, and whether we lived or got slaughtered, it was my country, so I wanted to fight for it and die if we had to die," the general said. "Sala Phou Khoun was hopeless . . . but we still had to fight, even if it was even any chance at all."

Vang Pao expected a bloodbath. As April ended, communist forces from North Vietnam and Laos launched an overwhelming attack on the junction. They unloaded artillery on the defenders for nearly three days. With no airpower and few big guns of their own, the junction's defenders could do little. Some of the Hmong retreated from the junction under the cover of the night into the mountains; a small group of these men would stay in the hills, fighting a guerilla war, for decades. By April 22, communist troops had overrun Sala Phou Khoun and marched on toward Vientiane.

With Sala Phou Khoun now in enemy hands, the communists had basically won. They just had to decide when they officially wanted the keys to the ministries in Vientiane.

As Sala Phou Khoun fell, the North Vietnamese and Pathet Lao troops controlled the path to the entire country. The joint communist forces took town after town, junction after junction. They moved openly on most roads, with no fear of counterattack. The Lao communists' radio station, preparing for a final offensive on Vientiane, broadcast bulletins calling Vang Pao and his men enemies who must be "wiped out . . . They were the main perpetrators of the barbarous, notorious crimes against the Lao people."[5]

Prime Minister Souvanna Phouma had stayed on through the creation of the coalition government—even as the national army and communist forces continued to fight. Realizing the end was near, he called Vang Pao to come to Vientiane in early May 1975. There Souvanna told the general that "the time for fighting is over." The prime minister wanted the city handed over peacefully to the Pathet Lao and the North Vietnamese; he did not want an orgy of final killing in the capital. Prominent government officials already were fleeing Vientiane, and by the time Vang Pao arrived for his meeting with Souvanna, small groups of pro–Pathet Lao residents of Vientiane, including some students, had begun holding regular demonstrations denouncing Souvanna and calling on the entire government to quit.

Though Vang Pao had quietly made an exit plan for asylum in the United States, he erupted at Souvanna. He was still willing to go to battle, even against overwhelming forces, even as communists marched to the capital. He defied the prime minister's order to stop fighting and called in air strikes—from the few Laotian planes that existed and were loyal to him—on communist forces heading for the major towns.[6] The strikes would do nothing to change the war. In public, Vang Pao tore off the medals given to him over the years by the king and by Laos's government. He returned to his base, telling his aides and the few CIA advisors remaining that he would lead his men into the hills for another fight with communist forces. He vowed to several aides that he would even launch the Hmong army's tiny air force against the capital, to bomb the government buildings still (for now) occupied by Souvanna Phouma, who had been Vang Pao's ally in the war for years.[7] "I think that was maybe the maddest I ever got . . . I could get angry [many times] but that was the angriest," Vang Pao reflected in 2006.[8]

The last CIA advisor in Long Cheng who was close to Vang Pao, Jerry Daniels, warned the Hmong leader that a decision to keep up the fight would mean a slaughter of his men, and probably of many Hmong civilians as well. Pathet Lao soldiers had a history of killing groups of captured Hmong soldiers, including some who had surren-

dered and believed they would be spared. The North Vietnamese–
Pathet Lao forces had artillery in the hills ringed around the Hmong,
and they could bombard them at will.[9] If Vang Pao fought on or
called in more air strikes at such a late stage, communist troops might
come down into Long Cheng and massacre people. Just the presence
of Vang Pao in Long Cheng could draw an attack, the general's advisors warned. Vang Pao should leave Laos immediately if he wanted to
survive and if he wanted to help the Hmong.

Vang Pao listened and cooled down. Then he went into his house
and cried for nearly an hour. He gave his CIA advisors the okay to begin
an evacuation, but he wanted all of the Hmong who had fought with
him to be airlifted to Thailand. This was highly unlikely, and the agency
men told Vang Pao so. Tens of thousands of Hmong had fought with
the general, and the CIA's senior leadership and the White House had
approved giving asylum only to Vang Pao and his immediate family.

In private, Daniels convinced the general to accept an evacuation of
himself, his family, and the Hmong most likely to be targeted by a postwar government. Communist forces could take Long Cheng at any time,
a fact that Vang Pao knew. Those who would be airlifted under this plan
would be men and women who could be identified as former officers in
the anti-communist army or clan leaders allied with Vang Pao.

In mid-May, Vang Pao and his closest circle of Hmong fled to
Thailand aboard a US helicopter; many thousands of other Hmong
civilians and soldiers who had fought with Vang Pao had battled to
get out in the US airlift. "Farewell, my brothers, I can do nothing
more for you; I would only be a torment for you" by making the communists more likely to target you, the general told a large crowd that
had gathered around him as he left.[10] To his family, just before they
boarded, Vang Pao said, "Take a close look at our country; this could
be our last time seeing our country, our land."[11]

In Thailand, the general seemed to return to his volatile self. He
cried and cursed and made grand, improbable plans to raise a new
army and take back Laos. He released messages urging Hmong to

stay in Laos rather than attempt to flee overland and risk hunger and death from communist forces.

The messages had little impact. Almost as soon as Vang Pao made plans to leave, word of his imminent departure spread quickly through the Hmong community. "It was pretty quick, panic. Thousands of Hmong wanted to get out—now," said one former intelligence agent who served in Southeast Asia.[12] Communist forces began to shell Long Cheng and other Hmong areas, adding to the chaos. It was "mass hysteria," reported the *New York Times*.[13]

When Vang Pao left, reporters noted, the remaining Hmong were left with no idea what to do but run. The once independent people had mostly turned over all their thinking about the future to the general.

The CIA clandestine officers still in Laos when Vang Pao fled, as well as some in the Far East division, pressed the White House to allow a large airlift of Hmong and other leading anti-communist fighters out of Laos, one similar to the airlift of Americans and Vietnamese from Saigon earlier in the year, as communist forces took over all of Vietnam and Americans and their allies fled the South Vietnamese capital. The answer came back: no such large-scale airlift was possible. Next, Daniels and other CIA officers pushed for an evacuation of at least two thousand Hmong whose lives were surely in immediate danger. Again: no. Only a few hundred more Hmong would be approved for evacuation. The word came down from the White House, remembered Ernest Kuhn, who was working at USAID in Laos when Vang Pao fled, that only "if you were Vietnamese you were [being] evacuated."[14] Congress passed a law helping Vietnamese, in Vietnam, Cambodia, and Laos, to flee and then get evacuated and resettled into the United States. "Laotians [including Hmong] were not protected," Kuhn remembered. This "really burned many people [left among the Americans in Laos] up."[15]

Daniels and some of the contractors and CIA operatives who had worked for years in Laos were not going to accept this answer. Without approval from the White House, pilots and clandestine officers began organizing flights into Laos to evacuate as many Hmong as they could carry. The pilots and clandestine officers could ferry only a handful at a time in the small turbo propeller planes, but the pilots flew and flew with little rest. By the end of August 1975, they had helped about twenty-five hundred Hmong get to safety in Thailand. Still, this was but a fraction of the Hmong who wanted to get out. The Americans had to close the doors of planes and begin to taxi, hard, before Hmong trying to climb on board fell back. Pilots had to push men and women aside to load those chosen for the flight: the ones that the CIA and the pilots believed would be in imminent danger after the war ended.

Many Hmong who could not get on the airlift packed anything they could and began to hike south and west toward sites where they could cross the Mekong River into Thailand. By August 1975, some forty-one thousand Laotians—twenty-five thousand of them Hmong—had fled to Thailand, mostly on foot, in anticipation of the final communist offensive.[16] A few wealthier Hmong paid for cars to drive them toward the Mekong; the rest frantically sold or dumped their horses, cattle, houses, motorbikes, and crops to any Laotians who would take them and started walking.[17] They toted blankets, tarps, bags of rice, and as much silver as could be carried.

Even if they made it to the river, though, crossing was by no means assured. In May 1975, only two weeks after Vang Pao left, a group of between two thousand and three thousand Hmong families clustered at Hin Heup, a bridge near Vientiane over the Nom Lik River. With little warning, communist troops near the bridge opened fire on the Hmong families, killing hundreds.[18] Some of the soldiers attacked the families with machine guns, heavier guns, and knives. "Mortars hit us . . . Some soldiers charged, bayoneting people," recalled Vang Teng, a former officer in Vang Pao's army who had tried to flee over the bridge. "I turned to run and jumped over seven or eight bodies lying on the road."[19]

The United States gave Vang Pao asylum, along with a small circle of the general's closest aides and friends. Most of the rest of the Hmong who got out remained trapped in temporary Thai camps. Diplomats and Laotian government officials wondered whether the government in Vientiane could hold out even until the end of the year. It would not.

————

To the US diplomats and aid workers in Laos at the time when communist forces swept across the land in their final offensive, the situation in the country, though hardly placid, seemed much calmer than in neighboring Vietnam or Cambodia. In Vietnam, communist forces had taken Saigon while US helicopters frantically evacuated Americans and some leading South Vietnamese political figures from the country, in an operation that was, at the time, the biggest helicopter evacuation in US history. Images of American diplomats, journalists, and other American and Vietnamese nationals frantically fleeing from the area near the US Embassy in Saigon made headlines around the world and became iconic. In Cambodia, the communist Khmer Rouge marched into Phnom Penh, emptied the city of most of its residents in April 1975, and began a wave of killings that would last for four years. The US Embassy in Phnom Penh closed its doors.

By contrast, as communist soldiers moved into Laos's biggest towns in the spring of 1975, the US Embassy did not close, though the size of its staff was reduced sharply. As the war in Vietnam came to a close, with the North Vietnamese army taking Saigon at the end of April, North Vietnamese leaders authorized communist forces to take the rest of Laos. Hanoi had been wary of allowing the Pathet Lao to take Vientiane until North Vietnamese forces were done fighting at home.

In May, after Souvanna had publicly called for peace, telling Laotians not to resist the Pathet Lao, Laotian and Vietnamese communist forces moved through the larger towns of southern Laos and began installing trusted officials in the government in Vientiane, especially in important posts such as the Defense Ministry.[20] Throughout the summer of 1975, the Pathet Lao did not yet take over the Vientiane government completely, which added to the sense of continuity and tranquility in the capital, at least compared with the bloody chaos in Phnom Penh and Saigon. In August Pathet Lao troops entered Vientiane with no fanfare, mostly sneaking into the city and never claiming to capture it. Though the troops kept arriving, the Pathet Lao continued to publicly support the coalition government that remained in place in the capital: a combination of technocrats with experience in previous Laotian governments and officials sympathetic to the Pathet Lao.

Still, with government officials and businesspeople fleeing, the value of Laos's currency, the kip, crashed.[21] Some communist supporters briefly attacked USAID offices in Luang Prabang and other towns. But the attackers did not harm USAID officials, and the US Embassy in Vientiane would stay open through Laos's communist takeover and up to the present day, though US officials in Laos after 1975 had little contact with top Laotian government leaders.

"They [the communists] gave a party to celebrate [the king's] overthrow," recalled diplomat Thomas Corcoran, who was in Laos from 1975 to 1978. The king was allowed to "take his leave in a very polite way."[22]

The postwar environment was not as polite in Laos as Corcoran thought. In December 1975 the Pathet Lao troops who had entered Vientiane now announced their presence, declaring that they were taking over the government. They installed a communist, authoritarian government. The Pathet Lao, with North Vietnamese advisors, dismissed any remaining technocrats with links to former governments and ending the fiction that a non-communist, coalition government might remain in power in Vientiane. Souvanna Phouma had stayed on in the coalition government, but he now quit, and the king abdicated, ending the Laotian monarchy.

Some of the Pathet Lao figures who had commanded the communist forces along with North Vietnamese officers but had rarely appeared at any meetings with Souvanna or other non-communist leaders in the past now came out of hiding and entered Vientiane as well. Souvanna's half brother, Prince Souphanouvong, had been the public face of the Pathet Lao during the war. The prince was not, in fact, among the most powerful leaders within the Pathet Lao organization, but he was a charismatic man, popular with a Laotian public that had little idea who really led the communists, so the prince made a perfect front man during the war. On December 2, 1975, the new regime, led by new prime minister Kaysone Phomivane, who had for decades commanded the communist troops but allowed the prince to be portrayed as the leader of the Pathet Lao, announced that the Lao People's Democratic Republic had been founded. (The prince was given the ceremonial title of president in the new republic, but Kaysone and his allies wielded all the real power.) The new government would have an intimate relationship with Hanoi, allowing Vietnam to station troops in Laos.

Most of the urban Laotians who had not yet fled to Thailand now tried to get across the Mekong. The communist government set up prison camps, where they sent officials, politicians, and soldiers who had served the other side during the long civil war.

The camps were not outright killing machines of the order of Khmer Rouge death camps, but they were extremely harsh. The king might have been allowed a send-off party, but in a prison camp, he was then essentially left to wither from hunger and illness until he died—probably in 1980, although his passing was never officially confirmed.[23] Tens of thousands of Laotians were sent to the prison and reeducation camps, where they had to forage for food in the forest to survive and do hard, slave-like labor all day long. In camps for the most prominent former officials, jailers meted out only a hundred grams of rice to each prisoner daily, and kept some in darkness day and night. Prisoners "fought to take out the [chamber] pots because it was the only sunlight they would get," said one former detainee.[24] Some prisoners were beaten to death inside the camps or taken outside the prisons, into the forest, to be summarily executed.[25] But the camps and their atrocities were largely ignored by the world, since Laos was no longer considered significant to the Cold War.

Along with the middle-class urban Laotians, a second wave of Hmong flight began in late 1975 and early 1976. Of all the people who supported the anti-communist side in Laos's civil war, the Hmong remaining in Laos were immediately the biggest targets for the communists. Because the Hmong had been by far the most effective fighters on the government side, many former communist soldiers had memories of friends and comrades who had been killed by Vang Pao's men. The Hmong left in Laos remained much more of a possible threat than the other non-communist soldiers, who had mostly vanished before the final fight for Vientiane.[26] The leaders of the communist forces, mostly lowland people, also were not immune from the ingrained prejudice against hill tribes that had been part of Laotian culture for centuries. As a result, the Hmong continued to flee Laos in large numbers. By the end of 1976, there would be at least one hundred thousand Hmong in camps in Thailand—the exact number was unclear—and almost all of them wanted to come to the United States, since the Thai government did not want to let them out into Thai society. "The Thais are becoming very obnoxious over the fact that the Hmong are not moving to other countries," Jerry Daniels, the CIA officer who had helped with the evacuation, wrote.[27]

At least four hundred thousand Hmong were left in Laos at the end of 1976. More would flee in 1976, 1977, and 1978, but those who remained were often treated horrifically by the new regime. The Hmong were singled out so severely for imprisonment, summary execution, and other abuses that some specialists on Laos called the postwar policy genocide.[28] Communist forces starved to death Hmong who they knew had worked closely with Vang Pao, putting them in holes in the ground with no food.[29] Men who had served in

Vang Pao's army were put in detention camps and tortured repeatedly, with the communists cutting out parts of their flesh and working them all day long with minimal food or water.

The US government was not highly supportive about the idea of settling thousands of Hmong in the United States—the Gerald Ford and Jimmy Carter administrations passed legislation allowing in some Indochinese refugees, but most of the first people resettled were from South Vietnam and had more connections in the United States than the Hmong did. "The Hmong were viewed as kind of stepchildren," said former diplomat Gunther Dean. "They were pretty unsophisticated, and it was seen as really hard to get them to adapt to the US, and they came from a war that few people in America knew much about, so it wasn't like there was a huge public outcry to help them."[30]

Few US officials had prepared for the possibility that tens of thousands, let alone hundreds of thousands, of Hmong would try to follow Vang Pao to Thailand and then to the United States. Few Americans, other than those still serving in Laos, had an idea of the desperate state of many Hmong. Most of the Americans at the State Department and the CIA who had worked with the Hmong during the war had been pulled off to other jobs, and had little interest in getting involved again in Laos issues. "It seems like the US government shouldn't have been that shocked with all the Hmong fleeing, after all that time we worked with them [the Hmong] and the fact that they had been on the losing side of the war, but that's the truth: most people in the US government were shocked, and the people who knew something about what was going on were working in areas that had nothing to do with Laos or the Hmong," said Gunther Dean.[31]

Overall, Laos suffered badly after the end of the war. About 25 percent of the country's people had fled their villages or towns, and people wandered across Laos looking for food and safety and relatives. The withdrawal after 1975 of Western aid, which had made up most of the government budget, hit hard, and communist allies could not make up the difference. The new Lao People's Democratic Republic government had little experience in economics or international affairs; Kaysone and his allies had lived for decades in caves and other hideouts to avoid being captured by the national army or bombed by US planes. Also, the new government had silenced, driven into exile, or killed many of the smartest businesspeople in the country. The country had little of value to export.

And although the war was technically over, its legacy remained. Roads, buildings, runways, and virtually every other type of infrastructure had been ravaged. Arable land had been decimated. Worst, the unprecedented bombing campaign had left the country littered with unexploded ordnance. Demining was—and still is—a slow, laborious, and expensive process. It could take decades, even centuries, for all of the unexploded ordnance to be removed from Laos.[32]

In January 1976 Bill Sullivan was, geographically, relatively close to Laos. From the US Embassy in the Philippines, where he had become ambassador in the summer of 1973, Sullivan could look out onto the brilliant sunset over Manila Bay and the remnants of the city's Spanish colonial quarter. In Manila's old colonial quarter, Intramuros, horse-drawn carts pulled tourists around the remaining paella restaurants and crumbling walls and cathedrals.[33] Manila was only a six-hour flight from Laos, with a stop in Bangkok, and the embassy in the Philippines was quickly becoming central to managing refugees fleeing Indochina. The embassy had been forced to set up a refugee processing center in its grand ballroom, to deal with all the Vietnamese washing up on Philippine shores after the collapse of Saigon. Sullivan personally sheltered the former ambassador from South Vietnam to Manila in the US ambassador's residence.

Yet Bill Sullivan spent little time following events occurring in the newly inaugurated Lao People's Democratic Republic. He did not particularly seek out cables about Laos or have much contact with the diplomats, like Corcoran, who were still in Laos in 1975 and 1976. He did not weigh in on internal State Department discussions about how to handle the collapse of Laos's non-communist government in 1975, including debates about whether to maintain diplomatic relations with Laos after the communists took control. Sullivan's former aides say that he rarely, if ever, spoke about Laos. Since most of the Laotian refugees were fleeing across the border to Thailand from landlocked Laos rather than putting out to sea, Sullivan ran across few former Laotian acquaintances while he was posted in Manila.

Unlike Poe or Lair, Sullivan had never set down any ties in Southeast Asia. Laos had been his job, and the United States' interests in Laos were waning. Almost no one at the State Department cared about Laos now.

Sullivan also found it hard to hide his disappointment that he had not received an even more prestigious posting. Being named ambassador to the Philippines, a former American colony, a treaty ally, and a country of strategic importance to Washington, was a reward, but he had hoped for more. Sullivan had believed that, having helped negotiate the peace accords with North Vietnam, he would also serve the Nixon administration as ambassador to Hanoi while residing in the Philippines. This would have made him the first US ambassador to North Vietnam—a career apex for even the most distinguished Foreign Service officer. Perhaps eventually, Sullivan thought, he would spend most of his time in Hanoi. Washington and Hanoi would normalize relations, the war would end, and Sullivan would eventually move to Hanoi, giving him a truly landmark position.

Sullivan had not made up this idea. Hanoi had intimated that such a posting was possible, and he had believed that during the negotiations, the North Vietnamese had agreed to him becoming the first American ambassador to Hanoi.[34] Of course, after the United States pulled out of Vietnam, the deal that Sullivan had helped negotiate collapsed. The 1973 Paris Peace Accords had not only provided for US forces to withdraw from Vietnam but also called for both the North Vietnamese and South Vietnamese militaries to remain in place, not taking more territory until Vietnamese leaders determined a democratic way to decide the fate of South Vietnam and the whole country. Both Hanoi and Saigon disregarded the promise to keep their armies in place. The stronger North Vietnamese army would quickly gain more ground, and US officials blamed Hanoi for disregarding pledges made in the agreement. Hanoi's forces eventually took over the entire country. "All thought of 'normalizing' our relations with Hanoi through the establishment of an embassy vanished," Sullivan wrote.[35] Relations between Washington and Hanoi remained icy for decades, and Sullivan did not get his landmark posting in Hanoi.

Even if Bill Sullivan had been interested in talking about Laos in 1975 and 1976, he would have found few other people, in the Foreign Service or most of the American foreign policy establishment, who wanted to talk to him about the war, about refugees, or about Laos's future. Although the US Embassy in Vientiane remained open, it was no longer the hive of activity that it had been in Sullivan's time. The embassy had only about thirty staff—in 1969 it had hundreds—and Washington had not posted a permanent ambassador to Vientiane again after the previous one, Charles Whitehouse, had left in 1975.[36] There was virtually nothing to do for entertainment in Laos, which made it highly unattractive, and diplomats knew they were going to have few interactions with Laotian leaders. The French cafes and the open-air bars by the Mekong that diplomats had loved were shuttered; the embassy in Vientiane essentially encouraged diplomats to travel frequently in order to stay sane.

Laos became a posting for junior diplomats with no other choices, dead-enders, or Foreign Service officers who truly loved being there and did not care about how a Laos stint might hurt them on the career ladder. As this shift occurred, the pool of Foreign Service Laos experts in Washington diminished. The whole constellation in Washington of people who had made a living in some way related to Laos—policy experts who had been paid to analyze Laotian communist forces, USAID specialists on Laos, contractors, CIA Laos analysts—

collapsed. In Washington, conversations about the country basically ceased. One diplomat who served numerous tours in Laos after developing a great interest in the culture and people, noted that, after 1975, it was easy to get repeated postings in Vientiane, even though the State Department normally tries to rotate its diplomats, to stop them from the "going native." "Absolutely no one wanted to go there [to Laos,]" the diplomat recalled, laughing. "It was obscure . . . career suicide."[37]

The Ford White House and the senior leadership of the State Department paid pretty much no attention to cables coming from Vientiane now. Congress, which had exploded in a fury of hearings in the early 1970s about the secret war, civilian casualties, and the administration's concealment of the Laos operation, also mostly ignored Laos. While Lyndon Johnson and Richard Nixon had enjoyed personal relationships with their ambassadors in Vientiane, after 1975, Corcoran, the interim ambassador in Vientiane, had virtually no interaction with senior members of the Ford and Carter administrations. He got few congressional visits either. "We did have a few [American] visitors," he recalled. But the only White House official who visited, he admitted, was President Jimmy Carter's antinarcotics specialist. The antidrug czar came to Laos, had breakfast and lunch in Vientiane, and then left.[38]

After the fall of Saigon, Vientiane, and Phnom Penh in 1975, the spread of communism in Southeast Asia halted; communists made no real inroads toward taking over Thailand, Indonesia, the Philippines, or other countries where conservative dictatorships, backed by the United States, repressed dissent harshly. The domino theory that one country after another would fall to communism, which originally prompted the Eisenhower administration to intervene in Laos, no longer seemed to hold in Asia.

The lack of interest in Laos from Presidents Gerald Ford and Jimmy Carter was in many ways understandable. The war was over, there were no more American lives directly at stake, and Carter had come into office without any particular background in foreign affairs. The American public generally wanted to forget about Indochina altogether. But to the Laos veterans in the US foreign policy community, the total shift in just a few years, from thinking that Laos was of critical importance to leaving the country in the hands of a tiny group of mostly junior Foreign Service, was disturbing. "We [the United States] didn't have a lot of history before World War II in foreign policy, and we had a short attention span," said Gunther Dean. "But of all the places where interest [in Washington] rose and fell, I think Laos was the [sharpest change] . . . It tells you how artificial a lot of the interest was, if it didn't last . . . It was interest that was created out of ideas, not interest based on whether Laos was really important to America . . . or the world, or real analysis."

Chapter 18

Laos and the CIA: The Legacy

AT THE CIA, HOWEVER, THE LAOS WAR WAS NOT FORGOT-
ten. Richard Helms had been director of central intelligence during
the height of the operation, but the director in 1975, the year the war
ended, was William Colby. Like Helms, Colby had played a central
role in the operation during his time at the Far East division in the
early 1960s. When, in 1962, President Kennedy had wavered on how
to handle the breakdown of the Geneva deal, Colby had strongly advocated shipping arms to Vang Pao's men and advising the Hmong.
"My arguments became more forceful [by the last months of 1962],"
Colby recalled.[1] Like Helms, Colby considered the Laos operation a
success, no matter the final ending of the US adventure in Indochina.

The message delivered by the directors, for posterity, was that
Laos was the "war we won," as Helms wrote in his memoir—that in
Laos the agency had proven itself in warfare and had held off communism far more effectively than even the US military.[2] The CIA did
"a superb job" in Laos, Helms said.[3] He did not dwell on how the Laos
war had impacted the agency's clients in Laos. Colby wrote that the
"Hmong, Air America, and the CIA performed so magnificently in
Laos" and contended that the secret war in Laos had occupied seventy thousand North Vietnamese troops who might otherwise have
fought Americans in Vietnam.[4] An internal classified CIA retrospective of Helms's tenure as director backed up what the former director

said, suggesting that most senior CIA figures shared Helms's assessment of the secret war. The retrospective concluded: "In the opinion of many officers in the CIA Clandestine Service, the paramilitary programs that the agency operated in Laos . . . were the most successful ever mounted."[5]

After 1975, too, the roster of Laos war alumni in the agency was vast, since the operation had, at its peak, employed so many CIA clandestine operatives and contractors. Since Laos was treated, inside the agency, as a success story, having paramilitary experience in the secret war often helped clandestine officers get future postings. By contrast, although the US Embassy in Vientiane had, in the late 1960s, one of the largest contingents of Foreign Service officers in Asia, Laos experience did not particularly help one rise up in the State Department.

Although the agency keeps secret the identities of its station chiefs in various countries around the world, over time the information often leaks out. After 1975, men with Laos experience took over CIA stations all over the world and senior jobs in agency headquarters. Richard Holm, who worked as a young CIA case officer in Laos, would take over the large CIA Paris station. Ted Shackley would go on to become the associate deputy director for covert operations. Daniel Arnold, the last CIA station chief in Vientiane before the communist takeover of Laos, became the chief of the evaluations and plans department of the agency's Directorate of Operations, another powerful position in Washington.

Many clandestine officers who had worked in Laos brought to other posts a belief that the agency could now handle warfare. Indeed, several of the agency's own initial classified retrospectives emphasized not only that Momentum had been successful in bleeding North Vietnam and prolonging the United States' ability to fight in Indochina but also that the operation had given the agency warfighting skills.

The mid-1970s were, in many ways, a time of retrenchment and playing defense for the CIA. A congressionally appointed committee, led by Senator Frank Church, launched a wide-ranging investigation into the CIA's activities around the world and inside the United States. The committee's findings led to legislation passed in the late 1970s that established new ways for Congress—and through Congress, the American public—to oversee the CIA. Jimmy Carter's appointee as director of central intelligence, Admiral Stansfield Turner, oversaw the elimination of eight hundred CIA jobs, in what was considered by many longtime covert operatives to be the worst moment in the agency's history.

In an era in the 1970s in which many longtime CIA clandestine operatives felt embattled, the agency's exploits in Laos took on even greater meaning within CIA headquarters. The Laos war was cited among many clandestine operatives as an example of why the agency would be needed even if its spying powers were curtailed. And despite these layoffs, and despite public anger over the revelations of CIA domestic spying that the committee produced, few of the agency's critics at the time focused on the expansion of CIA paramilitary power in the 1960s and early 1970s. Fred Branfman, the antiwar activist who had tried to expose the Laos war, said that in the late 1970s, the revelations of CIA spying on Americans dominated conversations about reforming the agency. The CIA's paramilitary programs, and the specifics of the CIA war in Laos were, he said, ignored by most antiwar activists after 1975, just as Laos was ignored by the foreign policy establishment after that year.[6]

"The way in which the CIA had allowed the president to have a war without really much public notice didn't get much attention in the Church Committee era, even among my circle," Branfman said. "Watergate and everything around Watergate and the domestic spying just took all the air out of anything else related to the CIA . . . It wasn't until a long, long time later, like after 9/11, that people paid more attention to how easy it was to make war without a declaration of war."[7]

Meanwhile, the paramilitary specialists who had served in Laos found their skills were still needed, despite the layoffs overseen by

Turner. After Ronald Reagan won the presidency in 1980, the program of CIA reforms was halted. Like Eisenhower and Kennedy, Reagan saw covert actions as effective ways to tip the balance of the Cold War. He publicly called on the United States to support "freedom fighters" anywhere in the world, and signed new executive orders that placed covert paramilitary action at the center of the administration's strategy for combating Moscow. Reagan's new director of central intelligence, William Casey, also was a powerful advocate for the CIA's paramilitary operations. Casey, a veteran of the World War II–era Office of Strategic Services, privately called the Laos operation a template for CIA operations in fighting communism. The new director of central intelligence pushed the agency's budget back to levels it had not seen since before the Ford and Carter administrations. Casey also helped convince Congress to remove restrictions on covert activities that it had implemented in the late 1970s.

In Afghanistan, where the Reagan administration launched a paramilitary program training and equipping mujahedin fighters against the Soviet-installed government, the operation bore a resemblance to the CIA's work with the Hmong, though Reagan did not give the mujahedin air support. Still, the mujahedin program had many similarities to Operation Momentum. The Reagan White House relied upon CIA paramilitary officers and Pakistani intelligence officers to move the arms to the rebels and to provide training for them in how to use antiaircraft missiles and other modern weapons, as well as in military tactics. CIA paramilitary officers, working with colleagues in Pakistan's intelligence outfit, also were given much of the job of helping the Afghan rebels plan attacks, just as in Laos the CIA had taken over this military advisory function from the uniformed US armed forces. The mujahedin bled Moscow: more than fourteen thousand Soviet troops lost their lives in Afghanistan, which Russian historians called "the Soviet Union's Vietnam."[8] The cost of maintaining the Afghan occupation was one factor that contributed to the ruin of the Soviet economy, a ruining that helped bring down the USSR.

Still, many of the mujahedin leaders did not understand that this bleeding of Moscow was the United States' primary interest in Afghanistan. Many of the Afghan tribal leaders, like Vang Pao and the Hmong clan chiefs, had little world experience before the world's conflicts came to them. After the Soviet Union collapsed in 1989, the United States government mostly lost interest in Afghanistan, at least until 9/11. Washington slashed aid for Afghan civilians, while also continuing to fund some of the militia leaders. But this aid was given largely out of inertia, according to several accounts of post-Soviet Afghanistan. The policy was nonetheless destructive. As Charles Cogan, who ran the CIA's operations in the Middle East and South Asia in the 1980s, recalled later, continued funding, with little thought, made it easier for the mujahedin to amass weapons and turn their guns on one another.[9] The heavily armed Afghan factions, loyal to one warlord or the next, battled one another. They leveled Kabul and other cities with shelling, paving the way for the rise of the Taliban, which was welcomed at first by many Afghans simply because Talib leaders promised to restore law and order.

In Central America in the 1980s, the lessons of Laos were applied even more directly, with many of the same CIA operatives who had overseen the secret war involved once again. The Reagan administration and Director of Central Intelligence William Casey heartily supported covert paramilitary action in the Western Hemisphere. In secret testimony to Congress in 1981, Casey told members that the agency had to undertake covert paramilitary support for anti-communists in Central America, of the kind undertaken in Laos, to protect the United States' security. If the Sandinista communists controlled Nicaragua, Reagan publicly warned, they could create a haven for anti-American militants just "two days' driving time . . . from Texas."[10] (Nicaragua is twelve hundred miles as the crow flies from the nearest Texas border point.)

Laos veterans, both inside the agency and in the network of contractors who worked with the CIA, took critical places running a new paramilitary support program for anti-communist fighters in Honduras and Nicaragua. Thomas Clines, the Shackley loyalist who had served at Udorn Air Base during the Laos war, had become the head of the agency's Nicaragua operations in the late 1970s, where he had started an operation, along with allies of the country's former dictator, to undermine Nicaragua's leftist government. Clines left the CIA in 1979 and went to work for an intelligence contractor started by his old boss Shackley. But in the 1980s, as the Reagan administration looked for ways to battle communism in Central America, Clines and his company were handed a central role in helping to arm the anti-communist Nicaraguan Contra forces. Outside of even the normal CIA channels, Clines and his firm reportedly helped build a network of companies that purchased arms from a range of dealers in Europe and then secretly transferred weapons to the Contras, and also eventually helped move money from arms sales to Iran to fund the Contras. Clines failed to report most of the money his company had made on the deal to anyone.[11] (Clines was found guilty of failure to report his income and was given a sixteen-month jail sentence, becoming the only Iran-Contra figure to see prison time.)

Richard Secord, an air force officer who, on loan to the CIA, had coordinated air strikes during the Laos war, became a central figure in the Iran-Contra operation as well. After the Laos war ended, Secord had continued to work on a range of covert operations with the agency and its contractors. He was recruited to the secret Central America operation by Oliver North, who was handling Iran-Contra while on Reagan's National Security Council staff. Secord reportedly helped establish secret bank accounts in Europe that could be drawn on for covert operations, including arming the Contras; he also reportedly helped take money intended for nonlethal aid to the Contras and secretly use it to ship weapons to the fighters.

Secord and Clines were just two of a number of Laos veterans who served in Central America. Raymond Doty, the CIA officer put in charge of actually managing Contra missions from Honduras, had gained his essential paramilitary experience training anti-communist forces in Laos.[12] Many of the pilots recruited to fly arms and non-lethal aid to the Contras were veterans of the agency's Air America operations in Laos. One former Air America employee, Felix Rodriguez, helped maintain the flow of funds for the Contras.

In the 1990s, as in the late 1970s, the CIA was downsized, although this time the cuts came because the end of the Cold War seemed to mean fewer threats to the United States rather than because of any public reaction to agency activities. The cuts led to the retirement of many older CIA clandestine officers.

Still, these cuts did not end the agency's paramilitary activities. In 1997 Director of Central Intelligence George Tenet launched a plan to enlarge the clandestine service's paramilitary branch, even as the overall size of the CIA was being slashed.[13] CIA paramilitary officers were sent into Somalia in 1992, as the country's government collapsed and a humanitarian and security disaster erupted, before American military Special Forces invaded the African nation. The paramilitary officers helped identify top targets among the many Somali warlords and helped plan attacks for the American soldiers.[14] The agency also put its paramilitary experience to use training Kosovar guerillas fighting against the Serbian government in the late 1990s, arming and training Iraqi exiles opposing the Saddam Hussein regime, and training other guerilla armies.[15]

The idea that the CIA should be involved in these types of military matters had, by the 1990s, become ingrained in the agency's culture. A more peaceful world, and even cuts in personnel, was not going to change this. The paramilitary branch of the agency had become as important to its mission as the division responsible for intelligence gathering, a shift from the early days of the agency, when paramilitary operations were an afterthought. Tenet, who had early in his tenure positioned the CIA to focus more on combating terrorism than it had in the past, believed that paramilitary operations would be critical to this redefined mission.[16]

After the terrorist attacks of September 2001, the agency's paramilitary operations were enlarged massively, clearly becoming the center of the CIA's activities. The shift begun in Laos had reached its natural end. Today intelligence gathering, though still important, is secondary in the agency's mission to kill enemies of the United States.[17]

The post-9/11 war on terrorism not only has been a massive undertaking, as the Laos war was. It also has replicated the executive power, the extreme secrecy, the creation of an alternative power center outside the US military, and the reliance on bombing that characterized the CIA's Laos battles.

According to documents released by the former contractor Edward Snowden, the CIA's requested budget in 2012 was $14.7 billion. The State Department's requested budget for that year was $14.2 billion. This is a staggering shift from the early years of the Cold War, when the State Department's requested budget for operations was routinely as much as five times larger than the CIA's. Other data suggest that the CIA's budget expanded rapidly in the ten years after the 9/11 attacks.

The Snowden budget documents reveal further that the CIA does still conduct spying and intelligence and analysis, its traditional functions, but that the agency spends much of its manpower managing drone strikes and many other aspects of paramilitary operations around the globe.[18] Other reporting, by the *New York Times*, revealed in 2015 that the CIA and Special Forces together had created a kind of global superelite paramilitary force. The force, which handled the operation that ultimately led to the killing of Osama bin Laden, reportedly has been handed responsibility for tracking and killing militants wanted by the United States government all over the world.[19] "When suspicions have been raised about misconduct [by Seal Team Six], outside oversight has been limited," the *Times* reported.[20]

In a further sign of the ascendance of paramilitary operations within the CIA, and the blurring of the lines between spies and soldiers, in early 2015 the agency's senior paramilitary specialist was made head of the CIA's entire clandestine service, which is responsible for nearly all overseas intelligence operations.[21] The operative had done multiple tours in post-9/11 Afghanistan, where the agency had helped arm and train forces fighting the Taliban, hunt down suspected militants, and launch air strikes from planes and drones. The operative—and the CIA station in Kabul in general—had formed a close relationship with Afghan president Hamid Karzai; the operative reportedly threw himself on top of Karzai to protect the leader when Karzai's position was accidentally bombed by an American plane.[22] Although only agency officials know for certain, intelligence analysts believed that this promotion marked the first time that a paramilitary expert had taken over the clandestine service.

The new head of the clandestine service will be conducting paramilitary operations on many fronts where the agency is already deeply involved in covert wars—from Yemen, to Somalia, to Afghanistan, to Mali, to Iraq, among other places. The CIA has seen its future, wrote the *New York Times*: "Not as the long-term jailers of America's enemies [or as a spying outfit] but as a military organization that could erase them."[23] The agency oversaw the creation of the Predator drone program, which led to the creation of a US government drone program, used for targeted assassinations, that includes a range of unmanned aerial vehicles. The CIA helps manage that program as well. The agency inserts its paramilitary specialists into places where the US government attempts to capture or kill suspected terrorists. It helps to vet recruits and train armies, from militias opposed to Syrian president Bashar al-Assad to Special Forces units in Afghanistan.[24] It supplies arms to these forces and to others.[25] It allows the American president, as in Laos, to conduct a broad range of warlike operations all over the globe, without ever worrying about putting large numbers of ground forces anywhere.

When the US government decided, in the summer of 2015, to bolster its campaign against the Islamic State in Syria, it turned to a parallel CIA apparatus that could avoid the normal military channels. "The CIA and US Special Operations forces have launched a secret campaign to hunt terrorism suspects in Syria as part of a targeted killing program that is run separately from the broader US military offensive against the Islamic State," US officials revealed in September 2015, according to the *Washington Post*.[26] "The clandestine program represents a significant escalation of the CIA's involvement in the war in Syria." The CIA's takeover of the Syria drone program occurred even though President Barack Obama stated publicly that he had hoped to move the agency back somewhat toward its older goal of spying instead of killing. And yet, beyond the CIA-led drone strikes in Syria, the agency was taking over the drone program, in the waning days of the Obama presidency, in other parts of the world like Yemen and Pakistan, according to several senior intelligence officials.

Members of Congress, who in the mid-1970s and late 1980s had questioned the CIA's killing programs overseas, also have mostly become used to the agency amassing vast war powers, a return to the lack of rigorous oversight common during the Laos war years. "About once a month," the *New York Times* reported in 2015, "staff members of the congressional intelligence committees drive across the Potomac River to CIA headquarters in Langley, Virginia, and watch videos of people being blown up. As part of the macabre ritual the staff members look at the footage of drone strikes in Pakistan and other countries and a sampling of the intelligence buttressing each strike, but not the internal CIA cables discussing the attacks and their aftermath." The congressional intelligence staffers, by and large, express what the *Times* called "unwavering support" for having the "CIA's killing missions . . . embedded" in the agency's mission.[27]

The post-9/11 war on terror also replicates the Laos war in another critical way: CIA activities go almost totally unwatched by the public and the media. The strategies used to keep most of the war on terror secret—prohibiting reporters from coming near CIA paramilitary operations, classifying even the most basic details of paramilitary campaigns, relying almost exclusively on technology, contractors, and local forces rather than US ground troops—would have been completely familiar to the CIA operatives running the Laos war.

Chapter 19

Aftermath

BILL LAIR HAD CHOSEN NEVER TO MAKE MONEY OFF HIS
CIA and Thai connections, though for years after the Laos war, he
continued to get offers for contract work from Thai businessmen and
from other former CIA officers. He rejected them all, just as he had
nixed the idea back in the late 1960s. Some of Lair's former colleagues
thought him crazy—and sad as well.

After his stint at the War College, Lair had taken a CIA desk job
in Bangkok, but one with far less power than he had enjoyed with
Operation Momentum. His job was mostly monitoring the narcotics trade in Thailand and the surrounding region; the drug trade had
continued to expand in Southeast Asia, and Bangkok was the main
station for monitoring and interdicting narcotics trafficking. He had
nowhere near the budget or the number of men under him that he
had enjoyed during Operation Momentum, and he mostly stayed in
Bangkok rather than flying around the region. Although Thai government officials still paid him polite heed, in part because his wife
was related to one of the most powerful Thai officials, he no longer
had the regular contact with top ministers that he had enjoyed during
his time running Momentum.

After a few years in Bangkok, Lair had hoped to find an agency
job with more power and responsibility. In the mid-1970s, with the
Indochina wars over for the United States, perhaps there was still
time for him to learn about another region of the world, or at least
move to CIA headquarters and do some kind of management job. For

a time, after all, he had overseen an operation that grew to number tens of thousands of men, and the CIA would come to view the Laos war as a great success, for empowering the agency and holding off so many North Vietnamese soldiers.

But when Lair looked for jobs at agency headquarters after the end of the Indochina War, he was told there were no positions available for him. Lair had clashed repeatedly with some of the most powerful men in the CIA, such as Ted Shackley, who continued to rise within the agency and seeded the CIA's clandestine operations division with his acolytes. Lair also had never abandoned his vision of Operation Momentum—a vision that was not the one ultimately embraced by the agency or the one celebrated for posterity. Lair had stuck to believing in a small footprint, and he had denigrated the bigger war, the introduction of more CIA operatives, and the agency's shift toward more paramilitary operations. And so, while men with Laos experience would be coveted assets within the agency in the 1970s, 1980s, and beyond, a man who did not get along with Ted Shackley, and who actually thought the bigger Laos war had been a failure, was not coveted property at CIA headquarters.

Even with all these strikes against him, Lair's fame for founding the operation and his contacts in Southeast Asia could have helped him build a profitable contracting business in Bangkok, but he refused this possibility once again. In 1976 Lair retired from the CIA.[1]

Lair returned to Texas. He rarely talked about his Laos war experiences, and he did not seek professional medical help even though he slept poorly, felt intense loneliness, and spent hours nearly every day brooding on how he had let Operation Momentum go wrong. Later, as it became apparent that Operation Momentum not only had failed to save the Hmong or stave off a communist takeover but also had provided a game plan for future large paramilitary operations, Lair rued the role he had played in the CIA's shift in mission as well. He rarely spoke to other CIA veterans. He had amassed some savings and had a pension, but he lost most of his money on an ill-timed investment in a horse-breeding operation.

In debt, Lair had to find other work. He had always liked driving, and so he took a job as a long-distance trucker, working in Texas and neighboring states, and pulling RVs to recreational vehicle showrooms all over the Southwest.[2] He found that the long solo drives, on open roads, could numb his mind and sometimes allow him to forget about Laos and the Hmong. A fifteen- or eighteen-hour day driving helped him sleep at night. At other times, he seemed embarrassed that a man who once could have been a leader of the CIA now struggled to make a living as a trucker.

By the 1990s and 2000s, Lair began to speak more about his experience in Laos, with a small handful of associates and historians. He began returning often to Laos and to Thailand, and he met with Hmong refugees. He attended Hmong American events in California and Minnesota and occasionally Washington, DC.[3] At Hmong events in the United States, Lair was always welcomed rapturously by older Hmong—some Hmong war veterans would introduce him as "father," though Lair hated the term. Younger Hmong Americans did not always treat him the same way; to them, Lair was a relic, or worse: a man who had entrapped the Hmong and led them to destruction. And when Lair returned to Thailand and Laos, the reception was not always so rapturous either. Some of the Hmong who had not been able to get to the United States lived in squalid camps in Thailand or squatted on the land of friendly Thais, Buddhist monks, and a few expatriates in Thailand. Those in Thailand were not Thai citizens, got few benefits, and were at the mercy of Thai police.[4] Many of the Hmong left in Thailand and Laos knew of the role Lair had played in launching the operation, and had heard rumors that he'd promised that Hmong who fought would be moved to Thailand and treated well, or settled in the United States, a pledge

Lair had never made. When they met with Lair, they often exploded at him, demanding to know why he had not delivered them to the United States.[5]

Lair felt it was his duty to maintain his Hmong connections, but he shied away from receiving awards and honors at Hmong events. If he had to give a speech, he kept it short. He was happy, he said, when mingling with war veterans meant he could relive just a bit of the camaraderie he had felt when he had first started to work with the Hmong.[6]

Lair lived for more than a decade after the terrorist attacks of September 2001, witnessing how killing became the center of the CIA's functions. He kept driving his truck, and when he no longer could drive far enough to make a living out of it, he would drive for hours through Texas in his own vehicle, just to be out on the road. After years of declining health, Lair died in the autumn of 2014. His passing was noted by many Hmong and some former CIA operatives, but it went mostly ignored by the world.

———

Almost thirty years after the war, Tony Poe seemed to have barely survived a lifetime of alcohol abuse, stress, and disinterest in his own health. He walked with a noticeable limp. He and his Laotian wife had settled in Thailand in the early 1970s before moving to the United States decades later. He was not popular with the Thai authorities, since for decades he had continued to try to help Hmong cross into Thailand. He suffered from diabetes, his feet were constantly swollen, and the weighty frame of a man who had been a fierce football linebacker as a teen had ballooned out, weighing heavily on his knees and legs. He still had shrapnel embedded in his body, and he drank a considerable amount.[7]

But Poe was hardly unhappy. He seemed content, and he relished talking about his past, unlike Bill Lair, whose voice sunk every time he discussed Momentum. Poe even seemed to relish talking about his own brutality and his descent into madness at Nam Yu. Despite a lifetime of alcohol abuse, Poe had vivid memories of the Laos war. No longer working for the CIA, he was free to swap stories with reporters for hours. He was disappointed with how the Hmong had been treated, and he still retained his old combination of disdain for Vang Pao and admiration for his military skills. But Poe had not started Operation Momentum, he had made no personal pledges to Vang Pao, and though he had gone insane for a time, he had not lived the rest of his life haunted by how the war had turned out, like Bill Lair.

For all his devotion to the men who fought with him, Laos had been one of a number of CIA paramilitary operations for Poe, and the Hmong were not even his favorite trainees. He had liked the Chinese Muslims he trained the best, for their informality and skill with weapons. He ranked the Hmong somewhere in the middle, among the people he had trained, for their skill as fighters. He had gotten along better with the Tibetans and their leaders, too, than he had with the Hmong fighters and with Vang Pao.

By 1970, Poe had finally made so many enemies in Laos that, although he still had many backers in the Far East division, his bosses had to remove him from the kingdom. Vang Pao increasingly tolerated no open criticism, not even from Americans, and Poe was inveighing against the general to everyone who stopped in Nam Yu. Vang Pao had pressured his agency handlers to get Poe out of the country; finally, in 1970, the CIA transferred him to Thailand. Poe was assigned to run a training camp where CIA operatives taught Thais and other allies in the region unconventional war tactics. At least eighty of Poe's loyalists apparently managed to sneak across the border to Thailand as well; they often joined Poe, heavily armed, at the training facility, following Poe's every move, and Poe claimed at least fifty of them had eventually made it to the United States as refugees.[8]

Despite the fact that Poe had essentially been forced out of Laos, the Thai trainees at the camp had heard a great deal about his legendary fighting skills. Even CIA operatives who resented Poe's manner admitted that many of the trainees worshipped him as a sage. After retiring from the agency in the mid-1970s, Poe survived on odd jobs in Thailand and his pension. Despite his checkered history, the CIA gave him a second Intelligence Star, an honor for extraordinary heroism, in 1975. A man who had been a real-life Colonel Kurtz, but in the mountains at Nam Yu with his private army instead of up a river, had been made a kind of model. Indeed, the Stars, and the way the agency held up the Laos war as an example, demonstrated to many younger agency officers who only knew of the Poe legend that the man's military skills had actually made him quite valuable. It was the second time he had been given the Star, having received one in 1959 for his skill in training Tibetans and Chinese Muslims. The agency did not give an Intelligence Star to Bill Lair.

Although Poe had never been a strategist or a deep thinker, nearly thirty years after the end of the Laos war, he could see that, though during the war some fellow CIA officers disdained him as mercenary, bloodthirsty, and outright crazy, his kind of paramilitary skill set had become essential to the CIA. In many ways, the agency actually had become more like him. In a way, Poe—minus the private army at Nam Yu and the severed ears and the heads on stakes—had become a template for a kind of paramilitary clandestine officer who filled the ranks of the agency and its contractors. The agency had few, if any, Bill Lairs anymore: clandestine officers who stayed in one place for decades, became almost locals, and cultivated extensive intelligence sources. It did have a large, growing pool of men who could be mistaken for American military Special Forces—many of the CIA's paramilitary specialists worked closely with Special Forces, and, indeed, were former Special Forces themselves. The agency's paramilitary operatives could be moved around the world, just like Tony Poe had been.

Poe did not live to see all the ways in which the CIA fought the global war on terrorism—he died in Northern California in June 2003. But he likely would not have been surprised to see paramilitary operations become the center of the agency's mission, with many aspects of the Laos proxy operation duplicated in other parts of the world. Poe also probably would not have been shocked that, in the 2000s, agency operatives became involved in a global game of detention and torture, that some of the agency men tasked to fight the war on terror devised ever more destructive ways to interrogate and even kill terrorism prisoners, or that agency headquarters had difficulty relieving operatives who became too brutal. It was hard to keep paramilitary officers—who were told to get results, no matter what—in the "cages" where Lair thought they should stay.

Poe, indeed, had embodied the ethos of doing anything to get results. One of the men who worked as Poe's aide during his time in Nam Yu said of Poe, "His motto was 'Kill all, burn all, and destroy all.' We never took prisoners; he ordered us to kill them and sometimes he would slit their throats."[9] Poe did not deny saying these words, and he first denied and then confirmed that he had ordered executions. "They'll write [when I die] Tony Poe the killer, the bad seed, he never got along with anyone . . . Now they have lots of Tony Poes [in the CIA] . . . They need a lot more people like me," he said.

In January 1979 the United States' relationship with Iran was deteriorating rapidly, and the Carter administration was scrambling to develop a new strategy. The US Embassy in Tehran had not been particularly helpful. Although protest against the increasingly isolated and autocratic shah had built throughout 1978, the embassy, headed by Ambassador Bill Sullivan, had mostly failed to anticipate that the imperious and often brutal shah might be toppled. In fact,

Sullivan had sent the State Department a cable expressing confidence in Shah Mohammad Reza Pahlavi. The shah, Sullivan wrote, was "the unique element which can, on the one hand, restrain the military and, on the other hand, lead a controlled transition [in Iran]."[10] (In his memoir, Sullivan called the shah "tender" but also a "starchy monarch whose secret police killed, tortured, and brutalized his subjects.")[11]

The protests had gotten larger and larger, and even Sullivan admitted later that the embassy had little intelligence on the demonstrations, or even what ordinary Iranians thought about most anything. Now, the shah was about to flee, and Islamic revolutionaries patrolled the streets of Tehran. Having stood by the shah until only weeks before his downfall, in the autumn of 1978 Bill Sullivan suddenly recommended to Washington that the United States find some way to work with the Islamic regime emerging in Iran. In a cable, he cautioned the Carter White House that the shah's position was precarious.[12] "He switched completely, from total confidence in the shah to acting like he had seen the Islamic Republic coming the whole time and having total confidence in his recommendations for how to handle an Islamic Iran," said one of Sullivan's aides in Tehran.

Sullivan had always been bold, and in Iran his style was no different from his approach in Laos. Now he advocated just as strongly that Carter deal with the Iranian Islamists as he'd once pushed Carter to stick with the shah. Sullivan would claim later in his memoir and in conversations with aides that the Carter administration simply would not listen to his new advice on Iran. If they had, he said, the White House could have worked with the new leaders of the Islamic Republic and avoided an escalation of hostilities.

But the ambassador's switch, from expressing total confidence in the shah to demonstrating total confidence in his plan to work with Islamists, unsettled Carter and his top aides. The president worried that he could not trust any advice Sullivan offered. In

February, after Ayatollah Ruhollah Khomeini had returned to Iran from exile in France, to a rapturous welcome, armed Islamic militants attacked the American Embassy and briefly took it over. The takeover could have easily disintegrated into a bloodbath. The militants had machine guns and other automatic weapons mounted on buildings facing the embassy, and they briefly opened fire.[13]

During the attack, Sullivan returned to his role as wartime commander, personally overseeing the marines defending the embassy and even at one point telling them where to lob tear gas and reinforce their ranks. Many of the embassy's employees believed that Sullivan's tough command kept order amid the takeover and prevented people from being killed. Although the militants who attacked in February pushed most of the embassy employees out of the compound at gunpoint, taking at least one hundred hostages temporarily, the attackers soon handed the embassy back peacefully and let go of the hostages. However, some embassy staffers were furious when Sullivan returned to Washington soon afterward, leaving behind only a skeleton crew at the embassy in Tehran. After Sullivan was gone, the men and women still at the embassy would almost all wind up as hostages the following November when more radical, determined militants took over the compound once more.

———

That Bill Sullivan was even serving as ambassador to Iran, a place he previously knew little about, demonstrated how he had continued to rise in Washington as the Laos war ended and administrations changed. Although the Hmong had fled, Vientiane had been taken over by communists, and the full details of the civilian casualties in Laos were becoming known by the mid-1970s, Sullivan's smooth handling of his testimony before Congress won him even more admirers within State and the CIA than he had before. "I don't think anyone could have done a better job of massaging, portraying the Laos war to Congress than Bill Sullivan," said former diplomat John Gunther Dean. "Congress and the public were angry about the years of secret war in Laos, and the bombing in Laos, but there was nowhere near the outcry there was on Cambodia . . . That was due greatly to how Sullivan defused Congress."[14] Anger within State about Sullivan's overseeing bombing, managing covert operations, and taking on other military operations that were highly unusual for an American diplomat dissipated. Within the CIA, the Laos war quickly took on an exalted status, both as an operation that effectively stalled the communist takeover in Southeast Asia and as an operation that remade the agency into a stronger, bigger beast. "He protected the agency, he protected State, so he protected himself," said one of Sullivan's former aides. People remember these things in Washington . . . If the situation in Iran had not deteriorated, he could have gone even higher."[15]

Sullivan was still a Democrat. After serving Nixon's and Ford's Republican administrations, he used his deep Democratic Party connections to continue his career under President Carter, and in late 1977, the new White House sent Bill Sullivan to be ambassador to Iran. Sullivan was surprised to be sent there, since he had no experience in the country, but Carter apparently wanted, most of all, an ambassador with extensive skill dealing with autocrats, and with thorny politics abroad and back in the United States.

Iran was now at the center of the American foreign policy universe, as Southeast Asia had been in the 1960s, and was a critical ally in the Middle East. Iran under the shah had close ties to Israel and to other American allies such as France and Britain. An ambassadorship to Iran was, without a doubt, one of the most prestigious Foreign Service jobs—up there with being ambassador to Moscow, Tokyo, or Riyadh, Saudi Arabia. In addition, President Carter personally liked the shah; on a visit to Iran in December 1977 and January 1978, the last by an American president, Carter toasted the Iranian autocrat, telling

him that he felt more of a "personal friendship" toward the shah than
he did toward any other world leader.[16]

Yet in Iran, Bill Sullivan's enormous confidence in his own skills,
which up until then had helped propel him into higher ranking jobs,
finally came back to hurt him. After Sullivan returned to Washington from Iran in early 1979, many of his State Department colleagues
praised him for handling the armed standoff at the embassy with no
American casualties, but he never regained the trust of President Carter after so rapidly switching his view of the situation in Iran. The fact
that, in the days just before Sullivan left the embassy, he had bluntly
nixed an idea floated by Carter's national security advisor to foment
a coup in Iran did not help him.[17] National Security Advisor Zbig-
niew Brzezinski's coup strategy was implausible, but Sullivan attacked
it so forcefully that Brzezinski became convinced Sullivan was not a
team player, and had to go. Carter later wrote that he should have
fired Sullivan for insubordination, as Sullivan repeatedly bashed the
White House's policy and refused to implement elements of it, but
that Secretary of State Cyrus Vance—one of Sullivan's connections in
the Democratic Party—convinced him not to.[18]

When Sullivan left Iran in early 1979, he would be the last American ambassador to the country. His career prospects, always so good,
had disintegrated. He retired from the Foreign Service and then
wrote a book about his time in Tehran.[19] In it, Sullivan concluded
that if the White House had followed his policy advice—at least, the
policy advice he embraced late in the day, to work with the Islamic
revolutionaries—the United States might have avoided breaking relations with Iran.

Throughout the 1980s, 1990s, and 2000s, Bill Sullivan wrote and
spoke often about his long career in the Foreign Service. He never
denied his unique role managing the war in Laos, and he expressed
little doubt that he had been right in how he handled the operation.
He claimed that he only did what was necessary to restrain the US
military from becoming directly involved in Laos, which would have

led to an even larger, more brutal war in the kingdom. Whether or not greater direct US military involvement would have actually enlarged the war is a question impossible to answer. What was clear was that the actual war was extremely deadly: On a per capita basis, many more Laotians were killed in the war than Americans or Japanese in World War II. (For example, in World War II, roughly 0.3 percent of the American population died, and approximately 3.75 percent of Japanese died; in Laos, as much as 10 percent of the population was killed in the war, a figure approaching the casualty rates of the countries that suffered the most in WWII, such as the Soviet Union and Poland.)

Sullivan had rarely visited Long Cheng or other Hmong redoubts when he was ambassador, and after retiring from the Foreign Service he defended his Laos record but made little attempt to communicate with Vang Pao, Bill Lair, or other prominent Laos war veterans living in the United States. "I tend to forget things or dismiss things from my mind so that I'm not haunted by them. If I were haunted by all my past life, I'd never be able to sleep quite as [well] as I do," Sullivan said. "So I don't keep things in mind."[20] The air war in Laos caused him "no personal anguish," Sullivan told one historian.[21]

In the late 1980s and early 1990s, as Vietnam and Laos, though still nominally communist, began to open their economies and reintegrate themselves with the world, Sullivan decided to help foster American reconciliation with Hanoi and Vientiane. Starting reconciliation was, to him, a natural sequel to his role in the peace talks with Hanoi, and to his attempts to be the first US ambassador to Hanoi. In the late 1980s, he met with one of his former North Vietnamese counterparts at the Paris peace talks and helped lay some of the groundwork for a restoration of America's relationship with its former adversaries. The reconciliation helped usher in a golden new age of American relations with Vietnam; the two countries, both worried about the rise of China, are closer strategically and economically today than at any time in decades.

Indeed, Sullivan's view that the legacy of the war should finally be buried made strategic sense. Yet to some Vietnam and Laos war veterans who had known Sullivan, his decision to suddenly play a role in fostering reconciliation brought up memories as well—memories that Sullivan seemed to believe in little more than Bill Sullivan. "Sullivan for years, he would defend the way the war in Laos was fought brutally as just saying it was right, we were fighting against an evil enemy, any means necessary," said Fred Branfman, the antiwar activist who helped expose the bombing of Laos. "Then he can just turn around and say, it's all forgotten . . . I always thought we should move on, restore ties with Vietnam and Laos, but that Bill Sullivan was in the middle of restoring ties, it's kind of horrible. What did he ever really believe in?"[22]

After coming to the United States in the mid-1970s, Vang Pao continued for years to live the existence of a major military and political leader who was still at war. Vang Pao lived surrounded by wives, ex-wives, and aides, first at a Montana ranch allegedly bought for him by the CIA and then at homes in Fresno, California, and Saint Paul, Minnesota. After a brief period in which he kept mostly quiet on his Montana ranch, spending his time hunting and fishing, he focused his efforts on raising money, supposedly to lead a war again in Laos. Vang Pao traveled to California, Wisconsin, Minnesota, and Washington, DC, among other locations, to preach that the Hmong needed to return to Laos and fight the communist government; during the Cold War, before the United States restored full relations with Laos, some Washington think tanks and politicians provided the Hmong leader with a platform to propose an unlikely armed return to Laos. In one speech at the conservative think tank the Heritage Foundation in the 1980s, Vang Pao told his audience that his organization would "mobilize all Laotian people, inside as well as outside of Laos, to overthrow the puppet regime."[23]

Even after the end of the Cold War, Vang Pao's organization, the Lao Family Community, and other informal associations linked to the general continued to raise money among Hmong Americans, with the proceeds supposedly to be used to fund a future fight to re- take Laos. Walking from house to house in Hmong neighborhoods, Vang Pao's men would ask for small contributions, always in cash. "City by city and district by district, Neo Hom representatives [repre- sentatives of Vang Pao] were assigned geographical areas from which to collect money by going house to house," the Twin Cities' *Star Tri- bune* reported in a comprehensive investigation of Vang Pao's organi- zation. "Over time, the organization raised millions of dollars, made in small individual cash payments."[24]

"We'd even get money, five bucks, ten bucks, from the poorest old women on welfare," said Tou Long Lo, Vang Pao's former son-in- law. "We'd threaten them to pay . . . People knew that in Laos, Vang Pao had killed, so threats worked." In exchange for the money, which eventually amounted to millions, donors would receive certificates promising them positions in a future Laotian government, which they mounted on their walls—alongside framed photos of Vang Pao.[25] "Parents paid for [the certificates] out of welfare checks," said Tou Long Lo. "Kids had nothing to eat."[26]

The certificates meant nothing, since Vang Pao never drew up any real plans to retake Laos, or strategies for how to form a future gov- ernment. "To become members of [Vang Pao's organization], fami- lies were required to pay $100 down and then $10 a month," reported the *Washington Post*.[27] "Those who paid $500 were given certificates [signed by Vang Pao] that they believe entitle them to return to Laos after the 'liberation,' with the understanding that their airfare will be free . . . Refugees paid $1,000 a month to hold their positions" in some future government of Laos.[28]

"It was just a scam," said Tou Long Lo. "Simple." Vang Pao and several of his closest associates denied ever pressuring Hmong to do- nate to the organization or scamming anyone.

The fund-raising might have even led to violence. In the early and mid-2000s, the police in Saint Paul, Minnesota, which has a large Hmong American population, repeatedly answered calls to normally quiet Hmong neighborhoods for firebombings and shootings that appeared like professional hits.[29] Many of the violent incidents had some apparent connection to Vang Pao and to the Lao Family Community. Many Hmong Americans, especially younger Hmong, believed that all the violence was due to fighting within Vang Pao's organization over power and control of the Lao Family Community's money.[30]

The violence and the allegations against his community organizations were not even the lowest points in Vang Pao's post-Laos life. In 2007 the Justice Department filed charges against Vang Pao and a group of associates for allegedly conspiring to buy heavy weapons and launch an attack, a kind of coup, against the government in Laos. The charges came with a possible sentence of life in prison.

Facing a storm of protest over Vang Pao's indictment from CIA veterans, members of Congress representing Hmong American dominated districts, and some lawyers who questioned the Justice Department's informants in the case, in 2009 the Justice Department dropped charges. In January 2011 Vang Pao died of complications from pneumonia. After another round of protests from Hmong Americans, congressmen and congresswomen from California and Minnesota, and some Laos war veterans, the US Army considered a request from Vang Pao's family to inter the Hmong leader at Arlington National Cemetery, making an exception to a policy that allowed only deceased US military to be buried there. The army ultimately denied the request.

Vang Pao's fall from revered national leader in Laos to alleged community shakedown artist in the United States only signified, to many younger Hmong Americans, the Hmong community's disastrous introduction to the United States, and the ongoing trauma that resulted from having to flee their homeland. The US government, having made few preparations for a loss in Laos, other than planning to grant Vang Pao and a few aides refugee status, had to improvise once a handful of CIA veterans, Southeast Asia activists in the United States, and church groups pushed Washington to let in tens of thousands of Hmong who had made it out of Laos and into Thailand. Eventually the Hmong community in the United States grew to over 260,000, a figure that is increasing rapidly—the population grew by 40 percent between 2000 and 2010—due to high fertility rates.[31]

"The Hmong were a nonpresence—we were embarrassed by them because we didn't want to talk about the Vietnam War anymore," said Stephen Young, a businessman in Saint Paul who worked with Hmong refugees for decades, and whose father was the American ambassador to Thailand in the early 1960s. Refugee resettlement specialists knew little about the Hmong's clan structures and history. Hmong settled in areas, like the Twin Cities and Fresno, California, where either clan and military leaders such as Vang Pao had come or where there appeared to be generous social welfare policies, but these regions frequently had little in common with the Hmong's rural, mountainous, agricultural homelands.

When the Hmong came to the United States, state and local governments played only a minimal role guiding their entry, instead mostly handing them welfare and then ignoring them. But unlike some other refugees, the Hmong badly needed help. Many Vietnamese refugees who fled to the United States after the communist victory in 1975 came from educated families in Saigon and quickly built businesses in the United States. The Hmong were probably the least prepared of any refugee group for integration into modern American life—even less prepared than Somali or Afghan refugees today. Most were illiterate, knew no English, had no capital, and had never been employed in any way other than subsistence farming and fighting. Shocked by years of war, upon arriving in the United States Hmong began dying young, dropping dead of unexplained illnesses or killing themselves. Fresno witnessed an epidemic of Hmong suicides, while the Twin Cities suffered outbreaks of Hmong gang violence. Even now, Hmong in the United States still lag badly behind most immigrants in nearly every category of health, wealth, and education. One study by the University of California at Los Angeles showed that a quarter of Hmong Americans in Fresno, California, relied on government cash assistance for survival, as compared with 3 percent of whites in Fresno and 10 percent of Asian Americans overall.[32]

––––––

Vang Pao never recovered from fleeing his homeland, either. While he avoided a trial, he died a bitter man who displayed only flashes of the energetic and visionary leader he had once been. His dark moods dominated his mind, and he never seemed to accept that he was unlikely to return to Laos. He seemed unable to understand younger Hmong Americans who saw themselves as Americans first, and who returned to Laos for visits only to be shocked by the country's poverty and uninterested in staying. "Vang Pao never moved on . . . His life was not here [in America]. His life was in Laos and trying to get back or re-create it," said Yang Dao, his biographer.[33]

Although older Hmong continued to venerate Vang Pao, younger Hmong Americans increasingly distanced themselves from the aging general. They had little interest in quixotic attempts to return to Laos and mount a revolution, and cared instead about how the Hmong American community was addressing gang violence, unemployment, suicide, and drug abuse.[34] The 1972 publication of historian Alfred McCoy's book on the narcotics trade in Southeast Asia, which had fingered Vang Pao as a major player, continued to resonate for years, helping to undermine the general's image both with some Hmong and with US politicians. McCoy's book, *The Politics of Heroin in Southeast Asia*, led to further investigations, including a 1988 PBS *Frontline* documentary that examined drug trafficking during the Laos war.[35]

The financial troubles of Vang Pao's community organization, the revelations in the mid-2000s that some Hmong were still fighting in Laos in a misguided belief that Vang Pao would come back to them, the rumors and charges and violence surrounding Vang Pao all contributed to a diminution of his status. Younger Hmong American leaders, more familiar with American culture and more attuned to the needs of younger Hmong, began to rise to prominence in the community. Although the general's six-day-long funeral in Fresno, California, in 2011 attracted thousands of people, if Vang Pao had died thirty years earlier, the Hmong community in the United States might have fallen apart, so central was the general to the lives of the Hmong who had fled Laos. Now the community continued on without him.

———

In 2007, more than thirty years after the United States pulled out of Indochina, a group of foreign journalists trekked into the mountainous interior of Laos and discovered that hundreds, perhaps even thousands, of Hmong fighters still hid in the jungles, their clothes ragged and their food supplies dwindling. They lived on small bits of rice they could cadge from sympathetic farmers, wild bamboo and yams, and small game they could kill. Many of the guerillas appeared to suffer from chronic illnesses and distended stomachs.

Although Vang Pao's organization in the United States had for decades promised to take Hmong American donations and fund fighters still active in Laos, this band of guerillas had never received anything from American supporters.[36] They were surprised to find out that Vang Pao's organization had raised millions of dollars in donations. Some thought Vang Pao had died years before. Some knew Hmong who had made it to the United States and hoped to join them, though the guerillas had little idea how they would get out of Laos.

The last Hmong guerillas did not know much of how the world around them had changed, either. Communism had all but died

around the world, even if Laos's regime was still nominally communist. By the mid-2000s, the Soviet Union was long gone, China had
become a capitalist free-for-all, Vietnam had befriended the United
States again, and Laos and the United States had restored normal relations as well. American diplomats met regularly with Laotian government leaders, although Laos's government remained an autocratic
regime, and warmer US-Laos relations made it harder for Hmong
fleeing Laos to claim refugee status and enter the United States.
(During his administration, President Barack Obama would visit
Laos, becoming the highest-ranking American official to travel to the
country since the war.) Even the government of Laos, while highly
repressive, had embraced capitalism. It had welcomed foreign inves-
tors, joined the World Trade Organization, and built massive casinos
along Laos's borders, where Chinese gamblers could come to blow
their cash on craps and prostitutes shipped in from Myanmar and
Thailand.[37]

But these Hmong guerillas had not changed much. Many had
lived through the war, and then the postwar period, when the world
ignored Laos and the Laotian government savagely attacked the
Hmong left behind. Several had shrapnel and bullets stuck in their
bodies. Since the guerillas had little ammunition to spare, they
mostly hid in jungle camps hours from the nearest roads, and would
emerge from the brush to launch occasional attacks on Lao government forces, which often tracked down the Hmong and slaughtered
them in return. The guerillas moved their camp every few weeks.[38]

Most of the group of guerillas, which numbered less than a hundred and included boys young enough to have been the grandsons
of Vang Pao's fighters, had little hope their lives would change. They
knew that, even after 1975, thousands more Hmong had been killed
in Laos's jungles. They had contacted several other groups of Hmong
guerillas but did not know how many Hmong were still in the jungle,
fighting.

Some of the guerillas fought for fear that if they handed in their arms, they would be killed. "If I surrender, I will be punished," one of the guerillas told a reporter.[39] The story of their dismal state sparked no outcry in the United States. Still, some of these left behind Hmong believed that, if they held out long enough, the United States would notice once again, and send in new bombers and helicopter gunships to help them finally win their war against communism. After all, they said, wasn't that what US leaders had promised them? Eventually, if they kept up the fight, their deliverance would come.[40]

Acknowledgments

This book could not have been written without the generous assistance and wise advice of many people. Heather Schroder championed the book throughout the entire process. At the Council on Foreign Relations, James Lindsay and Richard Haass read drafts of the work and offered critical and insightful comments. I also wish to thank Paul Stares at CFR for his counsel. Elizabeth Leader, Andrew Lim, Hunter Marston, James West, Anna-Sophia Haub, and Darcie Draudt contributed important research, translation, and analysis. Patricia Dorff and the CFR Publications and Library Departments worked to bring it to publication. Elizabeth Economy offered essential guidance. Susan Weill provided diligent research assistance. I am also grateful to Michael Montesano, William Young, Ralph Boyce, and all the experts on Laos, the former combatants in Laos, and the Laotian, Hmong, and Thai civilians who gave up their time to speak with me.

I would like to thank the Starr Foundation for their generous funding, which helped me research and write this book.

At Simon & Schuster, I am grateful to Priscilla Painton and Sophia Jimenez for their essential assistance in shaping the book.

Shira provided not only counsel and advice throughout but also love.

Notes

Chapter 1. Baci

1. Author interview with Vang Pao, Saint Paul, MN, November 2006. Author phone interview with Bill Lair, November 2010.
2. Ibid.
3. "The President's News Conference of April 7, 1954," in *Public Papers of the Presidents of the United States: Dwight D. Eisenhower, 1954* (Washington, DC: National Archives, 1955), 381-90.
4. Leslie Gelb with Richard Betts, *The Irony of Vietnam: The System Worked* (Washington, DC: Brookings Institution Press, 1974), 183.
5. Stephen Pelz, "When Do I Have Time to Think? John F. Kennedy, Roger Hilsman, and the Laos Crisis of 1962," *Diplomatic History* 3, no. 2 (April 1979): 216-23.
6. Gelb with Betts, *Irony of Vietnam*, 28-29.
7. Author interview with Joseph Lazarsky, Alexandria, VA, February 2006.
8. Joseph Scott, "Memorandum From the Deputy Director for Coordination, Bureau of Intelligence and Research to the Special Group," January 17, 1964, in *Foreign Relations of the United States 1964-1968, vol. 28: Laos* (Washington, DC: Government Printing Office, 1998), 1-5. Also John Prados, *Lost Crusader: The Secret Wars of CIA Director William Colby* (New York: Oxford University Press, 2003), 158. Also author interview with Vang Pao, Novermber 2006.
9. Mai Na M. Lee, *Dreams of a Hmong Kingdom: The Quest for Legitimation in French Indochina, 1850-1960* (Madison: University of Wisconsin Press, 2014), 1-18.
10. Author interview with Vang Pao, Saint Paul, MN, November 2006.
11. Ibid.
12. Jane Hamilton-Merritt, *Tragic Mountains: The Hmong, the Americans, and the Secret Wars for Laos, 1942-1992* (Bloomington: Indiana University Press, 1992), 92.
13. Ibid., 92-93. In the book, Lair is identified as "Colonel Billy," but it is obvious that the reference is to Lair.
14. Peter Dale Scott, *American War Machine: Deep Politics, the CIA Global Drug Connection, and the Road to Afghanistan* (Lanham, MD: Rowman & Littlefield, 2014), 304.

15. Author interview with Vang Pao, Saint Paul, MN, November 2006.

16. "The UXO Problem in Laos: Statistics," Mines Advisory Group (MAG), accessed October 2014, www.maginternational.org/the-problems/the-uxo-problem-in -laos-statistics/#.VN7iVi6whD0.

17. Ibid.

18. Ibid.

19. B. Hugh Tovar, "Chronicle of a Secret War," *International Journal of Intelligence and Counterintelligence* 8, no. 2 (Summer 1995), 248.

20. Ibid.

21. Author phone interview with Bill Lair, January 2011.

22. Thomas Ross and David Wise, *The Invisible Government* (New York: Random House, 1964), 151.

23. "Notes of Conversation Between President-Elect Kennedy and President Eisenhower, January 19, 1961," in *Foreign Relations of the United States 1961– 1963, vol. 24: Laos Crisis* (Washington, DC: Government Printing Office, 1994), 19–21.

24. Walt Haney, "The Pentagon Papers and United States Involvement in Laos," in Noam Chomsky and Howard Zinn, eds., *The Pentagon Papers, Vol. 5: Critical Essays* (Boston: Beacon Press, 1972), 260.

25. Fredrik Logevall, *Embers of War: The Fall of an Empire and the Making of America's Vietnam* (New York: Random House, 2012), 344–46.

26. For more on the overall Thai commitment to the Indochina War, see Richard Ruth, *In Buddha's Company: Thai Soldiers in the Vietnam War* (Honolulu: University of Hawaii Press, 2010).

27. Christopher Robbins, *The Ravens: The Men Who Flew in America's Secret War in Laos* (New York: Crown, 1987), 126.

28. Department of Defense, *The Pentagon Papers: The Defense Department History of United States Decisionmaking on Vietnam*, Senator Gravel Edition, sec. 1, vol 2 (Boston: Beacon Press, 1971), 1–39.

29. "Christian A. Chapman Oral History," March 3, 1990, Association for Diplomatic Studies and Training Foreign Affairs Oral History Project, 20–21, www.adst.org/ OH%20TOCs/Chapman,%20Christian%20A.toc.pdf, accessed January 2012.

30. Author interview with Willis Bird Jr., Bangkok, August 2007.

31. Robert Dallek, *An Unfinished Life, John F. Kennedy, 1917–1963* (New York: Little, Brown, 2003), 144–56 and 244–57.

32. Some of this map was false, or at least overstated: the Laotian and Vietnamese communists had gained territory in Laos but not to the extent that Kennedy suggested at his press conference. For more on the conference, see Seth

Jacobs, *The Universe Unraveling: American Foreign Policy in Cold War Laos* (Ithaca, NY: Cornell University Press, 2012).

33. "Transcript: Press Conference: March 23, 1961" in *Presidential Papers: President's Office Files—Press Conferences* (Boston: John F. Kennedy Presidential Library and Museum, 1961).

34. Richard Secord, *Honored and Betrayed: Irangate, Covert Affairs, and the Secret War in Laos* (New York: John Wiley and Sons, 1992), 61.

35. Martin Stuart-Fox, *A History of Laos* (Cambridge, UK: Cambridge University Press, 1997), 144–46.

36. "Statistical Information about Fatal Casualties of Vietnam War," National Archives, April 29, 2008, accessed December 2014, www.archives.gov/research/military/vietnam-war/casualty-statistics.html#water.

37. Ibid.

38. "Decades after Vietnam War, Laos Grapples with Unexploded Bombs," Reuters, September 5, 2006, www.reuters.com/article/us-vietnamwar-laos-bombs-iduskcn11b1jx.

39. Mark Mazzetti, *The Way of the Knife: The CIA, a Secret Army, and a War at the Ends of the Earth* (New York: Penguin Press, 2013), 8–20.

40. "Robert Amory Jr. Oral History Interview," February 9, 1966, John F. Kennedy Library Oral History Program, 9.

Chapter 2. The CIA's First War

1. For example, see Thomas Ahern, *Undercover Armies: CIA and Surrogate War in Laos, 1961–1973* (Washington, DC: Central Intelligence Agency Center for the Study of Intelligence, 2006, partially declassified, February 2009).

2. The Thai Ministry of Defense published a lengthy report on Thailand's combat in Indochina: Ministry of Defense, *Prawatiikkanrop khong thahan thai nay songkhram wiet nam*, or *The History of the Thai Military in the Vietnam Wars* (Bangkok: Amarin Printing and Publishing, 1998).

3. For example, see Ruth, *In Buddha's Company*.

4. Author phone interview with Fred Branfman, January 2013.

5. Ibid.

6. Richard L. Holm, "Recollections of a Case Officer in Laos, 1962–1964," *Studies in Intelligence* (unclassified) 47, no. 1 (2003): www.cia.gov/library/center-for-the-study-of-intelligence/csi-publications/csi-studies/studies/vol47no1/article01.html, accessed January 2010.

7. *The Ravens: Covert War in Laos*, dir. Kirk Wolfinger (Portland, ME: Lone Wolf Documentary Group), 2003, 6:57–7:25.

Chapter 3. Vang Pao, Bill Lair, Tony Poe, and Bill Sullivan

1. Throughout the book, I refer to the hill tribe as the Hmong, but in some older publications quoted here, they are referred to as *Meo*, a term used to describe the Hmong in the past and considered insulting by many Hmong.
2. Author phone interview with Tony Poe, March 2001.
3. *History Undercover: The Search for Kurtz*, History Channel, Adrian Levy (New York: documentary, January 2001), 33:25–34:40.
4. Matt Isaacs, "Agent Provocative," *SF Weekly*, November 17, 1999, www.sfweekly .com/sanfrancisco/agent-provocative/Content?oid=2137417, accessed January 2014.
5. Author phone interview with Tony Poe, March 2001.
6. Charles Davis, *Across the Mekong: The True Story of an Air America Helicopter Pilot* (Charlottesville, VA: Hildesigns Press, 1996), 183.
7. Author phone interview with Tony Poe, February 2001.
8. Ibid.; also, Richard Ehrlich, "Death of a Dirty Fighter," *Asia Times*, July 8, 2003, www.atimes.com/atimes/Southeast_Asia/EG08Ae02.html, accessed January 2012.
9. Tim Weiner, *Legacy of Ashes: The History of the CIA* (New York: Doubleday, 2007), 292.
10. Author phone interview with Tony Poe, February 2001.
11. Ibid.; also, Roger Warner, *Shooting at the Moon: The Story of America's Clandestine War in Laos* (Hanover, NH: Steerforth Press, 1996), 142.
12. Charles Weldon, *Tragedy in Paradise: A Country Doctor at War in Laos* (Bangkok: Asia Books, 1999), 147.
13. Ibid.; also Warner, *Shooting at the Moon*, 144–46.
14. Weldon, *Tragedy in Paradise*, 147.
15. Ibid.
16. Ibid.
17. "Bill Lair Oral History," December 11, 2001, Bill Lair Collection, Vietnam Center and Archive, Texas Tech University, 1–10.
18. Ibid.; also, author phone interview with Bill Lair, December 2009.
19. "Bill Lair Oral History," December 11, 2001, 1–10.
20. Ibid., 51.
21. Ibid., 51–52.
22. Ibid., 58.

23. Edwin Stanton, "Spotlight on Thailand," *Foreign Affairs*, October 1954, 79–80; also, Terence Gomez and Michael Hsiao, eds. *Chinese Business in Southeast Asia: Contesting Cultural Expectations, Researching Entrepreneurship* (Surrey, UK: Curzon Press, 2001), 96–98.

24. Timothy Castle, *At War in the Shadow of Vietnam: US Military Aid to the Royal Lao Government, 1955–1975* (New York: Columbia University Press, 1993), 12–13.

25. Stanton, "Spotlight on Thailand," 79–84.

26. Thailand and Laos are not only geographic neighbors but also very close culturally.

27. Author interview with Vint Lawrence, Norfolk, CT, November 2006.

28. Author phone innterview with Bill Lair, January 2011.

29. Thomas Lobe, *United States National Security Policy and Aid to the Thailand Police* (Denver, CO: University of Denver Press, 1977), 23–25.

30. Author phone interview with Bill Lair, January 2011.

31. Ibid.

32. For example, see James Scott, *The Art of Not Being Governed: An Anarchist History of Upland Southeast Asia* (New Haven, CT: Yale University Press, 2009).

33. Neil Sheehan, *A Bright Shining Lie: John Paul Vann and America in Vietnam* (New York: Random House, 1988), 133.

34. For example, see Jonathan Nashel, *Edward Lansdale's Cold War* (Amherst: University of Massachusetts Press, 2005).

35. Sheehan, *A Bright Shining Lie*, 133–49.

36. Author phone interview with Bill Lair, January 2001.

37. Lee, *Dreams of a Hmong Kingdom*, 1–18.

38. Alfred McCoy with Leonard P. Adams and Cathleen B. Read. *The Politics of Heroin in Southeast Asia* (New York: Harper and Row, 1972), 268.

39. Stuart Methven, *Laughter in the Shadows: A CIA Memoir* (Annapolis, MD: Naval Institute Press, 2008), 67. Although Methven, who served in Laos and worked with Vang Pao, took rudimentary steps to hide the identities of people he referred to in his book, their real identities are obvious; he describes Vang Pao in detail and refers to him as "Pang Vao."

40. Stuart-Fox, *History of Laos*, 77.

41. Yang Dao and Jean Larteguy, *La Fabuleuse Aventure du Peuple de L'opium* (Paris: Presses de la Cité, 1979), 154–60.

42. Paul Hillmer, *A People's History of the Hmong* (Minneapolis: Minnesota Historical Society Press, 2010), 113.

43. Charlie Weitz, quoted in *The Most Secret Place on Earth* (Gebrueder Beetz Film Production: Marc Eberle, director, 2008).

44. Yang and Larteguy, *La Fabuleuse Aventure du Peuple de L'opium*, 154–60.

45. Hillmer, *People's History of the Hmong*, 22–39.

46. Author phone interview with Yang Dao, October 2008; also, author interview with Vang Pao, Saint Paul, MN, November 2006.

47. Yang and Larteguy, *La Fabuleuse Aventure du Peuple de L'opium*, 154–60.

48. Ibid.; also, author interview with Vang Pao, Saint Paul, MN, November 2006.

49. Lee, *Dreams of a Hmong Kingdom*, 28.

50. Author interview with Vang Pao, Saint Paul, MN, November 2006.

51. Warner, *Shooting at the Moon*.

52. William M. Leary, "CIA Air Operations in Laos, 1955–1974: Supporting the Secret War," *Studies in Intelligence* (unclassified) (Winter 1999–2000): 71–86.

53. Author phone interview with Tony Poe, February 2001.

54. Author interview with Ralph Boyce, Bangkok, February 2006.

55. Author interview with William van den Heuvel, New York, March 2006; also, "Ambassador Leonard Unger Oral History," May 10, 1989, Association for Diplomatic Studies and Training Foreign Affairs Oral History Project, 22–28.

56. "Ambassador Leonard Unger Oral History," May 10, 1989, 22–24.

57. Haney, "The Pentagon Papers and United States Involvement in Laos," 272–73.

58. Ibid., 257.

59. Tom Yarborough, *Da Nang Diary: A Forward Air Controller's Gunsight View of Flying with SOG* (Havertown, PA: Casemate, 2013) 37.

60. Haney, "The Pentagon Papers and United States Involvement in Laos," 272.

61. Castle, *At War in the Shadow of Vietnam*, 78.

62. Ibid.

63. William Sullivan, *Obbligato: Notes on a Foreign Service Career* (New York: W. W. Norton, 1984), 211.

64. Keith Quincy, *Harvesting Pa Chay's Wheat: The Hmong and America's Secret War in Laos* (Cheney, WA: Eastern Washington University Press, 2000), 233.

65. Jacob Van Staaveren, *Interdiction in Southern Laos, 1960–1968* (Honolulu: University Press of the Pacific, 2005), 231.

Chapter 4. Laos Before the CIA, and the CIA Before Laos

1. Richard Harris Smith, *OSS: The Secret History of America's First Intelligence Agency* (Guilford, CT: Lyons Press, 2005), 3.
2. Author interview with Elizabeth McIntosh, Reston, VA, February 2007.
3. Franklin Roosevelt, "Address at the Annual Dinner of White House Correspondents' Association," March 15, 1941, American Presidency Project, University of California, Santa Barbara, www.presidency.ucsb.edu/ws/?pid=16089, accessed December 2014.
4. Alan Brinkley, "Why Were We in Vietnam?," *New York Times Book Review*, September 7, 2012, 1.
5. Ibid.
6. George F. Kennan (penned as *X*), "The Sources of Soviet Conduct," *Foreign Affairs*, July 1947, 566–82.
7. This was a supposition later shown to be, at best, flawed, and Kennan himself later disavowed the tough language of force and containment that he used in the *Foreign Affairs* piece, saying that the United States at the time was looking for an enemy to justify American power and preeminence, and that he fulfilled this Manichean worldview by painting the Soviet Union as inherently evil and impossible to deal with through diplomacy.
8. "The National Security Act of 1947," Office of the Historian: US Department of State, 1 November 2013, https://history.state.gov/milestones/1945-1952/national-security-act, accessed January 2015.
9. Weiner, *Legacy of Ashes*, 28–31.
10. Ibid., 27–28.
11. Sheehan, *A Bright Shining Lie*, 133.
12. Weiner, *Legacy of Ashes*, 26.
13. For more on Dulles's relationship with Wolff, see Michael Salter, *Nazi War Crimes: US Intelligence and Selective Prosecution at Nuremberg* (Abingdon, UK: Routledge-Cavendish, 2007).
14. Ibid.
15. Clayton Laurie, "A New President, a Better CIA, and an Old War: Eisenhower and Intelligence Reporting on Korea, 1953," *Studies in Intelligence* 54, no. 4 (December 2010): 1–8.
16. Stephen Kinzer, *The Brothers: John Foster Dulles, Allen Dulles, and Their Secret World War* (New York: Times Books, 2013), 32–47.
17. Jonathan Mirsky, "The Dalai Lama and the CIA," *New York Review of Books*, September 23, 1999, www.nybooks.com/articles/archives/1999/sep/23/the-dalai-lama-and-the-cia/, accessed January 2011.

18. Mikael Dunham, *Buddha's Warriors: The Story of the CIA-Backed Tibetan Freedom Fighters, the Chinese Invasion, and the Ultimate Fall of Tibet* (New York: Tarcher, 2004), 70.

19. Hillmer, *A People's History of the Hmong*, 128.

20. Author phone interview with Bill Lair, November 2010.

21. Author interview with Campbell James, Newport, RI, January 2007.

22. Author interview with Joseph Lazarsky, Alexandria, VA, January 2007.

23. L. Britt Snider, *The Agency and the Hill: CIA's Relationship with Congress, 1946–2004* (Washington, DC: Central Intelligence Agency Center for the Study of Intelligence, 2008), 260.

24. Ibid., 260–65.

25. Stuart-Fox, *A History of Laos*, 44–60.

26. Lee, *Dreams of a Hmong Kingdom*, 87.

27. M. A. Lavalee, "Notes Ethnographiques sur Diverse Tribus du Sud-Est de l'Indochine," *Bulletin de L'Ecole Française d'Extreme Orient*, no. 1 (1901): 311–12; also, Alfred W. McCoy, "French Colonialism in Laos, 1893–1945," in *Laos: War and Revolution*, Nina Adams and Alfred W. McCoy, eds. (New York: Harper, 1970), 79.

28. *Laos: War and Revolution*, Nina Adams and Alfred McCoy, eds. (New York: Harper, 1970), 91–92; Lavalee, "Notes Ethnographiques," 311.

29. Hamilton-Merritt, *Tragic Mountains*, 55.

30. Author interview with Denis Gray, Bangkok, January 2007.

31. Mervyn Brown, *War in Shangri-La: A Memoir of Civil War in Laos* (London: Radcliffe Press, 2001), 189.

32. Arthur Blanchette, "Life Along the Mekong," in *Canadian Peacekeepers in Indochina, 1954–1973: Recollections*, Arthur Blanchette, ed. (Kemptville, Ontario, Canada: Golden Dog Press, 2001), 56–58.

33. Logevall, *Embers of War*, 345–46.

34. Ibid., 345–46.

35. Ibid., 382–92.

36. Ibid., 345.

37. Paul F. Langer, "The Soviet Union, China, and the Pathet Lao: Analysis and Chronology," RAND Corporation paper, January 1972, 19–21.

38. Pierre Asselin, *Hanoi's Road to the Vietnam War, 1954–1965* (Berkeley: University of California Press, 2013), 51–53, 64.

39. William J. Rust, *Before the Quagmire: American Intervention in Laos, 1954–1961* (Lexington: University Press of Kentucky, 2012), 82–95.

40. Ibid., 97–98.

41. Author interviews with Laotian doctors, Vientiane, January 2001.

42. Hamilton-Merritt, *Tragic Mountains*, 90.

43. Paul Lewis and Elaine Lewis, *Peoples of the Golden Triangle: Six Tribes in Thailand* (New York: Thames and Hudson, 1984), 116–18.

44. George W. Long and J. Baylor Roberts, "Indochina Faces the Dragon," *National Geographic*, September 1952, 327.

45. Geoffrey C. Gunn, *Rebellion in Laos: Peasants and Politics in a Colonial Backwater* (Boulder, CO: Westview Press, 1990), 151–60.

46. Kenneth Conboy and James Morrison, *Shadow War: The CIA's Secret War in Laos* (Boulder, CO: Paladin Press, 1995), 59.

Chapter 5. The CIA Meets Laos

1. Logevall, *Embers of War*, 281–345.

2. Davis, *Across the Mekong*, 133.

3. Perry Stieglitz, *In a Little Kingdom* (New York: Routledge, 1990), 12–13.

4. Igor Oganesoff, "Living It Up in Laos," *Wall Street Journal*, April 8, 1958, A1.

5. Sutayut Osornprasop, "Thailand and the American Secret War in Indochina, 1960–1974" (dissertation for the doctor of philosophy, Corpus Christi College, University of Cambridge, November 2006), 106–10.

6. Ibid.

7. Brown, *War in Shangri-La*, 159. Also Jim Wilbanks, ed., *The Vietnam War: The Essential Reference Guide* (Santa Barbara, CA: ABC-CLIO, 2013), 135.

8. *Laos: A Country Study*, Andrea Matles Savada, ed. (Washington: GPO for the Library of Congress, 1994), http://countrystudies.us/laos/27.htm.

9. Conboy and Morrison, *Shadow War: The CIA's Secret War in Laos*, 95–99.

10. Evan Thomas, *The Very Best Men: The Daring Early Years of the CIA* (New York: Simon & Schuster, 2006), 279.

11. Brown, *War in Shangri-La*, 64–68; also, Jacobs, *Universe Unraveling*, 129–35.

12. Brown, *War in Shangri-La*, 64–68.

13. Arthur J. Dommen, *Conflict in Laos: The Politics of Neutralization* (Santa Barbara, CA: Praeger, 1971), 165.

14. Author phone interview with John Gunther Dean, September 2009; also, "Memorandum of Discussion at 434th Meeting of National Security Council," *Foreign Relations of the United States, 1958–1960; East Asia Pacific Region—Cambodia, Laos*, vol. 26 (Washington, DC: Government Printing Office, 1992), 920–22.

15. Arthur Schlesinger Jr., *A Thousand Days: John F. Kennedy in the White House* (New York: Houghton Mifflin, 1965), 330.

16. Logevall, *Embers of War*, 33–34 and 72–73.

17. Rust, *Before the Quagmire*, 14.

18. Jacobs, *Universe Unraveling*, 107–8.

19. Ibid.
20. Ibid.
21. "William H. Sullivan Oral History Interview," June 16, 1970, John F. Kennedy Library Oral History Program, 3.
22. Jacobs, *Universe Unraveling*, 158.
23. Schlesinger, *Thousand Days*, 297–301; also, "Robert Amory Jr. Oral History Interview," February 9, 1966, 9.
24. Rust, *Before the Quagmire*, 60.
25. Thomas, *Very Best Men*, 279.
26. "Christian A. Chapman Oral History," March 3, 1990.
27. Thomas, *Very Best Men*, 279; also, Rust, *Before the Quagmire*, 263–65.

Chapter 6. Operation Momentum Begins

1. Author phone interview with Bill Lair, February 2011; also, Conboy and Morrison, *Shadow War*, 59–60; Warner, *Shooting at the Moon*, 21.
2. Sutayut Osornprasop, "Thailand and the Secret War in Laos, 1960–1974," in *Southeast Asia and the Cold War*, Albert Lau, ed. (New York: Routledge, 2012), 196.
3. Warner, *Shooting at the Moon*, 32–33.
4. Leary, "CIA Air Operations in Laos," 71–86.
5. Author phone interview with Bill Lair, January 2011.
6. Leary, "CIA Air Operations in Laos," 71–86.
7. Author phone interview with Bill Lair, January 2010.
8. Conboy and Morrison, *Shadow War*, 61.
9. Author interview with Vang Pao, Saint Paul, MN, November 2006.
10. Author phone interview with Bill Lair, January 2010; also, author phone interview with Hugh Tovar, February 2006.
11. Author phone interview with Bill Lair, February 2010.
12. "Bill Lair Oral History," December 11, 2001, Part 2, 134.
13. Author phone interview with Bill Lair, January 2011.
14. Author interview with Vang Pao, Saint Paul, MN, November 2006.

Chapter 7. Kennedy Expands Momentum

1. Roland A. Paul, "Laos: Anatomy of an American Involvement," *Foreign Affairs*, Vol. 49, No. 3, April 1971, 33.
2. Pelz, "When Do I Have Time to Think?," 216–18; also, author phone interview with Bill Lair, January 2010.

3. Xiaoming Zhang, "China's Involvement in Laos During the Vietnam War, 1963–1975," *Journal of Military History* 66, no. 4 (October 2002): 1142–51; also William Rust, *So Much to Lose: John F. Kennedy and American Policy in Laos* (Lexington: University Press of Kentucky, 2014), 117.

4. Ibid.

5. Ibid., 116.

6. "News Conference: April 24, 1963," in *Public Papers of the Presidents of the United States: John F. Kennedy, 1963* (Washington, DC: National Archives, 1964), 349.

7. Martin Goldstein, *American Policy Toward Laos* (Rutherford, NJ: Fairleigh Dickinson University Press, 1973), 250–52.

8. 1951 Travel Journal, Box 11, Book 2, October–November 1951, 116ff, John F. Kennedy Personal Papers, John F. Kennedy Library.

9. Rust, *So Much to Lose*, 115.

10. "Memorandum for the President: Plan for Possible Intervention in Laos, Together with Discussion For and Against Such Action," May 4, 1961, declassified March 1998, W. Averell Harriman Papers, Library of Congress, Box 483, series B.

11. "Winthrop G. Brown, Oral History Interview," February 1, 1968, John F. Kennedy Library Oral History Program, http://archive2.jfklibrary.org/JFKOH/Brown,%20Winthrop%20G/JFKOH-WGB-01/JFKOH-WGB-01-TR.pdf, accessed January 2014, 24–26.

12. Pelz, "When Do I Have Time to Think?," 216.

13. Rust, *Before the Quagmire*, 264.

14. Dommen, *Conflict in Laos*, 189.

15. David Halberstam, *The Best and the Brightest* (New York: Ballantine Books, 1993), 438.

16. Xiaoming Zhang, "China's Involvement in Laos During Vietnam," 1157.

17. Keith Quincy, "Warlord," *Hmong Studies Journal* 3 (Winter 2000): 6–8.

18. "Memorandum from Michael V. Forrestal of the National Security Council Staff to President Kennedy: Washington, June 18, 1963," *Foreign Relations of the United States, 1961–1963*, vol. 24: *Laos Crisis* (Washington, DC: Government Printing Office, 1994), 1021–30.

19. Quincy, "Warlord," 6–8; also, author phone interview with Bill Lair, January 2010.

20. Yang and Larteguy, *La Fabuleuse Aventure du Peuple de L'opium*, 154–60.

21. Gayle Morrison, *Hog's Exit: Jerry Daniels, the Hmong, and the CIA* (Lubbock: Texas Tech University Press, 2013), 72.

22. Tony Kennedy and Paul McEnroe, "The Covert Wars of Vang Pao," *Star Tri-*

bune, July 3, 2005, www.network54.com/Forum/218837/thread/1120488377/last-1120488377/The+covert+wars+of+Vang+Pao.

23. Author phone interview with Bill Lair, November 2009; also, Hamilton-Merritt, *Tragic Mountains*, 90–92.

24. Quincy, "Warlord," 36–42; also, author interview with former Hmong combatants, Washington, DC, January 2010.

25. Ibid.

26. Douglas Blaufarb, *The Counterinsurgency Era: U.S. Doctrine and Performance, 1950 to the Present* (New York: Free Press, 1977), 154.

27. Terry Grandstaff, "The Hmong, Opium and the Haw: Speculations on the Origin of their Association," *Journal of the Siam Society* 67, no. 2 (1979): 70–79.

28. "Guns, Drugs, and the CIA," *Frontline*, PBS, May 17, 1988, produced and written by Andrew and Leslie Cockburn, www.pbs.org/wgbh/pages/frontline/shows/drugs/archive/gunsdrugscia.html.

29. Ibid.

30. McCoy, *The Politics of Heroin in Southeast Asia*, 289–91.

31. Author phone interview with Bill Lair, December 2007.

32. "Guns, Drugs and the CIA," *Frontline*, May 17, 1988.

33. Hillmer, *A People's History of the Hmong*, 111.

34. Author interview with Vint Lawrence, Norfolk, CT, November 2006; also, Robbins, *The Ravens*, 46–47.

35. Lewis, *Peoples of the Golden Triangle*, 122; also, author interviews with former Hmong soldiers, Saint Paul, MN, March 2007.

36. Quincy, "Warlord," 41–50; also, author interview with Vint Lawrence, Norfolk, CT, November 2006.

37. Hillmer, *A People's History of the Hmong*, 112–13; also, author interview with Hmong war veterans, Saint Paul, MN, December 2006.

38. Author interview with Vang Pao, Saint Paul, MN, November 2006.

39. Author phone interview with Vint Lawrence, March 2007.

40. Ahern, *Undercover Armies*, 115.

41. Ibid., 138–39.

42. Ibid.

43. Ibid.; also, author phone interview with Bill Lair, January 2010.

44. Ahern, *Undercover Armies*, 174–75.

45. John Prados, *Safe for Democracy: The Secret Wars of the CIA* (Chicago: Ivan R. Dee, 2006), 357; also, author interview with Vang Pao, Saint Paul, MN, November 2006.

46. Author interview with Vang Pao, Saint Paul, MN, November 2006.
47. Weiner, *Legacy of Ashes*, 255.
48. Arthur Keller, "In Afghanistan, Less Can Be More," *New York Times*, March 10, 2009, www.nytimes.com/2009/03/10/opinion/10keller.html, accessed January 2013.
49. Dommen, *Conflict in Laos*, 105.
50. Leary, "CIA Air Operations in Laos," 75–76.
51. Ibid.
52. Author interview with Vang Pao, Saint Paul, MN, November 2006.

Chapter 8. The Not-So-Secret Secret: Keeping a Growing Operation Hidden

1. Arthur J. Dommen, "Laos in the Second Indochina War," *Current History*, December 1970, 327.
2. Author phone interview with Bill Lair, September 2010; also, author interview with Macalan Thomson, Bangkok, January 2007.
3. Author interview with Vint Lawrence, Norfolk, CT, November 2006.
4. Author phone interview with Fred Branfman, January 2012.
5. Ibid.
6. Robert M. Hathaway and Russell Jack Smith, *Richard Helms as Director of Central Intelligence, 1966–1973* (Washington, DC: Central Intelligence Agency Center for the Study of Intelligence, 1993), 177.
7. Ibid., 176–80.
8. Ibid., 184.
9. "Bill Lair Oral History," December 13, 2001, 109–11; also, author phone interview with Bill Lair, January 2010.

Chapter 9. Enter the Bombers

1. Author phone interview with Bill Lair, January 2011; also, Castle, *At War in the Shadow of Vietnam*, 132.
2. Castle, *At War in the Shadow of Vietnam*, 132.
3. Ibid., 90.
4. Ibid.; also, author phone interview with Larry Devlin, November 2006.
5. Castle, *At War in the Shadow of Vietnam*, 79.
6. Ibid., 88–89.
7. Billy G. Webb, *Secret War* (Bloomington, IN: Xlibris, 2010), 112–13.

8. Hamilton-Merritt, *Tragic Mountains*, 176; also, author phone interview with Bill Lair, March 2011.

9. Hamilton-Merritt, *Tragic Mountains*, 176.

10. James E. Parker, *Codename Mule: Fighting the Secret War in Laos for the CIA* (Annapolis, MD: Naval Institute Press, 1995), 23.

11. Ahern, *Undercover Armies*, 180.

12. Author phone interview with Bill Lair, August 2009.

13. "Ernest C. Kuhn Oral History," March 25, 1995, Association for Diplomatic Studies and Training Foreign Affairs Oral History Project, Foreign Assistance Series, 62.

14. James C. Linder, "The War in Laos: The Fall of Lima Site 85" (declassified), *Studies in Intelligence* 38, no. 5 (1995): 79–88.

15. Author phone interview with Bill Lair, November 2010.

16. Author interview with Vang Pao, Saint Paul, MN, November 2006.

17. Logevall, *Embers of War*, 270–71.

18. Ibid.

19. Hamilton-Merritt, *Tragic Mountains*, 97.

20. Ibid., 96–98.

21. Author interview with Tony Poe, Bangkok, January 2001.

22. Henry Kamm, "End of Laos War Has Brought No Peace to Thousands in Meo Clans," *New York Times*, July 13, 1975, A2.

23. Ibid.

24. Ahern, *Undercover Armies*, 179.

25. "1969," Air America notebooks, William M. Leary Papers, University of Texas at Dallas, 13.

26. Halberstam, *The Best and the Brightest*, viii.

27. Ahern, *Undercover Armies*, 191.

28. Ibid., 212.

29. Ibid.

30. Ibid., 191.

31. Ibid., 195.

32. Soutchay Vongsavanh, *RLG Military Operations and Activities in the Laotian Panhandle* (Washington, DC: US Army Center of Military History, 1981), 108.

33. "Document 187: Telegram from the Embassy in Laos to the Department of State, 21 June 1965," in *Foreign Relations of the United States, 1964–1968, vol. 28, Laos* (Washington, DC: Department of State), 371–72.

Chapter 10. The Wider War

1. For more information, see Ted Shackley with Richard A. Finney, *Spymaster: My Life in the CIA* (Dulles, VA: Potomac Books, 2006); also, author phone interview with Bill Lair, November 2007.

2. "Ambassador James R. Lilley Oral History," May 21, 1998, Association for Diplomatic Studies and Training Foreign Affairs Oral History Project, 25.

3. David Corn, *Blond Ghost: Ted Shackley and the CIA's Crusades* (New York: Simon & Schuster, 1994), 134.

4. Warner, *Shooting at the Moon*, 186; also, author phone interview with Bill Lair, November 2007.

5. Corn, *Blond Ghost*, 153.

6. Ibid.

7. Ibid., 161.

8. Hathaway and Smith, *Richard Helms as Director of Central Intelligence*, 75.

9. Ibid., 75.

10. Ibid.

11. Sullivan, *Obbligato: Notes on a Foreign Service Career*, 211.

12. Author interview with Vang Pao, Saint Paul, MN, November 2006.

13. The exact number of men in Vang Pao's army at any time was hard to pinpoint, since soldiers came and left so routinely to plant, see their families, and perform other duties.

14. Author interview with Macalan Thomson, Bangkok, Nov 2006.

15. Anne Fadiman, *The Spirit Catches You and You Fall Down: A Hmong Child, Her American Doctors, and the Collision of Two Cultures* (New York: Farrar, Straus, and Giroux, 1997), 136.

16. Parker, *Codename Mule*, 2–3.

17. Ibid.

18. C. A. Kammerer et al., "Vulnerability to HIV Infection Among Three Hilltribes in Northern Thailand," in *Culture and Sexual Risk: Anthropological Perspectives on AIDS*, Han ten Brummelheis and Gilbert Herdt, eds. (New York: Routledge, 1995), 64–65.

19. Author interview with Macalan Thomson, Bangkok, January 2007; also, Fadiman, *The Spirit Catches You*, 137.

20. Author interview with Vang Pao, Saint Paul, MN, November 2006.

21. Fred Branfman, "Laos: No Place to Hide," *The Bulletin of Concerned Asian Scholars* 2, no. 4 (Fall 1970): 23.

22. Ibid.; also, author phone interview with Fred Branfman, December 2013.

23. Quincy, "Warlord," 16–17.

24. Kennedy and McEnroe, "The Covert Wars of Vang Pao."

25. Author phone interview with Yang Dao, January 2009; also, Quincy, *Harvesting Pa Chay's Wheat*, 269.

26. Sullivan, *Obbligato: Notes on a Foreign Service Career*, 214.

27. Author interview with Vang Pao, Saint Paul, MN, November 2006.

28. Thomas Vang, *A History of the Hmong: From Ancient Times to the Modern Diaspora* (Morrisville, NC: Lulu.com, 2013), 54–60.

29. Author phone interview with Tony Poe, February 2001.

30. Author phone interview with Bill Lair, November 2009.

31. "Bill Lair Oral History," December 12, 2001, 118.

Chapter 11. Massacre

1. Timothy Castle, *One Day Too Long: Top Secret Site 85 and the Bombing of North Vietnam* (New York: Columbia University Press, 1999), 81–90. Also author interview with Vang Pao, November 2006.

2. Bernard B. Fall, *Hell in a Very Small Place: The Siege of Dien Bien Phu* (Philadephia: J. B. Lippincott, 1967).

3. Conboy and Morrison, *Shadow War*, 185.

4. James C. Linder, "The War in Laos: The Fall of Lima Site 85" (declassified), *Studies in Intelligence*, 38, no. 5 (1995): 79–88.

5. "Telegram from the Embassy in Laos to the Department of State," Document 322, in *Foreign Relations of the United States, 1964–1968, vol. 28: Laos* (Washington, DC: Government Printing Office, 1998), 639–40.

6. Castle, *One Day Too Long*, 82.

7. Ibid., 81–90; also, Conboy and Morrison, *Shadow War*, 183–200.

8. Author phone interview with Bill Lair, January 2010; also, Ahern, *Undercover Armies*, 287–300; Corn, *Blond Ghost*, 155.

9. Castle, *One Day Too Long*, 81–90; also, Conboy and Morrison, *Shadow War*, 183–200.

10. Arne Kislenko, "A Not So Silent Partner: Thailand's Role in Covert Operations, Counter-Insurgency, and the Wars in Indochina," *Journal of Conflict Studies* 24, no. 1 (2004): 23.

11. "1968," Air America notebooks, William M. Leary Papers, 3.

12. Author phone interview with Tony Poe, February 2001.

13. Davis, *Across the Mekong*, 57; also, author phone interview with Bill Lair, January 2011.

14. Davis, *Across the Mekong*, 150.

15. Ibid., 21.

16. Joe F. Leeker, *The History of Air America, 2nd ed.: Air America in Laos I: Humanitarian Work* (Dallas: University of Texas at Dallas, 2013), 12–28.

17. William M. Leary, "CIA Air Operations in Laos, 1955–1974: Supporting the Secret War," *Studies in Intelligence* (unclassified), Winter 1999–2000, 71–86

18. Hamilton-Merritt, *Tragic Mountains*, 175.

19. Ibid.

20. Author phone interview with Bill Lair, March 2012.

21. Hamilton-Merritt, *Tragic Mountains*, 175.

22. Author phone interview with Bill Lair, March 2011.

23. Corn, *Blond Ghost*, 138; also, author phone interview with Bill Lair, January 2011.

24. Author phone interview with Bill Lair, January 2011; also, Corn, *Blond Ghost*, 138.

25. Corn, *Blond Ghost*, 164; also, author phone interview with Bill Lair, January 2011.

26. Soutchay, *RLG Military Operations and Activities in the Laotian Panhandle*, 27.

27. Haney, "The Pentagon Papers and United States Involvement in Laos," 268.

28. "Memorandum from the President's Assistant for National Security Affairs to President Nixon: 12 November 1969," in *Foreign Relations of the United States, 1969–1976, vol. 6: Vietnam, January 1969–July 1970* (Washington: Government Printing Office, 2006), 481–83.

29. Author interview with Campbell James, Newport, RI, January 2007.

30. Author phone interview with Bill Lair, January 2011.

31. Ibid.; also, Corn, *Blond Ghost*, 157.

32. Ibid.

33. "Bill Lair Oral History," December 12, 2001, 118.

34. Ibid., 120.

35. John Prados, *Lost Crusader: The Secret Wars of CIA Director William Colby* (New York: Oxford University Press, 2003), 158.

36. Ibid.

37. Author phone interview with Bill Lair, March 2011.

38. Ahern, *Undercover Armies*, 301.

39. Author phone interview with Bill Lair, March 2012; also, author interview with Ralph Boyce, Bangkok, March 2006.

40. Author phone interview with Bill Lair, January 2008.

41. Ibid.

Chapter 12. Going for Broke

1. Hamilton-Merritt, *Tragic Mountains*, 204; also, author interview with Vang Pao, Saint Paul, MN, November 2006.

2. Author interview with Vang Pao, Saint Paul, MN, November 2006.

3. Leary, "CIA Air Operations in Laos," 71–86.

4. Author interview with Vang Pao, Saint Paul, MN, November 2006.

5. Captain Edward Vallentiny, "The Fall of Site 85," Air Force Project Checo report, 9 August 1968, www.ojc.org/powforum/checo, accessed October 2015.

6. Ibid., 22.

7. Castle, *One Day Too Long*, 120.

8. Ibid., 124–25.

9. Ibid.

10. Hamilton-Merritt, *Tragic Mountains*, 186.

11. Author phone interview with Bill Lair, January 2011.

12. Author interview with Vang Pao, Saint Paul, MN, November 2006; also, author email communication with Fred Branfman, December 2013.

13. Peter Dale Scott, "Laos: The Story Nixon Won't Tell," *New York Review of Books*, April 9, 1970.

14. Seymour Hersh, "Kissinger and Nixon in the White House," *Atlantic Monthly*, May 1982, 61–68.

15. Hathaway and Smith, *Richard Helms as Director of Central Intelligence*, 3–18.

16. Stanley Kutler, *The Wars of Watergate: The Last Crisis of Richard Nixon* (New York: W. W. Norton, 1992), 16–28; also, Hathaway and Smith, *Richard Helms as Director of Central Intelligence*, 3–18.

17. Hathaway and Smith, *Richard Helms as Director of Central Intelligence*, 10.

18. For the definitive account of Nixon's friendship with Muhamad Yahya Khan, see Gary J. Bass, *The Blood Telegram: Nixon, Kissinger, and a Forgotten Genocide* (New York: Vintage, 2013).

19. "Insults Fly on Nixon Tapes," *Guardian* (UK), June 29, 2005, www.theguardian.com/world/2005/jun/29/india.usa, accessed January 2014.

20. Daniel Ellsberg, *Secrets: A Memoir of Vietnam and the Pentagon Papers* (New York: Penguin, 2003), 414.

21. Leary, "CIA Air Operations in Laos," 71–86; also, Raphael Littauer and Norman Uphoff, eds., *The Air War in Indochina, rev. ed.* (Boston: Beacon Press, 1972), 79.

22. Seymour Hersh, "How We Ran the Secret Air War in Laos," *New York Times Magazine*, October 29, 1972, 18–19.

23. Bob Woodward, *The Last of the President's Men* (New York: Simon & Schuster, 2015), Kindle location 1660.

24. Ibid., Kindle locations 1805–1809.

25. Jussi Hahnimaki, *The Flawed Architect: Henry Kissinger and American Foreign Policy* (New York: Oxford University Press, 2004), 111.

26. "1969," Air America notebooks, William M. Leary Papers, 8–20.

Chapter 13. The Victory and the Loss

1. Author phone interview with Tony Poe, February 2001.
2. Adrian Levy and Cathy Scott-Clark, "America's Unknown Soldier," *Sunday Times Magazine* (London), October 25, 1998, 5.
3. Warner, *Shooting at the Moon*, 113.
4. Howard Lewin, *Sunsets, Bulldozers, and Elephants: Twelve Years in Laos, the Stories I Never Told* (self-published, 2005), 120.
5. Ehrlich, "Death of a Dirty Fighter."
6. Peter Waldman, "Fighters Stay Loyal to 'Tony Poe,' Leader of America's Secret War," *Wall Street Journal*, January 12, 2000, A1.
7. Author phone interview with Tony Poe, February 2001.
8. Ibid.
9. Ibid.
10. Ibid.
11. "Guns, Drugs and the CIA," *Frontline*, PBS, May 17, 1988.
12. Hillmer, *A People's History of the Hmong*, 144.
13. Leary, "CIA Air Operations in Laos," 71–86.
14. Sutayut, "Thailand and the American Secret War in Indochina," 196.
15. "1969," Air America notebooks, William M. Leary Papers, 14–20.
16. Ibid.
17. Victor Anthony and Richard Sexton, "The United States Air Force in Southeast Asia: The War in Northern Laos, 1954–1973," Center for Air Force History Report, 1993, 307.
18. "1969," Air America notebooks, William M. Leary Papers, 14.
19. Author phone interview with Yang Dao, November 2006. Hillmer also provides an account of this attack in *A People's History of the Hmong*.
20. "1969," Air America notebooks, William M. Leary Papers, 14.
21. Author interview with Vang Pao, Saint Paul, MN, November 2006.
22. Anthony and Sexton, "The United States Air Force in Southeast Asia," 307–8.
23. Ibid., 298.
24. Ibid., 292.
25. Alfred W. McCoy, "America's Secret War in Laos, 1955–1975," in *A Companion to the Vietnam War*, ed. Robert Buzzanco and Marilyn B. Young (New York: John Wiley, 2006), 296.
26. Author interview with Fred Branfman, December 2013.
27. Quincy, *Harvesting Pa Chay's Wheat*, 320.
28. Ibid., 319.
29. Ibid., 318–319.

30. Anthony and Sexton, "The United States Air Force in Southeast Asia," 314.

31. Quincy, *Harvesting Pa Chay's Wheat*, 319.

32. Author interview with former Hmong soldiers, Saint Paul, MN, December 2006.

33. Author interview with Vang Pao, Saint Paul, MN, November 2006.

34. Castle, *At War in the Shadow of Vietnam*, 106.

35. Richard Helms, "Memorandum for the President," October 11, 1969, declassified September 2010, Nixon Library papers, www.nixonlibrary.gov/virtuallibrary /releases/jul11/declass01.pdf, accessed January 2012.

36. "1969," Air America notebooks, William M. Leary Papers, 15.

37. Richard Helms, "Memorandum for the President," October 11, 1969, declassified September 2010, Nixon Library papers, www.nixonlibrary.gov/virtuallibrary /releases/jul11/declass01.pdf, accessed January 2012.

38. "1969," Air America notebooks, William M. Leary Papers, 15–22.

39. Douglas Blaufarb, *The Counterinsurgency Era: U.S. Doctrine and Performance, 1950 to the Present* (New York: Free Press, 1977), 165.

40. Quincy, *Harvesting Pa Chay's Wheat*, 345–47. Also "1970," William Leary Notebooks, University of Texas at Dallas Leary Collection, 1–22. Also Castle, *At War in the Shadow of Vietnam*, 106.

41. Morrison, *Hog's Exit*, 80.

42. Quincy, *Harvesting Pa Chay's Wheat*, 345–48; also, author phone interview with Hugh Tovar, September 2007.

43. Conboy and Morrison, *Shadow War*, 9.

44. Robbins, *The Ravens*, 283.

45. Author interview with Vang Pao, Saint Paul, MN, November 2006; Hillmer, *A People's History of the Hmong*.

46. Arthur J. Dommen, *The Indochinese Experience of the French and the Americans* (Bloomington: Indiana University Press, 2001), 935–36.

47. Robbins, *The Ravens*, 284.

48. Ibid.

49. "Minutes of the National Security Council Meeting, February 27, 1970," in *Foreign Relations of the United States, 1969–1976, vol. 6: Vietnam, January 1969–July 1970* (Washington, DC: Government Printing Office, 2006), 638–46.

50. Sheehan, *A Bright Shining Lie*, 617–18.

51. Quincy, *Harvesting Pa Chay's Wheat*, 345.

Chapter 14. The Secret War Becomes Public

1. *Executive Sessions of the Senate Foreign Relations Committee, Vol. 20: 1968* (Washington, Government Printing Office, 2010), 35–36.

2. Author interview with Vang Pao, Saint Paul, MN, November 2006.

3. Author interview with Vint Lawrence, Norfolk, CT, November 2006.

4. Sullivan, *Obbligato: Notes on a Foreign Service Career*, 232–34.

5. Ibid.; also, author phone interview with Fred Branfman, September 2013; Finney and Shackley, *Spymaster*, 231–35.

6. Gotz Bechtolsheimer, "Breakfast with Mobutu: Congo, the United States, and the Cold War" (thesis for doctorate of philosophy, London School of Economics, March 2012), 67–71.

7. Author phone interview with John Gunther Dean, August 2011.

8. Sullivan, *Obbligato: Notes on a Foreign Service Career*, 237.

9. Peter Braestrup, "Laotian Hill Tribesmen, with American Help, Harass Pro-Reds," *New York Times*, January 7, 1967, A6.

10. Ibid.

11. Many of the essays were collected in Fred Branfman, ed., *Voices from the Plain of Jars: Life Under an Air War* (New York: Harper and Row, 1972).

12. Karen J. Coates and Jerry Redfern, "Eternal Harvest: The Legacy of American Bombs in Laos" (Occasional Paper 49, Japan Policy Research Institute, Oakland, CA, June 2014), 1–4, www.jpri.org/publications/occasionalpapers/op49 .html.

13. Fred Branfman, "Beyond the Pentagon Papers: Pathology of Power," in *The Pentagon Papers, Vol 5: Critical Essays*, Noam Chomsky and Howard Zinn, eds. (Boston: Beacon Press, 1972), 303.

14. Author phone interview with Fred Branfman, December 2013.

15. Branfman, *Voices from the Plain of Jars*, 1–9.

16. Ibid., 39.

17. Ibid., 296.

18. Perry Stieglitz, *In a Little Kingdom* (New York: Routledge, 1990), photo inserts.

19. Branfman, *Voices from the Plain of Jars*, 1–9.

20. Ibid., 53–54.

21. *The Most Secret Place on Earth*, Marc Eberle, director (Berlin: Gebrueder Beetz, 2008), 12:26–12:30.

22. Ibid.

23. Author interview with MacAlan Thomson, Bangkok, August 2006; also, author phone interview with Fred Branfman, January 2013.

24. John Hart Ely, *War and Responsibility: Constitutional Lessons of Vietnam and Its Aftermath* (Princeton, NJ: Princeton University Press, 1993), 68–71.

25. Branfman, *Voices from the Plain of Jars*, 36–39.

26. Walt Haney, "The Bombing of Laos and the Browning of One Volunteer," paper presented at the Fifteenth Annual Meeting of the Association of Third World Studies, Central Connecticut State University, Hartford, CT, October 9–11, 1997, 6.

27. Haney, "The Bombing of Laos and the Browning of One Volunteer," 5–6.

28. *Hearing of the Committee of the Judiciary Subcommittee to Investigate Problems Connected with Refugees and Escapees, 91st Congress, 2nd Session, vol. 4: 7 May 1970* (Washington, DC: Government Printing Office, 1970), 26.

29. Haney, "The Pentagon Papers and United States Involvement in Laos," 276–77.

30. McCoy, "America's Secret War in Laos," 296.

31. Lewin, *Sunsets, Bulldozers, and Elephants*, 308–10.

32. Tim Craig and Craig Whitlock, "Afghan Response to Hospital Bombing Is Muted, Even Sympathetic," *Washington Post*, October 5, 2015, www.washingtonpost.com/world/afghan-official-hospital-in-airstrike-was-a-taliban-base015/10/04/8638af58-6a47-11e5-bdb6-6861f4521205_story.html, accessed October 2015.

33. For example, see "Laos: The Unseen Presence," *Time*, October 17, 1969, 39; "More Aid to Laos: A Report on What the United States Is Doing There," *U.S. News & World Report*, October 20, 1969, 16; and Henry Kamm, "U.S. Runs a Secret Laotian Army," *New York Times*, October 26, 1969, 1.

34. *Hearings on United States Security Agreements and Commitments Abroad, Kingdom of Laos, Vol. 1, Part 2, October 20, 22, 28, 1969, U.S. Senate, 91st Congress, 1st session* (Washington, DC: Government Printing Office, 1970), 367.

35. Ibid., 366.

36. Ibid., 500–18.

37. "Memorandum from the President's Assistant for National Security Affairs (Kissinger) to President Nixon, February 27, 1970," *Foreign Relations of the United States, 1969–1976, vol. 6: Vietnam, January 1969–July 1970* (Washington: Government Printing Office, 2006), 633–38.

38. *Executive Sessions of the Senate Foreign Relations Committee, vol. 20: 1968* (Washington, DC: Government Printing Office, 2010), 35–36.

39. Ibid.

40. *Hearings on United States Security Agreements and Commitments Abroad, Kingdom of Laos, Vol. 1, Part 2*, 369–70.

41. Haney, "The Pentagon Papers and United States Involvement in Laos," 277.

42. Ibid.

43. *Hearings on United States Security Agreements and Commitments Abroad, Kingdom of Laos, Vol. 1, Part 2*, 500–14.

44. *Hearing of the Committee of the Judiciary Subcommittee to Investigate Problems Connected with Refugees and Escapees*, May 7, 1970 (Washington: Government Printing Office, 1970), 59.

45. Ibid., 59–65.

46. Ibid.

47. Yarborough, *Da Nang Diary*, 24–25; also, author phone interview with Bill Lair, December 2012.

48. *Hearings on United States Security Agreements and Commitments Abroad, Kingdom of Laos, Vol. 1, Part 2*, 375.

49. Ibid., 394.

50. Haney, "The Pentagon Papers and United States Involvement in Laos," 265.

51. *Hearings on United States Security Agreements and Commitments Abroad, Kingdom of Laos, Vol. 1, Part 2*, 401–2.

52. Ibid., 520.

53. Ibid., 402–5.

54. Ibid., 458–59.

55. Ibid.

56. Ibid., 458.

57. Ibid., 485.

58. Ibid., 543.

59. Ibid.

60. However, flattery did not stop Kissinger from allowing a presidential order to have Sullivan's phone tapped along with those of several other Nixon aides, from 1969 to 1971, just to make sure that Sullivan wasn't leaking any information to reporters. See William Yardley, "William H. Sullivan, U.S. Ambassador to Volatile Laos and Iran, Is Dead at 90," *New York Times*, October 28, 2013, A14.

Chapter 15. Defeat and Retreat

1. Corn, *Blond Ghost*, 163.

2. Quincy, *Harvesting Pa Chay's Wheat*, 335–37.

3. Hamilton-Merritt, *Tragic Mountains*, 251–54.

4. Lowenstein and Moose, *Laos, April 1971: Staff Report*, 1.

5. Ibid.

6. Author interview with Vang Pao, Saint Paul, MN, November 2006.

7. Hugh D. S. Greenway, "The Pendulum of War Swings Wider in Laos," *Life*, April 3, 1970, 36.

8. Castle, *At War in the Shadow of Vietnam*, 111.

9. Author phone interview with Yang Dao, January 2008.

10. Ibid.

11. Quincy, "Warlord," 51; also, author phone interview with Yang Dao, January 2007.

12. Kennedy and McEnroe, "The Covert Wars of Vang Pao."

13. Hillmer, *A People's History of the Hmong*, 142–43.

14. Webb, *Secret War*, 119.

15. Author phone interview with Yang Dao, January 2008; also, Quincy, "Warlord," 42–50; author interviews with former Hmong soldiers, Saint Paul, MN, August 2006.

16. Author phone interview with Yang Dao, March 2008.

17. Quincy, *Harvesting Pa Chay's Wheat*, 335; also, author phone interview with Tony Poe, March 2001.

18. Author phone interview with Tony Poe, March 2001.

19. Ibid.; also, Levy and Scott-Clark, "America's Unknown Soldier," 6.

20. Ibid.

21. Levy and Scott-Clark, "America's Unknown Soldier," 6.

22. *History Undercover: The Search for Kurtz*, 33:25–34:40

23. Levy and Scott-Clark, "America's Unknown Soldier," 6.

24. Author phone interview with Tony Poe, March 2001.

25. Ibid.; also *History Undercover: The Search for Kurtz*, 33:25–34:40.

26. Ibid.

27. *History Undercover: The Search for Kurtz*, 33:25–34:40.

28. Ibid.; also Waldman, "Fighters Stay Loyal to 'Tony Poe,'" A1.

29. Ibid.

30. Levy and Scott-Clark, "America's Unknown Soldier," 4.

31. Ibid.

32. Levy and Scott-Clark, "America's Unknown Soldier," 4.

33. Lowenstein and Moose, *Laos, April 1971: Staff Report*, 11.

34. Author phone interview with Fred Branfman, November 2012.

35. Warner, *Shooting at the Moon*, 316–318; also, author phone interview with Fred Branfman, November 2012.

36. *The Most Secret Place on Earth*, 40:40–42:06.

37. Author interview with Vang Pao, Saint Paul, MN, November 2006.

38. "Statistical Information about Fatal Casualties of Vietnam War," National

Archives, April 29, 2008, www.archives.gov/research/military/vietnam-war /casualty-statistics.html#water, accessed December 2014.

39. Haney, "The Pentagon Papers and United States Involvement in Laos," 274.

40. "Minutes of the National Security Council Meeting, 27 February 1970," in *Foreign Relations of the United States, 1969–1976, vol. 6: Vietnam, January 1969–July 1970* (Washington, DC: Government Printing Office, 2006), 638–46.

41. Ibid.

42. Ibid.

43. Richard Nixon, "Statement About the Situation in Laos," March 6, 1970, American Presidency Project Archives, University of California–Santa Barbara, www.presidency.ucsb.edu/ws/index.php?pid=2902, accessed February 2015.

44. Ibid.

45. "Ambassador Winston Lord Oral History," April 28, 1998, Association for Diplomatic Studies and Training Foreign Affairs Oral History Project, 101–5, www.adst.org/OH%20TOCs/Lord,%20Winston.pdf, accessed May 28, 2015.

46. *The Most Secret Place on Earth*, 43:33–44:04.

47. Statistical Information about Fatal Casualties of Vietnam War," National Archives, April 29, 2008, www.archives.gov/research/military/vietnam-war /casualty-statistics.html#water, accessed December 2014.

48. "The Vietnam Veterans Memorial Search Engine," http://thewall-usa.com/ summary.asp, accessed December 2014; also, "Statistical Information about Fatal Casualties of Vietnam War," National Archives, April 29, 2008, www .archives.gov/research/military/vietnam-war/casualty-statistics.html#water, accessed December 2014.

49. Castle, *One Day Too Long*, 151–56.

50. Ibid.

51. Ely, *War and Responsibility*, 68–78.

52. Mark Mazzetti and Scott Shane, "Tapes by C.I.A. Lived and Died to Save Image," *New York Times*, December 30, 2007, A1.

53. Karl W. Eikenberry and David M. Kennedy, "Americans and Their Military, Drifting Apart," *New York Times*, May 26, 2013, www.nytimes.com/2013/05 /27/opinion/americans-and-their-military-drifting-apart.html, accessed January 2015.

54. Jaime Fuller, "Americans Are Fine with Drone Strikes. Everyone Else in the World? Not So Much," *The Fix* (blog), *Washington Post*, July 15, 2014, www .washingtonpost.com/blogs/the-fix/wp/2014/07/15/americans-are-fine-with -drone-strikes-everyone-else-in-the-world-not-so-much, accessed January 2015.

55. Castle, *At War in the Shadow of Vietnam*, 108–9.
56. Author interview with Vang Pao, Saint Paul, MN, November 2006.

Chapter 16. Skyline Ridge

1. William Leary, "The CIA and the 'Secret War' in Laos: The Battle for Skyline Ridge, 1971–1972," *Journal of Military History* 59, no. 3 (July 1995): 505–9.
2. Author interview with Vang Pao, Saint Paul, MN, November 2006; also, author phone interview with Yang Dao, October 2008.
3. Leary, "The CIA and the 'Secret War' in Laos," 505–9.
4. Ibid.; also, author interview with Vang Pao, Saint Paul, MN, November 2006.
5. Leary, "The CIA and the 'Secret War' in Laos," 505–9; also, James E. Parker Jr., *The Battle for Skyline Ridge: Timeline, 18 December 1971 to 4 April 1972* (self-published, 2013), Kindle edition, locations 2499–599.
6. Parker, *Codename Mule*, 48.
7. "1971," Air America notebooks, William M. Leary Papers, University of Texas at Dallas, 24.
8. Parker, *The Battle for Skyline Ridge*, Kindle locations 2499–599.
9. Ibid.
10. Ibid.
11. Ibid.
12. Ibid.
13. Parker, *Codename Mule*, 68–87.
14. Hamilton-Merritt, *Tragic Mountains*, 284.
15. Parker, *Codename Mule*, 66.
16. Quincy, *Harvesting Pa Chay's Wheat*, 345; also, author interview with Jack Shirley, Pattaya, Thailand, March 2002.
17. Author interview with Jack Shirley, Pattaya, Thailand, March 2002.
18. Parker, *The Battle for Skyline Ridge*, Kindle locations 2499–599.
19. Leary, "The CIA and the 'Secret War' in Laos," 505–9.
20. Parker, *The Battle for Skyline Ridge*, Kindle locations 2499–610.
21. "1971," Air America notebooks, William M. Leary Papers, 4.
22. Leary, "The CIA and the 'Secret War' in Laos," 505–9.
23. Parker, *Codename Mule*, 67; also, author phone interview with Hugh Tovar, September 2007.
24. Parker, *The Battle for Skyline Ridge*, Kindle locations 2520–689; also, author phone interview with Hugh Tovar, September 2007.
25. Ibid.
26. "1972," Air America notebooks, William M. Leary Papers, 12.

27. Leary, "The CIA and the 'Secret War' in Laos, 505–9.

28. "1972," Air America notebooks, William M. Leary Papers, 9.

29. Ibid.

30. Leary, "The CIA and the 'Secret War' in Laos, 505–9.

31. Author interview with Vang Pao, November 2006.

32. Quincy, *Harvesting Pa Chay's Wheat*, 348.

33. Ibid.; also, author phone interview with Hugh Tovar, March 2007.

34. Leary, "The CIA and the 'Secret War' in Laos, 505–9.

35. Ibid.

36. Author interview with Jack Shirley, Pattaya, Thailand, February 2002; also, Quincy, *Harvesting Pa Chay's Wheat*, 349–51.

37. Parker, *The Battle for Skyline Ridge*, Kindle locations 2520–689.

38. McCoy, "America's Secret War in Laos," 298–99.

39. Leary, "The CIA and the 'Secret War' in Laos," 505–9.

40. Parker, *The Battle for Skyline Ridge*, 2520–689.

41. Ibid.

42. McCoy, "America's Secret War in Laos," 299.

43. Author interview with Vang Pao, Saint Paul, MN, November 2006.

44. Quincy, *Harvesting Pa Chay's Wheat*, 308; also, author interview with Vang Pao, Saint Paul, MN, November 2006.

45. McCoy, *The Politics of Heroin in Southeast Asia*, 290.

46. William Sullivan, unpublished memoir, obtained by the author from the family of William Sullivan, 5.

47. Sullivan, *Obbligato: Notes on a Foreign Service Career*, 240.

48. "Thursday, October 12, 1969," H. R. Haldeman Diaries, Nixon Library, www .nixonlibrary.gov/virtuallibrary/documents/haldeman-diaries/37-hrhd -audiocassette-ac25b-19721012-pa.pdf, accessed January 2014.

49. Henry Kissinger, *White House Years* (New York: Little, Brown and Company, 1979), 1362.

50. Henry Kissinger, *Ending the Vietnam War: A History of America's Involvement in an Extrication from the Vietnam War* (New York: Simon & Schuster, 2003), 363–65.

51. Author phone interview with John Gunther Dean, January 2010; also, Mai Elliott, *RAND in Southeast Asia: A History of the Vietnam War* (Santa Monica, CA: Rand Corporation, 2010), 589.

52. Author interview with Vang Pao, Saint Paul, MN, November 2006.

53. Henry Kissinger, *Years of Upheaval* (New York: Little, Brown and Company, 1982), 22.

54. Ibid., 22–25.

55. Hillmer, *A People's History of the Hmong*, 152–54

56. Vang, *General Vang Pao*, 56.

57. Author interview with Vang Pao, Saint Paul, MN, November 2006.

58. Warner, *Shooting at the Moon*, 301.

59. Ibid.

60. Lee, *Dreams of a Hmong Kingdom*, 310–12.

61. Castle, *At War in the Shadow of Vietnam*, 123.

62. Ibid.

63. Leary, "CIA Air Operations in Laos, 1955–1974," 71–86.

64. George McArthur, "Laos War Still Real for Meo Tribal Leader," *Los Angeles Times*, August 1, 1974, A1.

65. Ibid.

Chapter 17. Final Days

1. Xiaoming Zhang, "China's Involvement in Laos During the Vietnam War, 1963–1975," *Journal of Military History*, 66, no. 4 (October 2002): 1161–62.

2. Author interview with Vang Pao, Saint Paul, MN, November 2006; also, Hillmer, *A People's History of the Hmong*, 150–54.

3. Morrison, *Hog's Exit*, 90.

4. Henry Kamm, "U.S. Involvement in Laos Is Virtually Over," *New York Times*, June 20, 1975, A1.

5. Dommen, *The Indochinese Experience of the French and the Americans*, 934.

6. Kamm, "End of Laos War Has Brought No Peace," A1.

7. Warner, *Shooting at the Moon*, 338. Also author interview with Vang Pao, November 2006.

8. Author interview with Vang Pao, Saint Paul, MN, November 2006.

9. Ibid.

10. Fadiman, *The Spirit Catches You and You Fall Down*, 139.

11. Vang, *General Vang Pao*, 263.

12. Author interview with Greg Davis, Alexandria, VA, August 2006.

13. Kamm, "End of Laos War Has Brought No Peace," A1.

14. "Ernest C. Kuhn Oral History," March 25, 1995, 113.

15. Ibid.

16. Brian Phelan, "Thailand: Plight of the Meo," *Far Eastern Economic Review*, August 29, 1975, 20–22.

17. Quincy, *Harvesting Pa Chay's Wheat*, 369–70; also Bounsang Khamkeo, *I Little Slave: A Prison Memoir from Communist Laos* (Cheney, WA: University of Eastern Washington Press, 2006).

18. Morrison, *Hog's Exit*, 133–34.

19. Hamilton-Merritt, *Tragic Mountains*, 360.

20. Stuart-Fox, *A History of Laos*, 167–79.

21. Walter LaFeber, "Laos: The Silent Surrender," *Far Eastern Economic Review*, May 23, 1975.

22. "Ambassador Thomas J. Corcoran Oral History," June 21, 1988, Association of Diplomatic Studies and Training Foreign Affairs Oral History Project, www.adst .org/OH%20TOCs/Corcoran,%20Thomas%20J.toc.pdf, accessed January 2014.

23. For more on the royal family, see Christopher Kremmer, *Bamboo Palace: Discovering the Lost Dynasty of Laos* (New York: HarperCollins, 2005).

24. Hamilton-Merritt, *Tragic Mountains*, 398.

25. For more on the camps, see Bounsang, *I Little Slave*.

26. Frederic Frommer, "Exiled Laos Prince Appeals to U.S.," *Washington Post*, February 24, 2000, www.washingtonpost.com/wp-srv/aponline/20000224/aponline180821_000.htm, accessed March 2013.

27. Morrison, *Hog's Exit*, 165.

28. Hamilton-Merritt, *Tragic Mountains*, 337–90.

29. Ibid., 372.

30. Author phone interview with John Gunther Dean, February 2009.

31. Ibid., February 2010.

32. For more information on demining in Laos, see "Lao National Unexploded Ordnance Program," www.uxolao.org.

33. Sullivan, *Obbligato: Notes on a Foreign Service Career*, 251.

34. Ibid., 248.

35. Ibid., 250.

36. "Ambassador Thomas J. Corcoran Oral History," June 21, 1988.

37. Author interview with US diplomat, Vientiane, May 2006.

38. "Ambassador Thomas J. Corcoran Oral History," June 21, 1988.

Chapter 18. Laos and the CIA: The Legacy

1. William Colby and Peter Forbath, *Honorable Men: My Life in the CIA* (New York: Simon & Schuster, 1978), 192–95.

2. Richard Helms, *A Look over My Shoulder: A Life in the Central Intelligence Agency* (New York: Random House, 2003), 262–65.

3. "Richard Helms Oral History," Oral History Program, Lyndon Johnson Library and Museum, September 16, 1981.

4. William E. Colby, "Heroin, Laos, and the CIA," *New York Review of Books*, November 22, 1990, 68; also, Kennedy and McEnroe, "Covert Wars of Vang Pao."

5. Hathaway and Smith, *Richard Helms as Director of Central Intelligence*, 74.

6. Author phone interview with Fred Branfman, August 2013.

7. Ibid.

8. For example, see Lev Dvoretsky and Oleg Sarin, *The Afghan Syndrome: The Soviet Union's Vietnam* (New York: Presidio Press, 1993).

9. Jonathan Steele, "Ten Myths About Afghanistan," *Guardian* (UK), September 27, 2011, www.theguardian.com/world/2011/sep/27/10-myths-about -afghanistan, accessed January 2015.

10. Alfonso Chardy, "Reagan Warns of a Second Cuba, Meets Nicaraguan Rebel Leaders, Presses Congress on Aid," *Philadelphia Inquirer*, March 4, 1986, A1.

11. David Rosenbaum, "Ex-CIA Aide Called a Principal in Iran Affair, *New York Times*, April 23, 1987, A1; also, Tim Weiner, "Ex-CIA Official Guilty in Iran-Contra Tax Case," *Philadelphia Inquirer*, September 19, 1990, A1.

12. William Leogrande, *Our Own Backyard: The United States in Central America, 1977–1992* (Chapel Hill: University of North Carolina Press, 2000), 310–11.

13. Bryan Burrough, et al. "The Path to 9/11: Lost Warnings and Fatal Errors," *Vanity Fair*, November 2004, 22–26.

14. Vernon Loeb, "The CIA in Somalia," *Washington Post Magazine*, February 27, 2000, www.washingtonpost.com/archive/lifestyle/magazine/2000/02/27/ after-action-report/3c474a43-ea21-4bf5-afc5-02820b8579e5/.

15. Aidan Laverty and Tom Walker, "CIA Aided Kosovo Guerilla Army," *Sunday Times* (UK), March 12, 2000, A1; also, David B. Ottaway and R. Jeffrey Smith, "Anti-Saddam Operation Cost CIA $100 Million," *Washington Post*, September 15, 1996, A1.

16. Burrough, et al., "Path to 9/11," 22–26.

17. For more on the growth of the CIA in the 2000s and 2010s and its paramilitary operations, see Mazzetti, *The Way of the Knife*.

18. Scott Shane, "New Leaked Document Outlines U.S. Spending on Intelligence Agencies," *New York Times*, August 30, 2013, A1.

19. Christopher Drew, et al., "Seal Team Six: A Secret History of Quiet Killings and Blurred Lines," *New York Times*, June 7, 2015, A1.

20. Ibid.

21. Greg Miller, "Top Paramilitary Officer to Lead CIA Spy Branch," *Washington Post*, January 30, 2015, A4.

22. Ibid.

23. Jack Goldsmith, "How Obama Undermined the War on Terror," *New Republic*, May 1, 2013, www.newrepublic.com/article/112964/obamas-secrecy -destroying-american-support-counterterrorism, accessed December 2014.

24. Jeff Stein, "Inside the CIA's Syrian Rebels Vetting Machine," *Newsweek*, November 21, 2014, www.newsweek.com/2014/11/21/moderate-rebels-please -raise-your-hands-283449.html, accessed January 2015; also, Declan Walsh, "Car Bomb Kills Eight Afghans from Unit Linked to CIA," *New York Times*, October 15, 2014, www.nytimes.com/2014/10/16/world/asia/car-bomb-kills -cia-trained-afghan-soldiers.html, accessed January 2015.

25. Ernesto Lodono and Greg Miller, "CIA Begins Weapons Delivery to Syrian Rebels," *Washington Post*, September 11, 2013, www.washingtonpost.com/world/national-security/cia-begins-weapons-delivery-to-syrian-rebels/2013/09/11/9fcf2ed8-1b0c-11e3-a628-7e6dde8f889d_story.html, accessed December 2014.

26. Greg Miller, "U.S. Launches Secret Drone Campaign to Hunt Islamic State Leaders in Syria," *Washington Post*, September 1, 2015, www.washingtonpost.com/world/national-security/us-launches-secret-drone-campaign-to-hunt-islamic-state-leaders-in-syria/2015/09/01/723b3e04-5033-11e5-933e-7d06c647a395_story.html, accessed September 2015.

27. Matt Apuzzo and Mark Mazzetti, "Deep Support in Washington for the CIA's Drone Missions," *New York Times*, April 25, 2015, A1.

Chapter 19. Aftermath

1. Author phone interview with Bill Lair, November 2007.

2. Ibid.; also, Warner, *Shooting at the Moon*, 396.

3. Author phone interview with Bill Lair, November 2007.

4. Author interview with Willis Bird Jr., Chiang Rai, Thailand, August 2007.

5. Author phone interview with Bill Lair, January 2008; also, Roger Warner, "Once Upon a Time in the C.I.A.," documentary trailer, www.dailymotion.com/video/xf7p65_once-upon-a-time-in-the-c-i-a_news, October 15, 2010, accessed March 2014.

6. Author phone interview with Bill Lair, January 2010.

7. Author phone interview with Tony Poe, March 2001. Also author interviews with Jack Shirley, January 2001 and March 2002.

8. Ibid.

9. Levy and Scott-Clark, "America's Unknown Soldier," 5.

10. William Branigan, "William Sullivan Dies at 90; Veteran Diplomat Was Last U.S. Ambassador to Iran," *Washington Post*, October 22, 2013, www.washingtonpost.com/world/william-h-sullivan-dies-at-90-veteran-diplomat-oversaw-secret-war-in-laos/2013/10/22/f13e628c-3b2f-11e3-b6a9-da62c264f40e_story.html, accessed December 2014.

11. Sullivan, *Obbligato: Notes on a Foreign Service Career*, 269.

12. Ibid., 268–71; also, author phone interviews with former Sullivan aides, February 2013.

13. Author phone interview with Victor Tomseth, January 2006; also, Sullivan, *Obbligato: Notes on a Foreign Service Career*, 274.

14. Author phone interview with John Gunther Dean, January 2008.

15. Author phone interview with former US ambassador, January 2013.

16. "William Sullivan Obituary," *Telegraph* (UK), November 14, 2013, www.telegraph.co.uk/news/obituaries/10450380/William-Sullivan-Obituary.html, accessed January 2014.

17. Sullivan, *Obbligato: Notes on a Foreign Service Career*, 269–74.

18. Jimmy Carter and Don Richardson, *Conversations with Carter* (Boulder, CO: Lynne Rienner, 1998), 243.

19. For more on this point, see William H. Sullivan, *Mission to Iran* (New York: W. W. Norton, 1981).

20. Warner, *Shooting at the Moon*, 389.

21. Ibid.

22. Author phone interview with Fred Branfman, August 2013.

23. Vang Pao, lecture to the Heritage Foundation, Washington, DC, March 19, 1987.

24. Kennedy and McEnroe, "Covert Wars of Vang Pao."

25. Joshua Kurlantzick, "Hmong Friends," *New Republic*, February 5, 2007, www .newrepublic.com/article/the-st-paul-warlord-hmong-friends, accessed January 2014.

26. Kennedy and McEnroe, "Covert Wars of Vang Pao."

27. Ruth Hammond, "The Great Refugee Shakedown—The Hmong Are Paying to Free Laos, but What's Happening to the Money?," *Washington Post*, April 16, 1989, B1.

28. Ibid.

29. Kurlantzick, "Hmong Friends."

30. Kennedy and McEnroe, "Covert Wars of Vang Pao."

31. Hmong National Development, Inc., "The State of the Hmong-American Community 2013," April 2013, www.hndinc.org/cmsAdmin/uploads/dlc/ HND-Census-Report-2013.pdf, accessed January 2014.

32. "Asian-American Subgroups Among Nation's Poorest," *Diverse: Issues in Higher Education*, http://diverseeducation.com/article/53790, June 6, 2013, accessed December 2013.

33. Author phone interview with Yang Dao, January 2008.

34. Dan Browning and Pam Louwagie, "Shamed into Silence," *Star Tribune*, March 23, 2012, A1.

35. "Guns, Drugs and the CIA," *Frontline*, PBS, May 17, 1988.

36. Author interviews with former Hmong combatants, Vientiane province, Laos, March 2007.

37. "Busted Flush," *Economist*, May 26, 2011, www.economist.com/node/18744577, accessed January 2015.

38. Thomas Fuller, "Old Allies, Still Hiding in Laos," *New York Times*, December 17, 2007, www.nytimes.com/2007/12/17/world/asia/17laos.html ?ref=hmongtribe, accessed February 2012; also, author interviews with former Hmong combatants, Vientiane province, March 2007.

39. Ibid.

40. Ibid.

Index

About the Author

Joshua Kurlantzick is a senior fellow for Southeast Asia at the Council on Foreign Relations (CFR). Mr. Kurlantzick was previously a scholar at the Carnegie Endowment for International Peace, where he studied Southeast Asian politics and economics and China's relations with Southeast Asia, including Chinese investment, aid, and diplomacy.

Kurlantzick has also served as a columnist for *Time*, foreign editor of the *New Republic*, a correspondent for the *Economist*, and a contributing writer for *Mother Jones*. His work has been published in *Rolling Stone*, the *New York Times Magazine*, *GQ*, *Harper's*, the *Atlantic*, the *Wall Street Journal*, the *Washington Post*, *Foreign Policy*, and many other publications.

He is the winner of the Luce Scholarship for journalism in Asia and was selected as a finalist for the Osborn Elliott prize for journalism in Asia.

For more information on Kurlantzick and CFR, please visit www .cfr.org/experts/asia-southeast-asia-democracy-human-rights/joshua -kurlantzick/b15522.